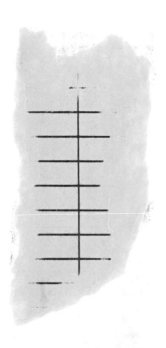

The West

The West

The History of a Region in Confederation

J.F. CONWAY

281570316

James Lorimer & Company, Publishers
Toronto 1983

ISBN 0-88862-661-4 paper
      0-88862-662-2 cloth

Cover design: Brant Cowie
Cover photo: NFB Phototheque

Canadian Cataloguing in Publication Data
Conway, John Frederick.
   The West

1. Canada, Western — Politics and government*
2. Federal-provincial relations (Canada) — Canada, Western.* I. Title II. Series: Canadian issues series (Toronto, Ont.).

FC3206.C66 1983   971.2   C83-099138-7

James Lorimer & Company, Publishers
Egerton Ryerson Memorial Building
35 Britain Street
Toronto, Ontario M5A 1R7

Printed and bound in Canada
6 5 4 3 2 1   83 84 85 86 87 88

Contents

For a Barnardo boy who escaped West....

Acknowledgements

The manuscript was read by Dr. R.M. Stirling, University of Regina, by Jim Lorimer and Ted Mumford, both of James Lorimer & Company, and by Sally Mahood. Their suggestions helped to produce a much improved book. Greg Ioannou enhanced the final product. To all five, and to my family for their patience, my thanks. Financial support for some of the research for this book was provided by the Social Sciences and Humanities Research Council and the President's Fund at the University of Regina.

Cross over the continent to the shores of the Pacific, and you are in British Columbia, the land of golden promise, I speak not now of the vast Indian Territories that lie between — greater in extent than the whole soil of Russia — and that will ere long, I trust, be opened up to civilization under the auspices of the British American Confederation. [Cheers]

Well, sir, the bold scheme in your hands is nothing less than to gather all these countries into one. . . . [Cheers].

Hon. George Brown, during
the Confederation Debates
in the Province of Canada's
Assembly, February 8, 1865.

1
Introduction

The West, today comprising the provinces of Manitoba, Saskatchewan, Alberta, and British Columbia, has always held a particular fascination for Canadians of other regions.

This was clearly true in the period leading up to Confederation. After all, the West was key to the successful establishment of a Dominion from sea to sea. The "Fathers of Confederation" — as our school children continue to be encouraged to call the businessmen who arranged the deal — knew only too well that the Canada they envisaged could be achieved only if the West were won and held.

The myth of the West as an almost limitless region of resource wealth, offering vast profits to investors, speculators, and entrepreneurs, played no small part in winning the support of the political and economic elites of the established British colonies in North America for London's planned colonial confederation. More modest variations on that myth were played to lure the settlers — farmers and workers — from Ontario, Atlantic Canada, the United Kingdom, the United States, and later, continental Europe, surrendering unhappy if certain circumstances for vague expectations of future prosperity in an often unforgiving land. Later, as the wheat boom established the conditions for the irreversible blossoming of the Western dream, wave upon wave of eager farmers, workers, businessmen, and professionals trekked westward to build lives they wanted but could not have in their home regions. Even today, especially during times of economic boom, the West often becomes the embodiment of hopes many had thought they had long surrendered to the harsh reality of compromise and making do.

Canada has never really come to terms with the West, nor has the West ever really come to terms with Canada. The West is a region that is hard to understand, full of contradictions, politically uneasy, economically vulnerable, chronically unhappy. The only insurrections in the history of Confederation both occurred in the West — the Riel Rebellions of 1869 and 1885. Farmers from the West, in alliance with their rural brothers and sisters in Ontario, led the only systematic, mass-supported political attack on the very economic foundations of the nation. Workers in the West at Winnipeg held the only general strike in Canada's history, and long before and long after set a standard for union militancy and political radicalism unmatched elsewhere in the Dominion. Political movements dedicated to a radical remaking of Canada's political economy were spawned in the West and sallied forth to try to win the hearts and minds of all Canadians.

The West has never been happy with its lot in Confederation. When times were bad, the West often rebelled openly, challenging the very founding principles of Confederation. When times were good, the voices of complaint and rebellion became only grudgingly more mute. They were never silenced. They are not silent today.

Canada needs the West. But does the West need Canada? Over the years, and even today, there has persisted a strong current of Western opinion that, in wondrously complex ways, has never conceded that the West needs Canada. In fact, that's as good a definition of "Western alienation" as any — there is a deep doubt among many Westerners about whether they need Canada, about whether Confederation gives to the West as much as it takes from the West. Many Canadians, especially Ontarians, can't understand that key fact. Westerners are not just complaining about the tariff, or about transportation policy, or about oil prices, or about this, or about that: the thing that unites all such specific grievances is an abiding Western suspicion that Confederation has been and continues to be a bad deal for the West.

Clearly, the West has been central to the Canadian story. Today, just as throughout our history, crises rooted in the West consume a great deal of the nation's political time and attention. This is understandable. The West, though sparsely populated, is a geographically sprawling region endowed with enormous resource riches. The West occupies about 48 per cent of the land mass of Canada, excluding the Yukon and the Northwest Territories. The gross domestic products of the four Western provinces usually make up about one-third of Canada's Gross National Product (GNP).[1] The West earns about 55 per cent of Canada's farm cash receipts, produces about 78 per cent of the value of Canada's mineral production, and, in 1982, received about 45 per cent of all new capital invested in Canada. About 25 per cent of Canada's GNP is earned through exports and 83 per cent of these exports are resources, raw and semi-finished. The

West, as a major resource region, is therefore central to Canada's continuing economic dependence on the export of natural resources. The West is clearly geographically and economically vital to Canada.

On the other hand, only about 29 per cent of Canadians live in the West. Only about 18 per cent of factory shipments originate in the West (compared with 49 per cent in Ontario and 25 per cent in Quebec). The West elects 77 of 282 Members of Parliament, a fair share based on population. Yet, only two Liberals were elected in the West in 1980, both in Winnipeg, the most "Eastern" part of the West. The West has not been significantly represented in the federal government since the defeat of John Diefenbaker (except during Joe Clark's brief 200-day regime in 1979-80). The West's political clout, therefore, has been increasingly marginalized — the long-governing Liberals have been shut out, while the post-Diefenbaker Tories have badly fumbled their bids for office. In recent federal elections, other than the 1979 Clark win, the outcome was already determined long before Western ballots were counted, in effect symbolizing the region's sense of political impotence.

Westerners feel that the federal government would never have dared to treat Ontario or Quebec as the West was treated during the energy crisis of the 1970s. If Ontario had had the oil and natural gas, many in the West argue, Canadians would have been forced to pay world prices all along. Were the Crow rate (the low freight rates fixed in federal law for Western grain) as significant to Central Canada as it has been to the West, efforts begun in 1983 to abandon the rate would never have materialized.

But these contemporary examples of Western grievance and complaint are just that. They are seen by many in the West as simply the most recent examples of federal arrogance and Central Canadian self-interest so characteristic of the treatment of the West in Confederation. Therefore, while compromise and concession might temper Western anger, the anger remains today, just as it remained after each of the many concessions made to the West over the years — the breaking of the CPR monopoly clause in the 1880s, the Crow rate of 1897, the regulation of the grain trade, some tariff relief, the establishment of the Canadian Wheat Board, transfer payments to poorer provinces, and so on. Such concession and compromise always stopped short of redressing the structural sources of the West's unhappiness. Clearly, then, what are we dealing with is a contradiction historically rooted in the very political and economic structures of Canada, as the nation was established and developed. To understand the West, therefore, we must examine the place of the West in Confederation, politically, but more importantly, economically. We must therefore begin at the beginning. In order to understand the present, we must come to know the past.

This book provides a short political and economic history of the West in Confederation. It begins with the Riel Rebellions of 1869 and 1885 and ends with the energy and constitutional wars of the 1970s and early 1980s. The story of Western dissent is told through the most dramatic events characteristic of the West's uneasy place in Confederation. Above all, the book documents how Western Canadians repeatedly struggled to re-construct Canada's political and economic order, not only to redress the grievances of the region, but to bring more justice and economic security for all Canadians. It is a story of which all Canadians can be proud.

2

"The Last Best West": The West in Confederation, 1869-1913

Canadians continue to embrace a whole series of myths about Confederation. We talk of the "Fathers of Confederation," politely overlooking the self-seeking motives of the businessmen-politicians who conceived the plan. We speak of the "national dream," focussing on patriotism and other fine sentiments in an effort to elevate the bargaining and trade-offs that resulted in Canada to some higher, moral plane. Our history is "prettified," revised, often completely reconstructed. Even the London *Times* of 1865 revealed a clearer insight into Confederation than most Canadians today have, when an editorial said, referring to Confederation, "Half the useful things that are done in the world are done from selfish motives under the cover of larger designs."[1]

Background to Confederation

Three great events shaped the essence of Canada long before Confederation was even contemplated. These events ensured that Canada would remain a nation bedevilled by the English-French conflict, characterized by unremitting conservatism, and beset by a deep suspicion of popular movements and aspirations. The conquest of Quebec by Wolfe, the immigration of the fleeing counter-revolutionary United Empire Loyalists, and the defeat and repression of the 1837-38 Rebellions all had a great deal to do with determining the essential character of the Dominion which emerged in 1867. As they approached Confederation, Canada's rulers, encumbered by this legacy, were determined to contain and humble Quebec, to resist extreme democracy, and to view popular assertions as seditious. Confederation was never conceived as a plan to address the long-festering grievances of the Québécois; nor was it viewed as an orderly progression to popular democracy; nor, indeed, as a way to fulfill the yearnings of the people for nationhood. The plan was conceived by the business and political elites of the various British North American colonies, inspired by the elite of the colony of Canada, for no other reason than to assure their futures.

To understand the place of the West in Confederation, it is crucial to know the context in which Confederation was finally successfully brought about. The rulers of the united colony of Canada, the merchants and nascent industrialists, had staggered from broken dream to broken dream, from crisis to crisis, emerging each time with the same basic strategy. First, and until the loss of imperial preference, they had striven to build a commercial transportation system to service the great trade between North America and Europe. When American expansion blocked this aspiration, reciprocity with the U.S. was sought and won. Finally, when the reciprocity agreement was abrogated by the U.S. the only option left was Confederation and independence.

Each crisis had increased the public investment in the transportation system, the resulting debt constantly threatening bankruptcy; each crisis and each depression was met with the same response — secure a larger borrowing base, borrow more capital, invest in transportation, accelerate the export of staples, and, only incidentally, establish protection for a modest Canadian industrialization. The single-minded devotion to this strategy finally led to Confederation, the biggest borrowing base of all.

A somewhat reconstituted ruling class, more open to this "political dream of wonderful audacity,"[2] had emerged from the ashes of the 1837-38 Rebellions. Forced reluctantly to grant responsible government, cast adrift by Britain as free trade was embraced in the 1840s, the new ruling class became dominated by the "progressive Conservative" (in Sir John A. Macdonald's words)[3] elements of the hard tory merchant bloc that had ruled before, a rising group of industrial capitalists, landowners, railway and steamship entrepreneurs, and financial adventurers in the growing Canadian banking and insurance system.[4] This group, and their backers in the British Colonial Office, recognized that some form of federation was the only road to the survival of an independent British fact on the continent, as well as to the establishment of an expanded national economy upon which they could realize their aspirations. In the absence of such a British federation, American hegemony over a growing portion of the continent was inevitable. And in the absence of an enforced east-west national home market, the rising Canadian capitalist class would see their hopes dashed, confined by localism, undercut by American economic competition.

Confederation, therefore, was essential to this new, emerging ruling class in Canada, allied more or less uneasily with the local elites of the other British colonies in North America. Confederation was to be conservative in design and character. The moves toward protection would be modest, as hopes to establish reciprocity with the U.S. were not to be completely surrendered until 1878. The new regime would expand westward by rail and begin the construction of a national industrial economy through protection. This economic design required a political union of the colonies with a strong central government — the final political solution, as Sir John A. Macdonald had so eloquently put it, to "the dead-lock in our affairs, the anarchy we dreaded, and the evils which retarded our prosperity."[5] In one stroke, the union of the Canadas would be dissolved, the reform of representation by population introduced, and a federation established, transferring all the colonies' debts to the new Dominion, which would provide a stronger credit base for further borrowing for westward expansion.

The new union would not go too far down the treacherous road of democracy. As Macdonald had so candidly put it at the 1864 Quebec Conference, what was being established was "constitutional liberty as opposed to democracy."[6] The House of Commons would not be elected by universal male suffrage, but tied to British qualifications for electors. Indeed, the principle of adult suffrage was not to be won until women were granted the vote in the context of World War I. Furthermore, there was to be a Senate, just in case the Commons got out of hand, which would be "the representative of property."[7] As Macdonald said, "A large qualification should be necessary for membership of the Upper House, in order to represent the principle of property. The rights of the minority must be protected, and the rich are always fewer in number than the poor."[8]

As might be expected, these were fighting words to the reformers, and radical democrats resisted the Confederation scheme on the grounds that it threatened the rights of the Québécois and that its structure was too undemocratic and anti-popular. But such arguments were to no avail; the conservative design remained intact. As G.E. Cartier said, "The scheme... met with the approval of all moderate men. The extreme men, the socialists, democrats, and annexationists were opposed..."[9] The "extreme men" were probably in a majority, had there been a more perfect democracy, but their resistance was futile against the power at the disposal of the "moderate men," backed by the British government. Even with severely restricted suffrage, the elites of the colonies were reluctant to put the scheme to the electoral test. The Confederation scheme was widely popular only in Canada West (Ontario), and other regimes faced political controversy on the issue. Guile, arm-twisting, opportunism, and pressure from Britain were the tactics used most often to effect the union.

When Queen Victoria signed the BNA Act on May 29, 1867, Canada, now to be Quebec, Ontario, Nova Scotia, and New Brunswick, became the federal Dominion of Canada. It was a new variation on the old theme. The new federal government would borrow capital, or guarantee investments, in order to unite British North America from coast to coast through an expansion of the transportation system westward by rail. Ultimately, in the West, vast quantities of wheat and other natural resources would be extracted to join the similar flow from Central and Atlantic Canada to feed Europe's industrial markets, especially that of Great Britain. Central Canada, especially Ontario, would additionally prosper in a variety of other ways: railway promoters and forwarding interests would move grain and other resources to market and manufactures back; the protective tariff would lead to a growing industrialization to supply the national home market expanded by a vast immigration of settlers to build the West; retailers and wholesalers would benefit through the general commercial boom; financial empires would rise on the growing demand for credit. Atlantic Canada would benefit from a growing demand for coal, fish, and the products of its long-established industries. The strong central government would play the crucial role — it would finance railway development, promote immigration, construct a wall of protective tariffs, and acquire the Prairie West as a colonial possession, while continuing pressure on B.C. to join the federation. The job of the federal state was to "clear and prepare the way for the beneficient operation of the capitalist."[10] The West, especially the Prairie West, was key to the success of the whole project.

The Winning of the West

At the outset a distinction must be made between the Prairies and British Columbia. The Prairie region entered Confederation as a colonial possession of the Dominion government. B.C. negotiated the terms of Confederation as a fully fledged British colony. This distinction is crucial and goes much of the way in explaining why B.C.'s relations with Central Canada have rarely been as tumultous as the Prairies'. B.C. had to be wooed and won. The Prairies were simply purchased from absentee owners without consultations with the local people. B.C. seriously considered other options to Confederation. The Prairies were not permitted this luxury. Both were viewed by the architects of Confederation as politically and economically vital. London was particularly concerned about B.C. as the opening to the Pacific for both economic and military reasons. Pacific ports would be crucial for trade with the west coast of the U.S. and Asia. London's naval base at Esquimalt was central to British strategic interests in the Pacific. Both the Prairies and B.C. were viewed as potentially rich resource producing regions and as captive markets for Central Canadian industrial products. In that sense they shared a common fate in the basic economic design of Confederation.

Still, the Prairies, a vast underpopulated hinterland, were the cornerstone in the Confederation scheme, politically and economically. The tremendous economic opportunities envisaged by the architects of the new Dominion depended upon successful agricultural settlement of the Prairies. Even B.C.'s eventual place in Confederation depended upon events on the Prairies. Prior to Prairie settlement, the B.C. colony's production of minerals, lumber, and salmon largely went to foreign markets, the most important of which was California. The hopes arising from the increase in B.C.'s population during the gold rush of the 1850s, hopes that for some included B.C. going it alone, were dashed when the rush collapsed in the 1860s and B.C.'s population fell to just over 36,000 in 1871.[11] By 1881, development in B.C. had limped ahead, as even the Northwest Territories and Manitoba could boast greater populations. Prairie settlement, and the railway and tariff policies associated with it, became a prerequisite first, for B.C.'s entry into Confederation and its willingness to stay, and second, for B.C.'s prosperity in the new national economy. Therefore events on the Prairies were central. It was on the

Prairies that Confederation, both politically and economically, would succeed or fail. And success or failure on the Prairies would determine B.C.'s final decision about Confederation.

The most blunt statement on the place of the West in Confederation was made by Clifford Sifton, minister of the interior in Laurier's 1896 cabinet. In 1904 he said to a Winnipeg audience:

> We look in the near future to see upon these western plains, and in this western province and territories a great population...
>
> We look forward to other things. We look forward to the production of natural wealth of all kinds. In this great country we expect to see the wealth of the field, of the forest and of the mines exploited in vast quantities...
>
> What...will western Canada do for the Canadian organism? Sir, it will give a vast and profitable traffic to its railways and steamship lines. It will give remunerative employment to tens of thousands of men...[who] engage in the multitude of occupations which gather around the great system of transportation.
>
> It will do more. It will build up our Canadian seaports. It will create a volume of ocean traffic which shall place Canada in a short time — in its proper position as a maritime nation. It will furnish a steady and remunerative business to the manufacturers of eastern Canada, giving assured prosperity where uncertainty now exists. These are the things the west will do for the east. In a word, I may say it will send a flood of new blood from one end of this great country to the other, through every artery of commerce.[12]

Sifton was speaking at the height of the great expansion of the wheat boom, the final success of Confederation, and he was speaking primarily of the Prairie

West. Yet Sifton was articulating the long-standing plan regarding the place of the West in Confederation. What he said applied to B.C. just as much as to the Prairies.

What is now the Prairie West, as well as most of Canada's huge north, had been granted in 1670 by the British Crown to the Hudson's Bay Company. For two centuries the fur trade dominated the life of the region. The Hudson's Bay Company exercised not only an economic monopoly over the region, but ruled the inhabitants politically as well. There had been, therefore, a long legacy of resistance to all efforts at settlement — permanent agricultural settlement undermined the fur trade and threatened the continuing control of the fur-traders. Settlement was discouraged by a Company policy of outrageously high land prices combined with a rigid commercial policy that attempted to enforce the Company's monopoly on all economic activity.

These policies had failed to some extent on three fronts: a Canadian, Montreal-based fur-trading company, the North West Company, had emerged to compete with the British concern; the Métis (the offspring of marriages between European, mostly French, men and Indian women) had successfully challenged Hudson's Bay Company efforts to regulate their commercial dealings in the U.S.; and a trickle of white settlers had continued. Of course, both fur companies were very much concerned about the advent of permanent agricultural settlement, and resisted such settlement.

Most dramatically, in 1816 this resistance to settlement had resulted in the Northwest Company inspired massacre of settlers at Selkirk's colony, established in 1812 on land granted to Lord Selkirk by the Hudson's Bay Company (in which he held a large interest) in order to prove the merits of agricultural settlement in the Red River area. The subsequent merging of the Northwest Company with the Hudson's Bay Company in 1821, and Selkirk's death the year before, ensured that the fur-trading interest in the West was united in efforts to resist permanent settlement. The subsequent persisting decline in interest in settling in the region was not therefore surprising. Meanwhile the U.S. was rapidly expanding westward. The new Canadian government, therefore, was very anxious about a number of problems.

The local population was inevitably very small. As the 1871 census later revealed, due to the Hudson's Bay Company's resistance to settlement, as well as the greater attractiveness of settlement in the U.S., there were only about 1,600 white settlers in the region, as well as 9,800 Métis (the largest portion of whom were French-speaking), whose loyalty was suspect among Canadian politicians.[13] Clearly, such a vast territory could not be held with so small a population, especially if the U.S. actively pursued possession of some or all of the territories — and there were real reasons to fear U.S. intentions.

The main economic link from Red River was through the more convenient transportation route south. To the south Minnesota had become a prosperous and well-populated state as early as the 1850s. After the end of the American Civil War, the call for the annexation of the British North West had become popular among many prominent Americans, including politicians and journalists. In fact, in 1868 the Minnesota Legislature demanded the American annexation of the North West. During the Confederation year, 1867, the U.S. had purchased Alaska from Russia, an event that the New York *World* characterized as "an advancing step in that manifest destiny which is yet to give us British North America."[14] This American agitation for annexation, combined with the strengthening of the economic links between Red River and the U.S., caused great consternation among Dominion politicians.

Finally, the region had to be acquired from the Hudson's Bay Company. For many years the Company had resisted Canadian acquisition of the territory, making impossible demands for an agreement. Finally, a new leadership in the Company and vigorous pressure from the British government led to a resolution. In December 1867, Canada's Parliament formally asked Westminster to admit Rupert's Land and the North West Territory to the federation as a possession of the Dominion government. Final negotiations in London between representatives of the Canadian government, the British government, and the Company resulted in an agreement that gave Canada possession of the region in return for £300,000 in cash, one-twentieth of the "fertile-belt" in the region (about 7 million acres), and further land grants around the Company's many posts. In 1868 the British Parliament ratified the agreement and the Canadian government passed the legislation necessary to establish control over the area. In 1869 a Canadian governor was sent, proclaiming his authority over the West in December, 1869. At no time were the inhabitants of the region consulted.

The local people in the Red River region responded with something less than enthusiasm. The largely French-speaking and Catholic Métis feared for their language, education, and religious rights, as well as the long-term consequences for their nation of Canadian annexation. White settlers and the Métis shared a concern that their rights, particularly land rights, would be over-ridden without prior guarantees. Both wanted some form of responsible government and the prospect of exchanging the unhappy but known dictatorship of the Company for the distant and unknown dictatorship of Canada was viewed with some alarm. The vocal and arrogant agitations of the minority Canada Party, composed largely of recently arrived Canadians from Ontario who enthusiastically called for swift annexation of the district by Canada, did little to placate such fears. As well, a significant, if minority, opinion argued that American annexation of the region was a more logical prospect.

The first confrontation occurred when the Métis refused to permit William McDougall, the Canadian lieutenant-governor, entry into the district. Nevertheless he proclaimed his authority over the West in absentia. In response to such threatening arrogance, and under the leadership of Louis Riel, the Métis and a majority of white settlers united to declare a provisional government and to seek further negotiations with the Dominion.

The Dominion government was in no position militarily to crush the Red River insurrection, despite a desire to do so. The American giant watched, waiting, it was believed, for the slightest excuse for intervention. Moving an adequate military force quickly enough to engage the rebels was impossible for a number of reasons, besides the obvious geographical and logistical ones. The British government wanted a peaceful settlement. Quebec sympathized with the Métis. The prospects of the great Indian nations, mainly the Assiniboine and the Cree, allying with the rebels were appalling. And the Métis themselves were well-known as a potentially formidable military foe.

Therefore, the Dominion government negotiated and conceded just enough to reassure the region's inhabitants. In 1870 the province of Manitoba was established with most of the rights of other provinces, including responsible government and representation in the federal Parliament. Guarantees were established for the French language and for largely local control of education. Lands were set aside to meet Métis land claims. Finally, the uncertain land rights of the people on existing farms were guaranteed by an assurance that land acquired from the Hudson's Bay Company would be secure under the new regime.

The Dominion government made up for these humiliations in other ways, finally stealing by stealth what had been a significant victory for the Métis nation and their white allies. In the first instance, the size of Manitoba was tightly constricted to about 10,000 square miles, barely encompassing most of the settlements on the Red and Assiniboine Rivers. It became known as "the postage stamp province" and was the subject of some hilarity among easterners. Alexander Mackenzie, leader of the Liberal Opposition, said, "The whole thing has such a ludicrous look that it only puts one in mind of some incidents in Gulliver's Travels ... it [is] one of the most preposterous schemes ... ever submitted to the Legislature."[15] It was really not so preposterous; the remaining territory would be governed arbitrarily as a colonial possession.

Next, one of the most crucial demands of the Red River rebels, control of lands and resources as other provinces enjoyed under the BNA Act, was refused. The denial of such control made it impossible for the province to plan and influence the settlement process, to dispose of, and gain revenues from, timber resources, or, indeed, any resources that began to be developed. Furthermore, the province, powerless over lands and resources, could not ensure fair settlements of outstanding land claims of "old" settlers, Métis or white, or to determine priorities in opening areas of the province either for new farms or the expansion of existing farms. Control of lands and resources was "vested in the Crown, and administered by the Government of Canada for the purposes of the Dominion," in the words of the Manitoba Act. As well, the guarantee of 1.4 million acres of land for the setttlement of Métis land claims was administratively and politically circumvented by the issue of "scrip," a piece of paper entitling individual Métis to select land later, by deliberate delays in the final settlement of Métis land claims, by refusals to provide a fair census of Métis in the area, and by military and bureaucratic harassment. A heavy trade by land speculators ensured that much of the scrip issued was converted into ready cash, at drastically low prices, by many Métis as they saw their victory turned against them and left the region to move westward.

Finally, Dominion politicians succumbed overzealously to Ontario opinion, which was outraged at Riel's execution of Thomas Scott, an Ontario Orangeman. (The Orange Lodge, though originally rooted among militantly anti-Catholic Irish Protestants, had become, in Canada, the main Anglo-Saxon anti-French and anti-Catholic lobby.) Scott had defied the authority of the provisional government and had repeatedly attempted to provoke armed civil strife. Had he had his way, Red River would have experienced a blood bath and, in the ensuing military struggle, the West might have been lost for Canada. In what was Riel's only significant strategic political blunder, Scott was tried and executed, becoming a public martyr in Ontario. Riel was hounded into exile, denied the amnesty he was promised and barred from the seat he won in the House of Commons. Thus the leader of the Métis nation, and the man who ought to have been the first premier of Manitoba, had he wanted the job, was driven from his home and his people by the smug opinion leaders of Ontario who, above all else, viewed the West as their own. There was to be no place for rebels who did not embrace Ontario's vision for the West — especially Métis, French, and Catholic rebels. The last vestige of Riel's triumph was to be erased some twenty years later when the Manitoba legislature abolished French, both as an official language and as an acceptable language of education.

This was not an auspicious beginning for the West in Confederation, but the Dominion government had carried the day. The West was theirs, but for the vexation of the postage stamp province. The government moved quickly. Lord Wolseley's military excursion to the Red River district in 1869-70 asserted federal military intentions graphically. The Manitoba Act of 1870 was followed quickly by the Land Act of 1872, which provided for free homestead land grants as well as pre-emption rights. The Act creating the Royal North West Mounted Police was passed in 1873, establishing a federal paramilitary force to enforce law and order. And finally the North West Territories Act in 1875 established Dominion authority over the entire region not included in Manitoba. The stage was now set for the expansion of the Dominion westward, largely on the Dominion's terms.

Years of Failure, 1870-1896

The belief was that the establishment of law and order and the clarification of the political status of the region, together with the temptation of free land, would start a huge flow of immigrants to the West. But in the absence of a railway, and in the presence of more attractive alternatives in the U.S., the policy was a hopeless failure. In 1872, there were only 73,000 people (including Indians and Métis) in the entire Prairie region.[16] The year before, in the negotiations that brought B.C. into the federation, the Dominion had promised to complete the railway to the Pacific by 1881. The underpopulation of the Prairies made that commitment more imperative. And although the 1872 Land Act contributed somewhat to settlement, Canada continued to have difficulty retaining the immigrants who arrived from Europe. Canada even had trouble retaining her native born, as settlers came West from the older provinces, took a look around and continued south into the U.S. The situation became so alarming that by 1890 it was estimated that there were about one million ex-Canadians in the U.S., representing about 17 per cent of Canada's entire population.[17]

In a series of determined manoeuvres, the Dominion government tried to speed up settlement. In 1874-75, a new policy enjoyed some success by encouraging ethnic and/or religious group settlement. This was supplemented by the establishment of Colonization Companies made up of groups of capitalists who bought or were granted blocks of land and proceeded, through sharp practice and propaganda, to entice settlers to their lands. Yet immigration and settlement limped ahead. Success still awaited the arrival of the railway. Ironically, the first railway to arrive was not Canadian; in 1878 a U.S. line connecting Winnipeg with Minneapolis/St. Paul began to bring in the first large flow of settlers.

1878 was an important year for reasons other than the arrival of a U.S. railway in Winnipeg. That year saw the return of Macdonald and his Tories to power with a new mandate, having lost office in 1873 and the election of 1874, largely as a result of the "Pacific scandal." The reasons for Macdonald's victory were clear. Liberal Alexander Mackenzie's transportation policy was failing and discredited; settlement of the Prairie region was dangerously slow; railway routes south through the U.S. were ominously becoming accessible to Canadians who, when they were not using the system to come and go, were using it for their commercial traffic. Macdonald promised to finish the railway and to speed up settlement. As well, Canada had fallen into serious depression in 1873 (together with the rest of the world) and efforts to conclude some kind of reciprocal economic deal with the U.S. were unsuccessful. Therefore Canadian industrial capitalist opinion had finally clearly crystallized around the protective tariff road to domestic industrialization. Macdonald agreed and promised to turn the depression around with a new tariff policy. In brief, Macdonald and his Tories campaigned on what really amounted to a commitment to ruthlessly bring the original design of Confederation to successful if roughshod completion. The architect of Confederation was recalled to continue as its chief engineer.

After victory Macdonald proceeded to erect a formidable tariff wall and to pick up the pieces of his previous railway policies. The tariff wall was begun in 1879, and completed in 1887, imposing a tariff range of 10 to 40 or 50 per cent, depending on the degree of industrial processing. From 1879 onward the primary purpose of the tariff was no longer to generate revenue, but rather to deliberately intervene in the economy in order to foster domestic industrialization.[18]

Such an elaborate tariff wall only made sense if the other two elements of the Confederation scheme — settlement and transportation — were realized. Settlement clearly depended on the railway, and ultimately, the successful settlement of the West was key to the success or failure of Confederation. Macdonald moved quickly on the railway question as well. In October, 1880 a contract was signed with a group of capitalists and, after much controversy, the Canadian Pacific Railway Act was assented to in February, 1881. In exchange for building and operating a transcontinental railway, the CPR entrepreneurs received a massive Western empire, which laid the basis for the company's position today as the largest conglomerate in Canada. The terms of the contract still enrage Westerners.[19] In addition to about $38 million worth of completed railway, the CPR received a $25 million subsidy and 25 million acres of prime Western land. Of enormous significance, the company was given the power to locate the main line through the Prairies, as well as branch lines. This ensured that the CPR could locate rail lines in ways to enhance the return on their vast land holdings. Significant tax exemptions were granted and the CPR was guaranteed an effective monopoly for 20 years. It was the kind of deal usually only realized in the dreams of railway promoters.

The agreement ensured that a prominent, powerful, and international group of capitalists had a profound interest in the successful settlement of the region. Patriotism and nation-building were given dollar signs. The West must be filled not only to expand the domestic market for protected industrial capitalists, but also to make the CPR viable and increase the value of the vast tracts of land held by the Hudson's Bay Company (7 million acres) and by the CPR consortium (25 million acres). The railway interests, with the power to choose where to locate the rail lines, were able to manipulate the value of land in any settlement region. But hopes of vast returns on a protected, largely public, investment given outright to a group of economic adventurers, awaited the arrival of an elusive population. Although the line was completed from Montreal to Vancouver on November 7, 1885, the population still didn't come. America continued to be more attractive to settlers for a host of reasons.

British Columbia had watched the Prairie drama unfold with growing concern. There had earlier been great worry among Canadian politicians, and their London masters, about the penetration of American settlers in the valleys of the Fraser River. This concern increased with the gold rush after 1856, especially because the huge Pacific coastal region was virtually empty of white population. However, by the mid-1860s the gold rush was over and concern abated. In preparation for Confederation, the separate colonies of Vancouver Island and British Columbia were united in 1866 into one colony. Yet the B.C. colonial regime was not enamoured of Confederation and resisted it until the death of the anti-Confederate governor in 1869 allowed London to send a pro-Confederate replacement. The new governor succeeded and his Executive Council (there was no responsible government in B.C.) finally petitioned for admittance to Confederation. When the B.C. delegates arrived in Ottawa in the aftermath of the Red River fiasco, Dominion officials generously embraced the new province.

On July 20, 1871 B.C. joined Confederation as a full province, controlling its lands and resources (except for the railway right-of-way). Canada agreed that a transcontinental railway would be completed by 1881. The depression of 1873, the failures associated with the Pacific syndicate, and then Mackenzie's equivocal performance all upset the province; in 1876 the Legislature petitioned the Queen complaining of Canada's incompetence, threatening secession. This secessionist agitation continued throughout 1877 and 1878 and played no small part in Macdonald's return to power. B.C. was finally won over by Macdonald's apparent successes associated with his new tariff policy and the establishment of the CPR. But B.C. uneasiness continued.

The promised results had not materialized as quickly as expected. The railway had not been completed in 1881. The settlement policies on the Prairies had failed to bring the waves of farmers to stimulate B.C.'s lumber and fish industries. The absence of a railway meant that even the small Prairie market had remained closed to B.C. In 1881 products of the mine still accounted for 60 per cent of B.C.'s exports, and foreign markets remained predominant.[20] B.C.'s great staple industries — mining, forestry, and the fishery — grew disappointingly slowly. This increased the province's restiveness. The colony's "Fathers of Confederation" had been very blunt when they decided to enter Confederation. As one of them had said in 1870:

No Union between this Colony and Canada can permanently exist unless it be to the mutual and pecuniary advantage to this Colony to remain in the union ... The people of this Colony have, generally speaking, no love for Canada ... Therefore no union on account of love need be looked for. The only bond of Union outside of force — and force the Dominion has not — will be the material advantage of the country and the pecuniary benefits of the inhabitants.[21]

Even the completion of the CPR main line in 1885 brought only disappointing results, as the Prairies remained largely unsettled. By 1891 B.C.'s population had only grown to just over 98,000, still less than either Manitoba or the Northwest Territory.[22] B.C.'s vast treasure house of natural resources needed the labourers, the investors, and the booming markets promised by the new Dominion. These all awaited success on the Prairies.

Final Success: The Wheat Boom, 1896-1913

It was not until the United States' massive westward expansion was virtually completed that the immigration tide turned in Canada's favour. Macdonald did not live to see the final success of his efforts, dying in office in 1891.The Tories did not live to see it either, at least not in office. The continuing depression into the 1890s, the failure of the grand plans to bear profitable fruit, the controversies surrounding the give-aways that had been indulged in behind the patriotic screen of nation-building, the death of their leader — all these conspired to replace them in office in the election of 1896 with Laurier's Liberals.

In 1896 the Laurier Liberals inherited a Dominion government heavily in debt, with over one-half of the government's current outlay committed to debt charges and new development programs. The same held true for all provincial governments, except Ontario. This had occurred due to the prevailing, if dubious, political wisdom of the proper role of government — "the traditional role of government in British North America as an agency for creating conditions in which private enterprise might thrive"[23] was assumed by all but a few politicians, according to the Rowell-Sirois Commission report of 1940. The fly in the ointment was that vast sums had been expended on creating conditions, yet private enterprise had refused to thrive. The mood abroad was anything but hopeful and, according to the Rowell-Sirois Commission, there were "forebodings about the success of Confederation."[24]

In 1896 prosperity began to dawn as the "wheat boom" of 1896-1913 began.[25] The key to the boom lay in declining transportation costs and rising prices for wheat, which overnight made the production of Prairie wheat profitable. Free and cheap land further stimulated the process, providing a strong magnet for the land hungry from around the world. Add to this the fact that the American frontier was for all practical purposes settled, and the conditions for a massive jump in population and wheat production on the Prairies were amply fulfilled.

The subsequent speed of settlement and agricultural development was unprecedented in Canadian history. In 1896, 140 million acres were available for settlement — 60 million open free homestead, the rest for sale from private owners such as the CFR, the Hudson's Bay Company, land combines, and private entrepreneurs. From 1896 to 1913, over 1 million people moved into the three Prairie provinces, occupied lands increased by 7 times, and wheat produced leapt by more than 10 times.

For the first time the Confederation design was functioning as it ought to have from the beginning. By 1913 the value of wheat and flour exports alone were greater than the value of all exports in 1896. The Prairies filled up as population moved in and followed the railway to every corner to produce the new gold — wheat. In the 1896-1913 period it would not be an overstatement to say, as the Rowell-Sirois Commission did, "the settlement of the Prairies dominated the Canadian economic scene."[26]

But the production and export of wheat, and the resulting east-west railway traffic, was only one cornerstone of the original design. Out of the boom one element of the original capitalist designers of Confederation gained much — the investors in transportation, the speculators in land, the middlemen who dealt in the international grain trade, the banks and trust companies, the commercial wholesalers and retailers who dealt in commodities for consumption and production, all these benefitted. However that was only one segment of the eager group who watched the final fruition of their long-postponed dreams. The other major segment was made up of the industrial capitalists who had tied their star to a strategy of industrialization through protective tariffs. The role the West played here, too, was crucial — the immigration brought a vast new captive market.

In 1903 Wilfrid Laurier said,

> The best way you can help the manufacturers of Canada is to fill up the prairie regions of Manitoba and the Northwest with a prosperous and contented people,

who will be consumers of manufactured goods of the east.[27]

In 1905, he elaborated,

They [the Prairie settlers] will require clothes, they will require furniture, they will require implements, they will require shoes... they will require everything that man has to be supplied with. It is your ambition [he was speaking to the Canadian Manufacturers' Association] that this scientific tariff of ours will make it possible that every shoe that has to be worn in these prairies shall be a Canadian shoe; that every yard of cloth that can be marketed there shall be a yard of cloth produced in Canada; and so on and so on.[28]

Again, the industrial component of the original design was working beautifully, as the net value of manufacturing production almost tripled between 1890 and 1910. However, the largest proportion — 80 per cent — of this massive industrial expansion occurred in Central Canada — this fact, combined with the tariff policies, was to figure large, then and later, in Western grievances about Confederation.

Wheat brought the long-awaited boom to B.C. The province's population almost quadrupled from 1891 to 1911, to just under 400 thousand.[29] In 1900 76 per cent of B.C.'s lumber exports had gone by sea. In 1913, 90 per cent were leaving the province by rail.[30] B.C. had joined the new Dominion economy. Stimulated by Prairie demand, the production of lumber doubled between 1908 and 1911 alone.[31] Mining — especially coal and copper — boomed in response to the hunger of the expanding Canadian market. The fishery, especially the canned salmon sector, burgeoned. Growing industrial production, primarily in wood products and fish canning, attracted a vast immigration of workers. The fantastic growth in demand for lumber and mine products led to a boom in settlement and economic activity in B.C.'s newly opened vast interior. The vision promised by Dominion politicians to the colony in 1871 was finally realized.

By 1913, when the boom ended, the pattern was established irreversibly. B.C.'s place in Confederation was to exploit her treasure house of resources for national and international markets. The Prairie West's place in Confederation was to produce cereal grains, primarily wheat, for export to an international market. Any and all commodities derived from "the wealth of the field, of the forest and of the mine," as Clifford Sifton put it, were also to be "exploited in vast quantities" as development went forward. But then, wheat was king, wheat had made Confederation work.

The population, which had been begged, cajoled, lured, and even deceived, into coming to provide the labour, to settle the prairies, to raise the wheat, therefore, served other purposes of which they were initially unaware. They were, behind the walls of the protective tariff, the captive market for the manufactures of Central Canada. The agricultural population and the essential, if small in number, wage-earners who settled and rendered productive the Prairies, and the wage-earners and entrepreneurs who opened the mine and lumber camps of B.C., were all a commercial capitalist's dream come true. They were forced to buy dear and sell cheap.

This was particularly rankling for Prairie farmers, the most decisive element in the final success of Confederation. The protected manufactures they needed for production, for consumption, and even for amusement, cost them up to 40 or 50 per cent above what they would have paid had there been free trade. At the same time, the commodities they produced for a cash income — grains, especially wheat, and livestock — had to be forwarded through middlemen, each of whom took a share of the final price ultimately gained on the world market, as well as transported vast distances. From the Prairie farmers' point of view, in terms of their share of the final price, they were forced to sell cheaply indeed. Add to this the cost of credit needed to buy land, to purchase machinery, and to erect buildings, and even the ability and right to produce was subject to a tariff in the form of interest.

Granted, but for the small Prairie working class, the Prairie settlers were small capitalists who embraced the basic tenets of the system of private enterprise and extolled individualism and entrepreneurial ability. But they had been brought into being by big capitalists — the railway interests, the grain trade, the retailers and wholesalers, the industrialists, the banking, trust and insurance interests — for purposes beyond their control. Almost immediately there was a clash of interests.

In the first instance, some of the best lands of the vast region had been alienated to the Hudson's Bay Company, the CPR, colonization companies, and many other individual friends of the Dominion government. Hence they found that in order to expand and develop their holdings, they must purchase lands already owned. Indeed, the land sold exceeded the land acquired by free homestead in the West. As well, on a national basis four out of ten free homesteads failed from 1870 to 1927. And in Alberta from 1905 to 1930, 46 per cent of homesteads failed, while in Saskatchewan from 1911 to 1931, 57 per cent failed.[32]

Clearly, the myth of the Prairies as a land of free homesteaders is false. Second, they were at the mercy of a legislated railway monopoly, which charged excessive freight rates. Third, they were forced to buy all their manufactured necessities at prices mercilessly inflated by the tariff. More generally speaking, they were involved in a highly sophisticated capitalist agriculture concerned with the extensive industrial cultivation of cash grain crops for a distant market — a market to which they could gain access only through the railways and grain middlemen, and which paid prices over which they had no control.

Still, Confederation had worked and wheat had made it work. Yet it was to be precisely the underpinnings, the very economic foundation of Confederation — a transcontinental railway, a protective tariff, the settlement policies — and the special economic place assigned to the West in the newly constructed national capitalist economy, from which the settlers' grievances began to spring. And the grievances had been given expression by early settlers long before the wheat boom, and continued long after that boom had become a fond memory in the cruel cycle of boom and bust that came to dominate their lives.

3
Agitation and Rebellion: Riel and the Farmers in the 1880s

The acquisition of the Prairie West by the Dominion, which set the stage for the great wheat boom of 1896-1913, was not viewed with enthusiasm by many Westerners during the continuing depression. The agitations that had resulted in the 1869-70 Rebellion continued among agrarian settlers and Métis alike, though now the focus was on the effects of incorporation by the Dominion and the ongoing grievances of the region, rather than on the principle of incorporation itself. Indeed, angry echoes of discontent reverberated among Prairie settlers from the beginning. Part of the popular historical mythology of the Prairies holds that much of the complaining can be attributed to the harsh environment the settlers confronted and conquered. Nothing could be further from the truth. A close examination of the record shows that from the outset, the farmers' agitations had more to do with senators than seasons, with railway charges than grasshoppers, with land policies than frost, with tariffs than poor yields — indeed, with the many man-made calamities wrought by a distant political and economic system than with the natural disasters faced and overcome.

The Manitoba and North-West Farmers' Union had this to say to the Canadian people at their December 1883 convention:

> We have hopefully faced the hardships of isolation and of a vigorous climate, and have been and are still willing to contend manfully with the natural disadvantages of our new location.
>
> Now, however, that we have for the first time, a surplus of grain, we have discovered that the prices we obtain are not sufficient to cover the cost of production, and that we are face to face with the fact that notwithstanding all our labour and outlay we can barely subsist.
>
> No doubt a combination of unfavourable circumstances such as early and severe frosts, together with imperfect arrangements for saving and marketing grain, have this season aggravated the farmers' condition and contributed to his discontent. Yet the fact remains that those of us whose crops were untouched by frost and who were at the same time most conveniently situated as to markets, realized little or no profit on our produce.[1]

The organized farmers of Manitoba had other grievances: "excessive charges of a railway monopoly"; "an oppressive tariff which, however beneficial ... to the manufacturing Eastern provinces, cannot fail to be inimical to the interests of a purely agricultural country such as this"; and "the improper and vexatious ... administration of the public lands in Manitoba." The convention issued a Declaration of Rights with the following demands:
• provincial rights to charter railways to break the CPR monopoly and speed up branch line construction;

- Manitoba be given "absolute" control of lands and resources;
- abolition of tariffs on agricultural implements;
- a rail route to Hudson Bay;
- legislation granting authority to municipalities to construct grain elevators and warehouses, and mills; and
- establishment of government grain inspection.[2]

These last two demands represented an early effort to begin to take the storage, handling, and grading of grains out of the hands of the private grain trade.

The convention was trying to address the issues confronting settlers daily in their efforts to prosper. Federal settlement policies were a dismal failure — immigration was a trickle, emigration a real problem. The tariff cruelly inflated production and living costs. There were serious marketing problems as a result of a lack of adequate grain storage and of railway branch lines (many settlers were from 50 to 300 miles from the railway).[3] And when the farmers got their grain to market after bone-shaking wagon hauls, they found the grain merchants imposed fixed, low prices, and unreasonably low grades on the grain. Finally, land problems persisted as many settlers found Dominion control of lands frustrated their desire to expand their holdings. But these grievances were hardly novel.

Matters were brought to a head, stimulating the outbursts of sustained agitation in the 1880s, when serious economic problems crippled the early success of the farmers. As early as the 1870s, the superiority of Manitoba wheat was recognized. In 1878 over a million bushels were harvested and the first shipment of Manitoba wheat reached Great Britain. By 1885 almost 7 million bushels were harvested, and in 1890, over 16 million. Manitoba's share of Canada's wheat production leapt from 3 per cent in 1880-81 to over 38 per cent in 1890-91.[4] There had been a significant, even startling, increase in settlement in Manitoba and the Territory. By 1881 Manitoba boasted a population of over 62,000, by 1891, over 152,000. The North-West leapt from over 56,000 in 1881 to over 99,000 in 1891. Occupied farms in the region grew from just over 10,000 in 1881 to over 31,000 in 1891. Acres under crops grew 5 times — 250,000 to 1.3 million.[5] This general success in settlement and grain production, though far from the wildly optimistic hopes of federal politicians, was crushed by a fall in grain prices that set in almost as soon as the growth began.

The decade began well.[6] In 1881 a bushel of No. 1 Northern wheat brought a Fort William price of $1.34. By 1885 the price was 84 cents — a 37 per cent fall. This sharp fall in prices was heart-breaking for settlers who had only just begun to have some modest success. Their very success was being stolen by the price system. But the depression in prices was only part of the story. There was a general rise in the costs of production and living, some of which was due to deliberate federal action. For example, in 1883 tariffs on agricultural implements were upped from 25 per cent *ad valorem* to 35 per cent. Nature also took an additional toll — drought or early frosts hit every crop from 1883 to 1886.

But what rankled farmers most was the pricing system, which robbed them, and the freight rates, which squeezed them. In 1886 wheat sold for 81 cents at Winnipeg, 83 cents at Fort William, and $1.00 at Liverpool. At Brandon, the farmer could only get 53 cents. Grain middlemen who bought the wheat at Brandon could make a profit of 30 cents at Fort William, 28 cents at Winnipeg, or 47 cents at Liverpool. In 1886, it cost just under 20 cents to transport a bushel of wheat from Regina to Fort William, or just over 35 cents from Regina or Liverpool. Clearly the full blame for the big difference between the Brandon price and the other prices could not be completely laid on either transportation costs or the mysteries of international competition. The grain middlemen were taking a handsome share on each bushel, leaving less and less for the farmer. Clearly, too, the CPR was imposing excessive charges when in the same year it was possible to use the U.S. rail system to get a bushel of grain all the way from Duluth to Liverpool for between 12 and 18 cents a bushel. The grain merchants and the railways were clearly fleecing the farmers.

Prairie farmers were from the outset most angry at the policies and shady practices that deprived them of a just return on their crops: the prices they obtained, the tariff they were forced to pay, the excessive railway charges, the land policies, the lack of branch line construction, the absence of adequate storage. In summary, the problem was the lack of a responsible and responsive government that would serve and defend, or even take marginally into account, the farmers' real interests. The 1880s, therefore, witnessed a period of sustained and serious agitation on the Prairies. In the Saskatchewan region, the agitation culminated in the Riel Rebellion of 1885. In Manitoba, the agitation bordered on insurrection, as the settlers and their provincial government defied the federal government and the CPR. The settlers were definitely not listening to the advice of editorial writers, like that of the Saskatoon *Sentinel* who, on August 9, 1884, warned, "We want men of pluck and spirit out here, able to do lots and give their tongues a rest."[7]

In Manitoba, agrarian grievances crystallized

around the demand for the right of provincial governments to charter railways. Such a focus challenged not only the hated monopoly of the CPR, but federal authority in general. Indeed, the Manitoba government could not act on most of the other grievances since they were in federal jurisdiction. A provincial government could, however, speed up the construction of railway branch lines, an essential part of a solution to the farmers' marketing problems. The Manitoba government therefore incorporated the Manitoba South Eastern Railway. In 1882, the Dominion government disallowed the legislation. There was a local uproar at the "paralyzing policy of disallowance," as the Winnipeg *Free Press* described it.[8] Further provincial railway charters were passed and disallowed in a cat-and-mouse game between the province and Ottawa. Finally, backed by an aroused public opinion, the Manitoba government decided to build, as a public work, the Red River Railway from Winnipeg south to West Lynne, near the U.S. border, regardless of the consequences. The CPR threatened to withdraw its workshops from Winnipeg. There were rumours that federal troops would be sent in to stop construction. There were counter-rumours that local farmers were arming themselves. There was talk of insurrection, of annexation by the U.S., of secession, if the Dominion government and the CPR did not yield. The troops were never sent and the railway was begun in open defiance of the Dominion government and its laws. The CPR monopoly was finally broken a few years later.

Like the farmers of Manitoba, settlers in the Saskatchewan region began to organize and agitate. In 1883, a Settlers' Union was formed just east of Prince Albert. Their initial grievances included complaints about federal land policies and political corruption. Blocks of land had been granted to the Prince Albert Colonization Company, an Ottawa consortium of speculators, including a senator. This was done by the Dominion government without regard to the rights of the settlers who had already settled there, on or near the reserved land. "Old" settlers, as they were called, wanted guarantees that the farms they possessed would become theirs; some near the lands in question wanted to expand their holdings but the reserved land stood in the way. Other practices that outraged the settlers, white and Métis, had to do with timber. Officials from the East, usually friends of the government, received contracts for cordwood for the Hudson's Bay Company for around $8 a cord, which they then subcontracted out to locals for from 50 cents to $1 a cord. Even more rankling, settlers had to pay dues for the right to harvest timber for their own use for fuel, construction, and fencing.[9] Whites and Métis alike wanted the right to harvest timber and to contract directly. As meetings were held, however, the grievances and demands of the Settlers' Union went far beyond these initial annoyances to encompass those of their Manitoba brethren and more.

Meanwhile the Métis were agitating for a settlement of their land claims. Ever since the Territory had been annexed by the Dominion, the local Métis had petitioned Ottawa for a settlement of their land entitlements. As the years went by, and as many Manitoba Métis moved to live in the territory, concern grew because of what had happened in Manitoba, where armed confrontation had been necessary to secure the most meagre and unsatisfactory of settlements. In addition to demands for land guarantees, the Métis had regularly petitioned Ottawa for capital to help them begin farming to join the new economy being established in the West. They were ignored, and, as a result, their agitations became more and more frantic. Increasingly, the white settlers and the Métis recognized that they shared similar concerns and that united action might succeed where separate pressure had failed.

Thus a new movement, uniting Métis — French and English — and white settlers, emerged, largely led by the Settlers' Union. On February 25, 1884 a full platform was adopted encompassing all popular grievances in the Territory, including those of the Indians, who, as a result of a policy of deliberate neglect, faced starvation in the midst of appalling living conditions. A later meeting in the spring determined to invite Louis Riel back from exile to lead the agitation. Pleas from the Settlers' Union, in addition to those of Métis leaders, had a great deal to do with Riel's decision to return. Support for the agitation was overwhelming: the press supported it initially and even the Prince Albert Tories toyed with the idea of adopting the platform as their own. The agitational meetings took on the character of a prairie fire, as they spread throughout the Saskatchewan territory and into the Alberta region. By December of 1884 the demands had been exhaustively discussed and codified into the Bill of Rights sent jointly to Ottawa by the Settlers' Union and Riel. The demands were not unreasonable and had been made many times before: better treatment for the Indians; land settlement for the Métis; provincial status; representation in the federal Parliament; control of land and natural resources; changes in the homestead law and regulations; vote by secret ballot; tariff reductions; a railway to Hudson Bay.

The federal government did not respond. They did

not issue the expected invitation to send a Western delegation to Ottawa to negotiate. Macdonald claimed he never saw this petition; the overwhelming historical evidence is that this was a bold lie. Macdonald clearly wanted a confrontation. An election was looming, and he was in trouble. The CPR give-aways were again provoking serious public opposition. The continuation of the depression had turned his 1878 promise of prosperity into ashes. In order to take the additional steps necessary to finish the CPR and to silence his opponents, a crisis in Manitoba and the North-West Territory served his purposes very well. Perhaps, too, Macdonald sought revenge on Riel for the Manitoba crisis: had it not been for Riel Macdonald would not be facing continual harassment by that small province. Whatever his motives, he wanted a final showdown. Officials in Ottawa and on the scene pleaded with him to negotiate — to no avail. He awaited the inevitable.

As the ominous silence from Ottawa made clear, the movement in Saskatchewan would have to move beyond petitioning and negotiation. The petitions had been ignored. No one from Ottawa had offered to negotiate. Confrontation was in the air. Riel's arrival had already frightened the territory press, and many moderates among the white settlers, into silent neutrality, inactive sympathy, or open hostility. Only the bravest and most militant among the white settlers continued to support the movement. Even many English-speaking Métis had been scared off. Riel continued to beg for such support, so essential for final success of the campaign. On one occasion Riel sent a message to a Prince Albert meeting of settlers saying, "Gentlemen, please do not remain neutral. For the love of God help us to save the Saskatchewan."[10]

Riel's subsequent declaration of a provisional government, and the determination of the Northwest Mounted Police to put a stop to the rebellion, frightened off most remaining white settler support. Riel and the Métis, supported by a few Indians allies and a handful of white settlers, stood alone against the Dominion.

Riel had never wanted an open military conflict. Throughout the agitations he had expected negotiation. He had refused to make serious military preparations. When military action began, Riel refused to give Gabriel Dumont, the military commander of the Métis forces, a free hand to use hit-and-run tactics to harry the police and the troops.[11] As the final conflict approached at Batoche, the Métis capital, Riel insisted on staying in fixed position rather than scattering to begin a guerrilla war. Faced with inevitable defeat in a battle of fixed positions with the Canadian troops, Dumont nevertheless organized an admirable defence. Had Dumont been free to organize a serious military campaign from the outset, the Métis forces may well have been able to inflict sufficient casualties, as well as to prolong the conflict for weeks or perhaps months, putting further pressure on Ottawa to negotiate. In the event, the movement was decisively militarily defeated at Batoche and the Métis nation was crushed. Riel and eight Indians went to the gallows. Many others went to prison, while others, including Dumont, fled to sanctuary in the U.S. Still others trekked northward, where their descendants today live. Two white settlers, prominent leaders of the Settlers' Union, were acquitted. Canada, from sea to sea, had exacted its first payment in blood.

The results sent a crystal-clear message. The

Dominion government would not tolerate opposition to its plan for the West. Central Canada's vision, especially Ontario's, of the opening of the West would remain Canada's. The Indians were brought to heel by the executions and by the imprisonment of some of their proudest leaders. The Métis nation was defeated, their homes burned and looted, their people, especially their leadership, dispersed in what can only be described as an act of attempted genocide. In the ensuing hysteria, the farmers' movement was discredited as Macdonald blamed the Rebellion on their ceaseless agitations. Although responsible government and provincial status was refused to the North-West until 1905, some small concessions were made. The CPR monopoly was broken and provincial involvement in constructing branch lines was won. The crisis spurred the CPR to speed up branch line construction. Federal representation was won for the region in the House of Commons. But all this was really a pittance. The main issues raised were brushed aside and ignored as the Dominion relished its triumph.

Macdonald won his 1887 election, an election most observers believed he must inevitably lose before the uprising. Canada paid a heavy price for this cynical victory. The settlers in the West were deeply embittered by what happened — it was the beginning of a distrust of the federal government that was never to be extinguished. The people of Quebec were deeply embittered by Macdonald's pitiless and blind determination to hang Riel though, as he himself said, "every dog in Quebec bark in his favour."[12] Macdonald saw his chance to win solidly in English Canada and he was sure Quebec would forgive and forget, as it had forgiven and forgotten so often before. This time Quebec did not and to this day the Tory party pays the price for what was, in fact, a legal political murder.

The CPR speedily got the funds it needed, thanks to the Rebellion. Van Horne, CPR general manager and vice-president, jested that the CPR should erect a monument to Riel.[13]

Meanwhile, the farmers on the Prairies redoubled their agitations.

4

"The Man Behind the Plow": Agrarian Populism and the Farmer Governments

As the crisis of the 1880s unfolded in the West, the federal government, the CPR, and the private grain trade were taking the necessary steps to ensure the orderly and privately controlled export of Prairie grain. In 1883 the CPR mainline arrived at Winnipeg and the company completed its first lakehead terminal at Fort William. In 1884 the first shipment of Prairie wheat through the Canadian transportation system reached Europe. In 1886, federal government grain inspection was established at Winnipeg and Port Arthur. In 1887 the Winnipeg Grain and Produce Exchange began operations.[1]

Due to serious problems getting the 1888 crop speedily to market, the CPR offered local monopolies in grain handling to anyone willing to build modern grain elevators at key points on rail lines. These line elevator companies pursued their advantage through deliberate undergrading, unfair dockage, high storage charges, suspect weigh scales, and low prices. As well, farmers saw the speculators in the Grain Exchange filching their profits as prices were often depressed in the fall, when most farmers had to sell, and high during other times of the year when grain moved from storage to market. Government inspectors harshly suppressed farmers' grades and seemed to act more as agents of the grain merchants than public officials. Terminal elevators mixed low and high grades, selling the mixture at the higher price, in which the farmer did not share.[2] Such abuses lead to deep anger and bitterness among the farmers. As W.R. Motherwell, first Territorial Grain Growers' Assocation president and later a federal Liberal minister of agriculture, put it:

> While this sort of thing continued for twenty years it so calloused and hardened the people against everybody and anybody in authority that the farmers were willing to do almost anything to obtain redress... There are few... who know how near the people were to resorting to violence...[3]

The farmers, temporarily disoriented by the hysteria after the Rebellion, re-organized quickly.

The Patrons of Industry, already long active in the U.S. and in Ontario, began to organize at Portage la Prairie in 1891. Their official aim was clear and blunt: "to protect both farmer and employee against the over-powering influences of the financial and commercial classes."[4] The Patrons' 1892 Brandon convention endorsed the now-familiar demands of Prairie farmers, but added some new ones: farmer ownership of grain elevators and flour mills; provincial banks to loan money at five per cent; farmer representation on the Grain Standards Board. In that year their Prairie membership reached 5,000.[5] Of great significance was the fact that the Patrons in the West were allied with Ontario's organized farmers, active since the 1870s, and aspired to build a national organization from the outset. The Patrons made other innovations: they established consumer co-operatives for twine, coal oil, and coal; they unsuccessfully tried a binder twine production co-operative; they published their own newspaper; and they went directly into politics. In 1896 two of seven Patron candidates in the Manitoba election won office. In 1894 the Ontario Patrons had won 17 seats. As well, in the 1896 federal election the Patrons fielded 29 candidates, winning 3 seats; and in 1897 they won a federal by-election. Most significant, in terms of what was to come, the Patrons pioneered organized grain growers' co-operation by establishing a grain elevator at Boissevain in southeast Manitoba. They were the first farmers' organization to do so, although by 1898 individual local groups of farmers co-operatively owned 26 of the 447 elevators in the West. The Patron decision to go into politics had deeply split the organization and it disintegrated almost overnight — but they had shown the way.[6]

This continuing agrarian agitation gained some quick concessions from the new Laurier Liberal government. The Crow's Nest Pass Agreement of 1897 was a landmark. In exchange for building a rail line from Lethbridge through the Crow's Nest Pass to Nelson, B.C., the CPR, as usual, got a generous public subsidy. However, the new Liberal government demanded that the CPR help redress some of the farmers' grievances through significant freight rate reductions on grain and flour moving eastward, as well as on crucial industrial agricultural inputs, such as machinery and fuel, moving westward. This agreement established the principle of some statutory regulation of freight rates on the movement of grain. Most importantly, at the time, grain production became more viable by cuts in transportation costs. In 1899 a Royal Commission on the Shipment of Grain was appointed, reporting with amazing speed in 1900 that the farmers' grievances were well founded. Again, the federal government acted quickly, passing the *Manitoba Grain Act* that year. The Act, hailed as the "Magna Charta" of the grain producer, proclaimed what the farmers wanted. But the Act failed completely, its provisions for farmer access to load their own cars and fairer grading practices ignored with impunity by the CPR and the private grain trade. This growing disappointment was hardened on the question of the tariff. During the 1896 campaign Sifton had promised tariff relief: "Free coal, free oil, free clothing, and free implements you shall have if the Liberal party are returned to power."[7] Indeed, he had gone further at one point, no doubt in response to the cheering enthusiasm of his rural electors, promising that a Liberal government in Ottawa would "wipe off the statute book the villainous protection policy" that had "taken the heart's blood out of the people of Manitoba."[8] The Liberals declined to deliver this promise, even reneging on the limited list of free items. Only in 1907 were some small reductions made on certain items in response to Western demands. As a result, the farmers continued to view both parties with suspicion. A Tory government refused to act at all; while the new Liberal government, after great promises, only pretended to act in ways that were increasingly seen as either hesitant or useless.

Therefore the early years of the 20th century witnessed great changes in the agrarian agitation. The small victories squeezed from Laurier were viewed with contempt and, despite the wheat boom, the abiding conviction among Prairie farmers remained that a fair share of the return on their crops systematically failed to reach their pockets. The farmers quickly learned that many of their earlier specific demands had little to do with the structural problems they confronted. They had agitated for branch lines: now they had branch lines. They had agitated for better grain handling facilities: these were now available. They had agitated for government terminals: a small breakthrough had been made. They had wanted fairer grades: now they increasingly had these.

Inevitably they came to see more clearly that the primary sources of their grievances lay with the whole grain marketing system itself as well as with the general economic policies of the federal government. As a result the agitation developed two distinct if related thrusts. On the one hand, the farmers fought for changes in the marketing and handling of grain. On the other, the organized farmers developed a sustained populist offensive against the economic terms of the National Policy, the basis of Confederation, as well as against aspects of modernizing capitalism. It was in this context that new grain grower organizations were founded.

Thanks to the CPR and the private grain trade, the organizing went extremely well. In 1901 the farmers again experienced great difficulty getting their grain to market, due, they were convinced, to the CPR's manipulations and inefficiency. This year they publicly denounced it as the "Blockade of 1901," and went on the offensive, successfully taking the CPR to court at Sintaluta, Saskatchewan. The Territorial Grain Growers Association (TGGA) was founded that year at Indian Head. The Manitoba Grain Growers Association (MGGA) was founded in 1903. And with the creation of Saskatchewan and Alberta in 1905, the TGGA became the Saskatchewan association (SGGA), while competing farmer groups in Alberta finally united into the United Farmers of Alberta

(UFA) in 1909. That year all three Prairie associations joined the Canadian Council of Agriculture (CCA), uniting with the 9,000 farmers in the Dominion Grange of Ontario (later the United Farmers of Ontario). By the summer of 1910, when Laurier visited the Prairies, the Prairie organizations had over 23,000 members: 9,000 in Manitoba, 6,000 in Saskatchewan, and 8,500 in Alberta.[9] (In 1911, there were just over 40,000 occupied farms of over 50 acres in Manitoba, almost 95,000 in Saskatchewan, and about 60,000 in Alberta. The organized farmers were weakest in Ontario, where there were just over 148,000 such farms in 1911.[10]) Nationally, they now commanded a formidable organized force in excess of 30,000 farmers, and their influence was growing. In response, the private grain trade organized the North West Grain Dealers' Association and began to engage in price-fixing, as well as lobbying against the increasingly militant farmers.

The conflicting agitations, the claims and counter-claims, led to the establishment of yet another Royal Commission on the Grain Trade in 1906, which once again sustained the farmers' case. But the organized farmers did not rest on their laurels. Rather, they began a detailed inquiry of the Winnipeg Grain Exchange and the whole private grain marketing system. The conclusion of this investigation was a shock: rather than demanding legislative controls and penalties on the private grain trade, the farmers decided to organize a farmers' co-operative grain company to engage in marketing from farmgate to international market. In 1906, the Grain Growers' Grain Company (GGGCo) was founded and went to work to win farmers to a new and radical solution to their problems. Success was phenomenal — by 1910, 9,000 farmers marketed their grain through the company.

In efforts to maximize the return to the grain grower, the farmers were on the march to eliminate the grain middle-men through the construction of farmer-owned marketing companies to gain control of the storage and sale of the harvest. This struggle ultimately led to the establishment in the 1920s of the great Wheat Pools, which culminated in final victory. Today the Prairie Wheat Pools are among Canada's largest corporations and dominate the domestic grain trade. The pooling idea, whose seeds were planted by the GGGCo, finally ensured that farmers got the full market return for their crops, less a fair cost for marketing. The successes obtained by the organized farmers in the marketing area contributed to the self-confident thrust of their more political agitation. This agitation was nothing less than a national effort to reform the party system, to hold in check the advance of industrial capitalism, and to transform the root economic policies of the whole nation. Its focus was the protective tariff and it took on the character of a crusading class struggle.

The Agrarian Crusade, 1910-1930

In December 1910 the Canadian Council of Agriculture brought over 800 delegates from Ontario and the West to a "Seige on Ottawa." Parliament and the nation were presented with the Farmers' Platform of 1910, the clearest expression of organized agrarian thinking to that point, marking the opening salvo in the general political agitation. The demand for free trade was the centrepiece of the document. As well, the petition expressed the deep concern among farmers at

advancing rural depopulation as industrial capitalism
marched relentlessly forward:

> Believing that the greatest misfortune which can befall
> any country is to have its people huddled together in
> great centres of population, and that the bearing of the
> present customs tariff has the tendency to that condi-
> tion... the greatest problem which presents itself to
> Canadian people today is the problem of retaining our
> people on the soil, we come doubly assured of the
> justice of our petition.[11]

The platform also called for a series of specific reforms
and government interventions, most of direct interest
to farmers.

Laurier was impressed with what he had seen in the
West in the summer of 1910, and this early winter seige
helped convince him to make some concessions to the
farmers. In 1911, with one eye to the farmer agitations
and the other to eastern industrial capitalist opinion,
Laurier determined on a course of limited reciprocity
with the U.S. in an effort to strike a politically judicious balance between what were contradictory
claims. In late January, 1911 the federal government
announced a new trade agreement with the U.S. The
agreement was complex, establishing free trade in natural products and on a number of semi-processed
industrial commodities, as well as schedules involving
mutually agreed lower tariffs on specific items, especially farm machinery. The overall impact was
nowhere near what the farmers wanted, but as a result
of the implacable opposition of prominent capitalists,
the agreement caused a political furor, which led to a
Liberal defeat in the famous 1911 Reciprocity
Election.

The farmers saw the agreement as the first step in

dismantling the hated tariff economy. The Canadian Manufacturers' Association (CMA) agreed, but feared it as the prelude to more serious free-trade policies. The debate became near hysterical: supporters of the policy were accused of disloyalty, of treason, of selling out to the Americans. The opposition from commercial, banking, and industrial capitalists in Toronto and Montreal was so effective that prominent Liberals deserted Laurier. Even Clifford Sifton, that erstwhile Manitoban champion of free trade, broke with Laurier, joining the opposition. The Liberals reeled under the onslaught, failing either to confront the issues directly or to mobilize free-trade opinion effectively.

The results of the election were not only a defeat for Laurier but, it was thought, a final staggering blow to free-traders. The Tories swept Ontario, 73 seats to 13. The Liberals only narrowly won Quebec, 38 seats to 27. The parties split Atlantic Canada. The agrarians rewarded Laurier's small efforts, with 8 of Saskatchewan's 10 seats and 6 of Alberta's 7 seats. Yet Manitoba, under Sifton's influence, went Tory 8 seats to 2. And B.C., always solidly behind the National Policy in these early years, sent 7 out of 7 Tories to Ottawa. Of 221 seats, the Tories took 134. Once again Canada had voted for the National Policy. Free-trade, even the limited policy of Laurier, had failed to convince capitalists or workers.

Even the staunch free-trading farmers were deeply split, as the Manitoban results attested. Clifford Sifton's argument that free trade in natural products would hurt the farmer had been as effective there as similar arguments had been among B.C. farmers, fishermen, miners, and lumbermen. Sifton had painstakingly documented that prices gained by Canada's farm products in the U.S. would be, in many instances, far lower than those prevailing in Canada. Furthermore, he suggested that the Canadian meat packing industry would be destroyed, allowing U.S. packers to pay as little as possible for farm products in the future. Most importantly, he argued that the destruction of the autonomous, east-west Canadian grain market would deliver Canadian farmers forever into the hands of the U.S. grain merchants. In B.C. the suggestion that the loss of the Canadian east-west market in fish, minerals, and lumber would, in the long run, lead to lower prices and less industrial development in canning and wood products, was just as compelling.[12]

Yet the 1911 results did not discourage the organized farmers; on the contrary, they urged themselves on to greater efforts. As Edward and Annie Porritt, in a 1913 anti-tariff polemic published by the *Grain Growers' Guide*, declaimed:

> The victory of the Conservatives... forms the best possible proof of the immensity and difficulty of the task of education and liberation which still lies before the grain-growers of the West and the common people of Canada who do not belong to the small and privileged class which profits from protection.[13]

The farmers learned three clear lessons in 1911. First, they could not effectively influence either federal party when in power. Second, those who had all along argued for a peoples' party had won their point, though it took some additional time to win the argument. Third, the sources of the 1911 defeat sharpened the farmers' understanding of the powers ranged against them: The Canadian Manufacturers' Association, the banks and financial interests, the railways, the commercial interests. Further, the British nationalist hysteria generated during the anti-Laurier election showed farmers just how far their foes would go to secure victory. Politically the defeat furthered the discrediting of the two old parties, already well-advanced, by showing the Tories at their worst and by revealing that Liberal equivocation even in marginal efforts did not serve the farmers' cause well. Rather than retreating, therefore, the organized agrarians went on a new political offensive, staging a Second Seige on Ottawa in December, 1913, and declaring,

> in 1913 it is still the manufacturers of Ontario and Quebec, who through the power conferred on them by Conservative Governments, and continued after 1897 by the Liberals, levy toll to the full statutory limit on this population west of the Lakes; and likewise on the rural populations in Ontario and Quebec and the Maritime Provinces.[14]

1911 was an important year for the farmers for a reason other than the Laurier defeat. 1911 was a census year and the figures portended the decimation of rural Canada and the final triumph of urban industrial capitalism. The "greatest misfortune" that the 1910 Platform had so feared was on the immediate historical agenda. Nationally, rural population had fallen to just over 54 per cent.[15] More significantly, more and more of the labour force, about 66 per cent, were involved in non-agricultural occupations.[16] Moreover, the number of occupied farms had fallen dramatically in the older parts of the country, especially Central Canada.

Even on the Prairies, where the number of occupied farms continued dramatic increases, the rural share of population had fallen from 75 per cent in 1901 to 65 per cent in 1911.[17] These trends were bitterly lamented by the organized farmers and they blamed the tariff unreservedly. The 1916 version of the platform attributed "the declining rural population ... largely to the increased cost of ... everything the farmer has to buy, caused by the Protective Tariff, so that it is becoming impossible for farmers ... to carry on farming operations profitably."[18] Further, the sheltered industries in the cities served as magnets, drawing population to the higher wages and shorter hours made possible by the tariff. Clearly, the farmers believed, the abolition of the tariff would lead to a return of people to the countryside where work on the land or in the villages awaited as the unnaturally supported industries declined in the absence of protection.

The related themes of the economic injustice of the tariff and rural depopulation became cornerstones of the 1911 to 1921 agrarian political offensive. The sharpness and vigour of the movement surprised many. The political and economic critique of the forces oppressing the farmers, and all common people, was generalized. The two old parties were dismissed, increasingly seen as indistinguishable in their loyal service of vested interests. The critique turned to capitalism itself and parliamentary democracy, very much from the point of view of the small agrarian capitalist. Condemnations of the capitalist plutocracy, of the money power, of special interest, and of the New Feudalism became wide-spread.[19] Add to these the repeated attacks on the corruption of "partyism" as an enemy of true democracy and it becomes clear just how extensive the organized farmer critique became.

The farmers, in the words of one of their polemicists, supported measures that would "revolutionize the whole established commercial system" and denounced those "parasites" who took for themselves an "Unearned Increment." Demands that politicians support the proposals, and the politicians' refusals, led to denunciations of the "nose-pulling game of Party Politics." "A pitched fight between capitalistic groups and the people at large, led by the farmers" was envisaged. The farmers would triumph. "What chance will Special Privilege have against the public desire for Equal Rights?" Songs like "The Day of Right" (to the tune of the "Battle Hymn of the Republic") reverberated in community halls across the Prairies:

> The farmers of the prairie lands are massing in their might,
> Exulting in a Principle, a Cause for which they fight:
> The sacred cause of Justice, the establishment of Right
> And Equal Rights to all.

> CHORUS: Oh! 'Tis time to get together
> You will help us get together;
> Pledge we all to stand together,
> For the days of Peace and Right.

> The farmers of the prairie lands have right upon their side;
> Their platform is the people's, democratic, nation-wide;
> Their cause, the ancient cause for which brave-hearted men have died —
> Of Equal Rights to all.

> The farmers of the prairie lands know well the foe they fight,
> The Profiteers of Privilege, full armed with legal right;
> Against that giant bluff we aim to solidly unite
> For Equal Rights to all.[20]

The ultimate goal became "the establishment of GOD'S

KINGDOM upon earth."[21] If the national leadership of "the Man behind the Plow"[22] were embraced by all, it was asserted, "in the place of the deep furrows of dissension will be the level seed-bed of greater unity among men."[23]

The intensity of the agitation, and the success of the agrarian organizations, both accelerated with the bust of 1913, the war of 1914-18 and the post-war depression of 1920-23.[24] The wheat boom broke in 1913, beginning an unexpected depression. Wheat prices collapsed and drought slashed the crop of 1914. General industrial and construction unemployment skyrocketed. The export prices of other natural resources fell. Investment contracted. The depression showed signs of becoming deep, general, and long. Only the arrival of World War I saved Canada from economic calamity. Overnight the depression was replaced by a war-induced boom. Prices for Canada's natural resource exports rose — in the case of wheat, astronomically. Industrial production spiralled.

There was, however, a dark side to the boom for the agrarians, as manufacturing's share of the value of exports grew from 13 per cent in 1913 to 31 per cent in 1918, while agriculture's share fell from 55 per cent in 1913 to 48 per cent in 1918. There were other dark portents as the boom inflated farm production costs, pushed up the cost of credit, and ballooned the public debt. Generally farm prices, though good, zigged and zagged as production costs marched steadily upward. Yet the farmers achieved some remarkable successes, moving Canada from its pre-war place of third among world wheat exporters, to second by 1918, to first by 1923. Prairie acreage in field crops increased by 84 per cent between 1914 and 1920, while the Prairie population went up another 19 per cent.

Although the Prairies did well out of the war, Central Canada, as the focus of capitalist industrialization, did even better as industrial and finance capitalism grew to maturity. Growing urbanization confirmed the worst fears of the organized farmers when Central Canada emerged from the war as the industrial heartland of the nation. Paradoxically, the war therefore laid the basis for an aggravated sense of grievance and disillusionment. War profiteering, inflation, high interest rates, the unequal sacrifices demanded of agriculture (price controls were imposed on wheat), combined with cynical calls for patriotism, all were viewed as further evidence of the abject dishonesty and hypocrisy of the political system and the two old parties. The demands for a farmer-led peoples' party became irresistible. In 1916 the *Grain Growers' Guide* declared,

> The time has come when the Western representatives should represent Western people and Western views and cut off connections with the privilege-ridden, party blind, office-hunting Grit and Tory parties that make their headquarters at Ottawa.[25]

In 1916 another edition of the Farmers' Platform was issued by the CCA and it appeared that the farmers would enter the next election. The 1917 conscription election nipped the move in the bud, as the Union Government walked to an easy victory.

With the war's end the agrarians again went on the offensive. In 1919 a further edition of the Farmers' Platform was submitted to member organizations of the Canadian Council of Agriculture, and finally revised for the 1921 election. The document, called "The New National Policy," was more far-reaching and complete in its proposals than earlier editions.[26]

The tariff still occupied centre stage, standing accused of fostering combines and trusts which engaged in shameful "exploitation," of causing rural depopulation, of making "the rich richer and the poor poorer," of being the "chief corrupting influence ... in national life," and of lowering "the standard of public morality." Free trade was the principled panacea. The document also advocated a reformed tax system, a series of political reforms to deepen democracy, a more sympathetic approach to returned soldiers and trade unions, and public ownership of transportation and energy resources.

Armed with this policy the organized farmers marched into political action federally as the Progressive party. A large part of their arsenal was the postwar depression, which ravaged the Canadian economy. Between 1920 and 1923, wheat prices collapsed by 67 per cent. Real incomes dropped dramatically, exports fell off, and industrial unemployment almost tripled. Very quickly the organized farmers won some notable victories. In the 1919 election the United Farmers of Ontario (UFO) won the largest bloc of seats and formed a minority government. In 1921, the UFA swept to 14 years of secure majority rule. And in 1922, the United Farmers of Manitoba won majority power as well.

Most significant, however, were the national results of the 1921 federal election.[27] The Progressives won 65 seats with 23 per cent of the vote. They swept the Prairies: 11 of 12 seats in Alberta, 15 of 16 in Saskatchewan, and 12 of 15 in Manitoba (with popular votes of 57 per cent, 61 per cent, and 44 percent respectively). In B.C. they won 2 seats and 9 per cent and in Atlantic Canada, 1 seat with more than 10 per cent of the vote in each province. No seats were won in

Quebec. The Ontario results marked the Progressives' most impressive political achievement, 24 seats with 28 per cent of the vote. Thus the Progressives' biggest single bloc of seats and of votes came from Ontario, a fact often overlooked by those who focus on the massive popular support won on the Prairies in efforts to paint the Progressive movement as a regional rather than a national movement. The fact is that in 1921 there was no section of the nation, except Quebec, where the Progressives had not made a presentable showing, certainly enough to form the electoral basis for a new agrarian-led peoples' party with the ultimate capacity to govern. It was the organized farmers' finest hour in politics and they appeared to have reached the threshold of political success in turning the nation around. Yet the party faltered and collapsed almost overnight. Why?

Probably it is correct to say that the Progressive refusal of the chance to become the Official Opposition in Ottawa and thereby to adopt the party system ensured its failure. Yet no one should be astounded at that principled decision given the previous 20 years of agitation. It would have quite simply been impossible for the Progressives to have embraced the party system, having denounced it for years as a main source of evil and corruption in political life. Such a decision would have broken the Progressives on the day after the election. The problems were much deeper and were exhibited by the farmer governments in the provinces.

The federal Progressives were a loose coalition of the various provincial farmer organizations. There was no coherent, separate and united, national political organization. The federal agrarian Progressives were solely united around the New National Policy document, and there was little unity on other policy matters. Urban labour had only returned a handful of Progressive MPs, and they found little real sympathy for labour's plight among the more numerous agrarian MPs. The provincial farmer governments were wholly independent, able to pursue their courses with little or no input from either the federal organization or other provincial organizations.

After winning office, federal Progressive MPs, and the farmer provincial governments, rode off in all directions in a spectacle of disunity and policy incoherence that discredited them in the eyes of the electorate. In Ontario, the minority farmer government behaved as a typical party government and, when the rank-and-file organization refused to broaden out to include membership from other popular classes (like workers and teachers) to increase its base of support, its fate was sealed. The United Farmers of Manitoba government, always reluctant violators of political norms, despite its majority, gradually edged back into the Liberal fold, unclear about just what a farmers' government should be doing. In Alberta, the farmer government, its comfortable majority and tradition of militancy providing no excuse, imposed rigid cabinet government and party discipline on MLAs, failed to respond to demands for reform from its membership, and governed unimaginatively until 1935.

The organized farmers had no clear idea about what to do with power after getting it. There was no agreement on how to win the necessary support of the working class. Even the Labour MLAs invited into cabinet in Ontario and Alberta failed to influence the governments to become more generally responsive on labour, minimum wage, and social welfare policies. There was no agreement on the principles needed to guide practical political organization. Survival of the organizations in politics required that they move toward becoming general political organizations of farmers, workers and other sympathetic classes, with a more broadly responsive political program and an effective mechanism for continuing policy development. Such sentiments were unsuccessfully expressed by a minority.

The farmer governments, and the federal Progressive party, decided to remain decisively farmer oriented. There was no agreement on the role of the government in the economy. There was no real policy worth the name, except the principles and polemics of the New National Policy and vague notions of the need for sound, business-like, honest government. Before going political the organized farmers' coherence had had its source in their critique and lamentations; after going into politics, especially after notable victories, there was no coherence. During the federal elections of 1925, 1926, and 1930 their disintegration was as remarkable as their rise, and almost as speedy.

The Progressives had been truly a meteoric political phenomenon, entering and exiting the effective political stage in five years. Yet they had a significant impact: they wrung some significant concessions from the Liberal government and Canadian politics were never as certain as they had been prior to the agrarian onslaught. Most importantly, they won significant concessions for their agrarian base, which helps explain their demise.[28] In 1922 they won the restoration of the Crow's Nest Pass statutory freight rates, suspended in 1919. They also won significant tariff relief on agricultural implements and motor vehicles, some federal farm credit assistance, and the re-establishment of the Wheat Board (suspended in

1920). As well, the Progressives, especially their urban labour members, pushed the government toward the first hesitant steps in constructing the modern welfare state. Such concessions may have taken the edge off their popular support, but the fact is that the crisis in the Progressive party and in the farmer governments merely revealed a crisis at their base.

The united farmer organizations reached their peak in members in 1921, followed by rapid declines in the next year or two: in Ontario, 60,000 members to 30,000; in Alberta, 38,000 to 15,000; in Saskatchewan, 29,000 to 21,000; in Manitoba, 16,000 to 6,000.[29] The decreases were greatest in those provinces where power was won. It is ironic that at the height of what appeared to be their greatest political hour, the organized farmers were disintegrating. The farmers very quickly left overt political action. By 1923 the United Farmers of Ontario declared its withdrawal from politics, devoting itself to educational and co-operative work. And the Canadian Council of Agriculture withdrew support for national political action, leaving politics to provincial organizations, thus removing the national focus for the Progressives. These decisions ended the brief intrusion of the organized farmers into national politics, indeed, into provincial politics, except for the farmer regime in Alberta, a lonely shell that, in its rigid conservatism and unrelenting lack of imagination, reminded everyone of the failed promise.

There is no doubt that the return to prosperity after 1923 undercut the agrarian political offensive. Wheat production and exports regained and surpassed wartime highs. Prices were good, though still unstable from year to year. Nature wrought no general disasters. There was money to be made and hard work to be done. The boom of the 1920s accelerated the mechanization of Prairie agriculture as well as witnessing the final completion of the setttlement process. The organizational skills of the farmers after 1923 were focussed on building voluntary wheat pools at the provincial level, necessitated by the Manitoba Legislature's refusal to go along with the Wheat Board legislation passed by Ottawa, Saskatchewan, and Alberta. Increasing the return to the farmer through co-operative marketing seemed a more sensible expenditure of time than ceaseless political agitation. Great success rewarded the farmers' efforts when by 1930 the three Prairie Pools had almost 56 per cent of Prairie farmers under contract and controlled one-third of total Prairie elevator capacity.[30]

But it must be said that the most important grievances of the organized farmers remained unaddressed. True to its increasingly sophisticated political habit of granting just enough concessions to blunt the sharpness of any troublesome agitation, the federal government had astutely avoided conceding anything of real importance to the farmers.

The tariff, despite modifications, remained essentially intact. The near-complete reliance on grain production remained to plague Prairie prosperity. Rural depopulation continued and industrialization and urbanization accelerated remorselessly. Control of natural resources was denied the Prairie provinces until 1930, when settlement was completed. What security had been gained had been won by the self-organization of the Prairie farmers into co-operative pools. Control over the costs of production continued to elude the farmer. High interest rates continued to take much of the cream of any profits. Railways continued to impose their freight rates with impunity, save for the small measure of relief granted by the Crow Rate. Grain merchants made up for their setbacks in the domestic market by clinging to their shrinking share of the market, and diversifying their investments. The political clout of agrarian Canada, and of the Prairie West, continued to be virtually ignored but for this or that gesture of conciliation flung by the federal government. The prosperity of the 1920s turned out to have the substance of a house of cards.

During the first round of Prairie agitations, Riel and his efforts had won great sympathy in Quebec and deep hostility in Ontario. In this second round, the farmers had won significant support in rural Ontario and indifference in Quebec. The pattern of Canadian politics seemed ominously set. And Prairie grievances, once again, were locked up west of the Lakes.

5
Socialism and Syndicalism: The Rising of the Working Class, 1870-1919

As the farmers' agitations developed and matured, those of the West's working class led inexorably to the 1919 confrontation at Winnipeg and the aftermath of repression. The agrarian movement believed in small capitalism, yet yearned for basic reforms, and mounted a near-effective challenge to the party system and the National Policy. The Western workers' movement generally embraced varieties of socialism or syndicalism, anticipating the final overthrow of capitalism. The farmers dreamed of a society based on co-operation, reason and compromise, free of class conflict and special privilege. The workers agreed that this was a dream, asserting that co-operation, reason, and compromise had never got the workers anywhere. The farmers owned land, which they wanted to keep, expand, nurture, protect. The workers had no land, nor any hope of getting any; all they had was their labour to sell for a wage. The capitalist plutocrats may have coveted the farmers' land, imposed low prices on grain, charged high interest and freight rates, and squeezed them with the hated tariff. From the worker, all the capitalist wanted was labour, as much as could be had at the lowest possible wages, regardless of the risks to health or life for the workers.

The Western working class provided the vital labour essential to the settlement of the West.[1] They came in hundreds of thousands to take the jobs in the booming West. They worked in coal and hardrock mines. They built the towns and cities, the homes, schools, and hospitals. They dug the sewers. They laid the track for two transcontinental railways. They cut the trees, sawed the lumber, processed the pulp. They provided the year-round labour on the farm as well as joining the harvest trains for the few weeks of hard work each fall to bring in the Prairie crop. The jobs they found were in resource extraction, construction, transportation, manufacturing, and agriculture. Many of them were migrant, moving to where there was work, and, when the job was finished, moving on to the next mine, construction project, or logging operation. The same worker might cut pulp wood in Western Ontario in the winter, dig sewers in Winnipeg in the spring, mine coal in Alberta in the summer, join the Prairie harvest in the fall, and move on to a B.C. logging camp for the next winter. The "lucky" ones settled into the permanent jobs running the railway, working in the new cities in sundry occupations, digging in the more prosperous among the mines in Alberta and B.C.

Many had come with great expectations of a better life with more opportunity and prosperity, some even dreaming of owning a farm. What they found was low wages, high living costs, appalling living conditions, dangerous jobs, and ruthless employers. The coal mines of B.C. and Alberta were the most dangerous on the continent: from 1889 to 1908, 23 men died for every million tons of coal extracted in B.C. — the North American average was six fatalities per million tons. Things in the coal mines barely improved from

1908 to 1918, when over 12 men died in B.C. and Alberta for every million tons, while just under five per million died in the U.S.[2]

Many mines, coal and hardrock, were remote company towns or camps where workers were charged exorbitant fees for family shacks or space in a bunkhouse. Charges were deducted for weigh services, for non-existent medical services, and for blasting powder. Often miners were paid in scrip, acceptable only at the expensive company store. Frequently miners were paid a contract price that fluctuated with world prices and took no account of increases in the cost of living. Ten- or twelve-hour days and six-day weeks were commonly necessary to earn a living wage. Railway construction camps were often worse, work often harder, demanding 12 hours a day in a seven-day week. Workers arrived at the job site in debt for transportation charges and saw their pay packets reduced by costly room and board and high prices at the company store. Some foremen enforced work discipline with fists and threats, and some railway camps kept armed guards to protect railway property. Remote lumber camps were just as bad. Ten-hour days and six-day weeks were the norm and, again, workers frequently arrived in debt for travel costs. No matter how bad conditions were, workers were forced to work at least as long as it took to pay off the debt and to accumulate enough to travel on. Such camps and company towns were notorious for their poor food, their vermin-ridden quarters, and lack of even minimal sanitation. Those who escaped death or maiming in the dangerous work were often at risk as epidemics of typhoid fever and other infectious diseases attacked bodies already weakened by hard labour and poor food. Conditions in the working-class districts of the new Western cities were not much better. High rents, overcrowding, and minimal services turned such districts into ghettoes of impoverished humanity.

Resistance and rebellion, therefore, were not simply matters of justice, they were frequently matters of survival. Safer conditions, a living wage, decent food and living quarters, and security for the families of those maimed or killed, became matters of great concern. Workers from the mines of Vancouver Island to the manufactories and skilled trades of Winnipeg began to organize trade unions. By today's standards their demands were modest. The right to collective bargaining, decent wages, safer conditions, shorter work days, a day off in seven, workers' compensation for injured workers and the families of those killed on the job, were what they asked. The employers' opposition to unions was implacable and ruthless, buttressed by politicians and governments. Union sympathizers were fired and blacklisted. Strike leaders were jailed. Spies and detectives reported on union activities as well as acting as *agents provocateurs*. Strikes were met by machine guns and militia, and governments colluded with employers to bring immigrants in to scab. Striking railway workers lost their pension rights. Striking miners and their families were driven from their homes in company towns. The near-universal response among employers was that unions were seditious and treasonous, threats to the Canadian way of life, a short step away from flagrant insurrection. Government officials and politicians agreed, and lent their weight to the employers' side in what was already an unequal battle. An examination of the events surrounding two strikes, one in Winnipeg in 1906 and one on Vancouver Island in 1912, illustrates this unyielding attitude of business and government to trade unions in this era.

In March, 1906 the Winnipeg Street Railwayman's Union went on strike against the streetcar company, demanding higher wages, shorter hours, improved safety measures, and union recognition.[3] The strike had been provoked when the company arbitrarily fired two members of the union's negotiating committee. The company brought in scabs to run the streetcars, and private detectives to protect company property, resulting in widespread demonstrations of public support for the union. The demonstrations continued, disrupting the operation of the streetcars, and a number of instances of violence and property damage occurred. The company's subsequent demand that the militia be called out was acceded to by civic authorities. The militia was brought in, the Riot Act read, and the crowds dispersed by troops armed with rifles with unsheathed bayonets and at least one machine gun. Public support, a boycott of the streetcars in working-class districts, and mediation efforts by the clergy brought the strike to a speedy end. The workers were granted some of what they asked, but not clear-cut union recognition. And union recognition was the first demand in all early trade union struggles because not only did such recognition mean that employers would have to bargain for formal collective agreements, but union organization and activity among workers could not be punished by firings and blacklisting.

The 1912 strike of miners in the Nanaimo coal fields was merely another in a series of sharp clashes between capital and labour that began there as early as the 1850s. The Dunsmuir coal empire had been the major protagonist for capital, the United Mine

Workers of America for labour. James Dunsmuir, a
one-time B.C. premier, had publicly declared, "I
object to all unions... I want the management of my
own works, and if I recognize a union, I cannot have
that."[4] His remedy for all union activity among his
miners was simple: he "fired the heads of the union,"
"every time," as he himself admitted.[5] The mine
workers had been defeated in strikes in 1903 and 1905,
and union organization had disintegrated. However,
continuing problems with dangerous and poor working conditions, and low pay, combined with persisting
repression of union activity to precipitate a strike in
1912, this time against Canadian Collieries Ltd.,
which had bought out the Dunsmuirs.[6]

The strike began with over 3,000 miners out, but
quickly spread to involve over 7,000 miners in a two-
year strike (September, 1912 to August, 1914). In
efforts to continue production the companies brought
in immigrant labour to strike-break, had martial law
declared in the district, and imported special police to
protect the scabs. Several incidents of violence between strikers and scabs justified the final decision to
bring in the militia in August, 1913 to begin what was
to be a 15-month military occupation. The strike was
finally broken: 256 strikers were arrested, five were
sentenced to two years in jail, 23 to one year, and 11 to
three months. One striker died in Oakalla prison due
to a lack of medical attention. Although a public
campaign finally led to the pardoning of 22 of those
convicted, the battle had confirmed the deep chasm
separating capital and labour. As one of Dunsmuir's
partners had put it:

> The battle... is one of principles. It is labour versus
> capital, and... the question is: How far labour is to be

> supported in lawlessness?... Surely there can be no
> question whether the Government should support the
> law or not so long as capital has the law on its side,
> about which surely there is no doubt.[7]

Such implacable attitudes, and repeated defeats did
not deter the struggle for trade unions. Indeed the
workers in the West persisted, as they did all over the
world, and continued to organize and to agitate, confront the great myths and promises of their society
with the dreary reality of their labour and their lives.
On the Prairies, however, the polarization was muted
by the farmers. Capital and labour frequently squared
off in polarized confrontation, especially in Manitoba
and Alberta, but the farmers, often critical of both
sides, set the tone of Prairie politics. Both workers and
employers had to defer to the agrarian umpire on the
Prairies. This was not the case in B.C.

The Working Class in B.C.

The Western working class made its biggest mark in
B.C. The farmers there were too few to be significant,
and always conservative. The B.C. working class
therefore became the real opposition in the province,
the sole repository of a vision of an alternative, more
just society. Even as early as 1870 wage workers in
mining, trade, and manufacturing made up almost 69
per cent of the wage labour force, agriculture accounting for the rest. In 1872 products of the mine made up
75 per cent of B.C.'s exports, falling to 60 per cent in
1881.[8] B.C. was and remained a province of workers,
and their bosses, not of farmers. By the 1931 census
only six per cent of B.C.'s adult male wage workers
were involved in agriculture (there were only just over
26,000 farms), while nine per cent were in forestry and

fishing, six per cent in mining, 20 per cent in manufacturing (most resource-related in the wood, pulp and paper, fish-canning industries), and the rest in transportation, trade, finance, and service jobs.[9] It was, therefore, a province polarized between the capitalists, who owned the economy and dominated the political parties and the government, and the workers, who were virtually powerless.

The first trade unions in B.C. began to organize in the 1850s in what remained a bitter struggle. Employers showed no quarter, forcing the unions to re-double and intensify their agitations. In response to the implacable opposition of employers, and the seeming hopelessness of orderly change, B.C. workers became increasingly radical. Notions of revolutionary socialism emerged. The only solution to the workers' plight, it was argued, was political education and action until a majority of workers voted socialist. Although as early as 1882 trade unionists ran for office, it was not until 1898 that the Socialist Labour Party emerged, followed by a series of organizations, often working at cross purposes, until the Socialist Party of B.C. emerged. In 1900 the first socialist labour MLA was elected in Nanaimo. In 1903, three were elected, one Labour and two Socialists, giving them the balance of power between contending business groups. By 1912, two MLAs elected by the Socialist Party became the Official Opposition for a time. Despite repeated failures to find a third reform road, real politics in the province remained polarized between capital and labour. Out of this polarization there developed two thrusts in B.C. labour politics — radical socialism and syndicalism.

By 1904 the Socialist Party of B.C., as a result of its electoral successes, had been convinced to become the core for the Socialist Party of Canada (SPC). It was Marxist, militant, and revolutionary and it dominated socialist politics for almost a decade. The SPC propounded the doctrine of "impossibilism" in response to the bosses' intransigence. Their views could not have been more blunt and direct: capitalism could not be reformed; trade unions were largely useless efforts; the only solution was to build working-class consciousness leading to concerted political action and revolutionary change. The SPC were unique in the history of socialism, even of revolutionary socialism, demanding and wanting no reforms. Many B.C. workers flocked to the SPC banner because "impossibilism" explained the daily dismal reality — bosses granted no concessions and ought to be given none. Practically, however, SPC members and supporters were in the forefront of winning reforms and concessions of real significance to workers. For example, their early efforts led to the eight-hour day in mines and improved safety conditions. In terms of the ultimate goal, they remained impossibilists — capitalism had to be entirely overthrown.

Another stream of working-class thought emerged in B.C., more attuned to the reality of trade union struggle, and less directly politically oriented — syndicalism. The syndicalists were just as radical as the impossibilists, perhaps more so. In its purest form syndicalism conceived a coming together in one big union of all wage workers whereupon a general strike would bring down capitalism and the state in preparation for a genuine socialist democracy. They were militant, courageous, uncompromising. And they had great success because they began to win some immediate results — improved food, more adequate quarters, better pay. Pure syndicalism gave way to a more pragmatic variety — the general strike became not a tool of revolutionary transformation, but an industrial strategy to bring employers to their senses; the sympathetic strike became not a prelude to a general struggle for an anarchist utopia but a practical means of supporting fellow unionists on strike. As a result, syndicalism in Western Canada became an intelligent way to fight bosses unwilling to grant even the least concession of union recognition. Syndicalism in B.C. ceased to be solely a vision of the final revolutionary apocalypse. The general and sympathetic strike became tactics in the industrial guerrilla war that emerged between bosses who refused to recognize the unions which refused to disappear.

Unions like the Knights of Labour, the B.C. Loggers' Union, the Western Federation of Miners, and the United Mine Workers, as well as a series of unions in the construction trades and crafts, waged a series of bitter struggles for union recognition and collective bargaining rights. Though often ineffective in winning long-term recognition; such struggles forced employers to improve conditions. Effective strikes often hit employers hard, undermining their profits and giving their competitors an edge. Therefore, while often declining to deal directly with the unions, employers slowly began unilaterally to respond to what they decried as a wave of industrial terrorism. The union most feared by employers was the Industrial Workers of the World (IWW), which began organizing in Western Canada in 1906, obtaining an estimated membership of 10,000 by 1911.[10] The IWW's influence spread far beyond its own membership — their devotion and attacks on the "porkchoppers" of the older unions inspired workers, while impelling less militant union leaders to respond to persistent challenges for leadership.

Wherever there was a dispute, a strike, a particularly rotten boss, the IWW's organizers, sort of itinerant preachers of pure syndicalism, would appear. Few mines, logging camps, construction sites, or harvest trains of the era failed to contain at least some adherents of the IWW, if not a leading organizer. Miraculously mattresses and sheets appeared in bunkhouses, food became better, wages improved, coal scales became less dishonest. But these were small victories often won at great expense, and the basic rights of collective bargaining still eluded most unions in the West.

Yet failure and repression seemed not to discourage the workers, but only to push them further down the road of militancy and revolutionary thought. Commitment to the need for independent working-class political action, and to at least a modified form of syndicalism, became characteristic of virtually all Western trade union activists. Some were moderate labour supporters, others social democratic reformers, others revolutionary socialists, still others revolutionary syndicalists. But on a number of things they began to unite to form a coherent Western bloc in Canada's trade union movement: the need for independent working-class political action, the need for militant strike tactics, the need to organize on an industry-wide rather than a craft basis, and the utility of syndicalist forms of strike solidarity and struggle — the general and the sympathetic strike.

The Trades and Labour Congress of Canada (TLC) was a moderate and conservative trade union central based in the more traditional craft unions. These craft

unions represented workers with the traditional skills
— such as carpenters, plumbers, painters, and plaster-
ers — and argued that organization should be primarily along craft lines. Thus on a large construction site,
or in a large industrial plant, many unions representing the different skills would be active. The problem
this posed for most Western workers was simply that it
was irrelevant to the realities they faced, except perhaps in the larger Western cities where craft organization made some sense. However, this left out the
masses of unskilled and semi-skilled workers in the
West.

Western trade unionists therefore were among the
first in Canada to push industrial unionism — the
need to organize all workers on a job or in a factory
into one union, or, indeed, all workers in an industry
(miners, loggers, labourers) into one inclusive union.
Their experience had been that only a complete shut-
down served the workers' cause. They also argued that
a general strike in a whole industry — like coal mining
— might be necessary to win concessions. At least,
they argued, workers in various locals might want to
support the actions of striking brothers through a
series of sympathetic strikes, putting pressure on an
employer from other employers.

The TLC did not like this talk of general and sympathetic strikes. Increasingly committed to continental
or international unions, the TLC wanted all its
members to affiliate with American unions, most of
which were deeply conservative and anti-political. Not
surprisingly, the TLC was highly critical of independent working-class political action. This would divide
workers, they argued; the best political strategy was to
act as a pressure group on the existing parties and to
throw labour's support to the candidate or party

expressing most sympathy for labour's case. Generally, the TLC leadership became increasingly nervous about the growing militancy and revolutionary sentiment among their Western comrades. As a result, TLC conventions became scenes of increasingly fractious clashes between radical Western delegates, led by B.C., and the more moderate Central Canadian representatives. This polarization finally resulted in a deep cleavage in the TLC.

The Prairie Working Class

On the Prairies the working class was outnumbered by the farmers. In fact, Prairie farmers were the employers of thousands of workers, permanent and seasonal. For example, in 1913, there were an estimated 200,000 farmers on the Prairies, 49,000 farm wage labourers, 50,000 non-agricultural wage workers, and as many again involved in trade, finance, clerical, service, and professional work.[11] In 1921 B.C. may still have been a rural province, but it was not a province of farmers. By 1931, B.C. had become a decisively urban province and the farm sector remained very small, employing only 14 per cent of the gainfully occupied. On the Prairies agriculture remained dominant, employing a huge share of the gainfully occupied — in Saskatchewan and Alberta, a decisive majority. All other Prairie occupations, as Table 5-1 demonstrates, remained overshadowed by agriculture. The opposite was the case in B.C. Manitoba was the most working-class province on the Prairies, but even there agriculture remained the leading sector of employment. The Prairie working class therefore found their complaints constantly drowned in the clamour for reform from agrarian organizations.

As a result, only in Manitoba, especially Winnipeg,

Table 5-1

Urban and Rural Population Percentages, Number of Occupied Farms and Distribution of Workforce* in the West, 1921 and 1931

	Manitoba		Saskatchewan		Alberta		B.C.	
	1921	1931	1921	1931	1921	1931	1921	1931
Population								
Urban	43%	45%	29%	32%	38%	38%	47%	57%
Rural	57	55	71	68	62	62	53	43
No. of Occupied Farms	53,252	54,199	119,451	136,472	82,954	97,408	21,973	26,079
Occupations								
Agriculture	40%	35%	65%	60%	53%	51%	16%	14%
Mining	0.1	1	0.1	1	4	3	5	3
Forestry, fishing and trapping	0.3	2	0.3	0.2	0.4	1	8	7
Manufacturing	8	8	3	4	5	5	11	11
Construction	5	5	2	2	3	3	6	6
Transportation	7	8	4	5	5	6	8	10
Labourers	7	10	3	5	5	6	12	14
Clerical	9	7	4	3	5	4	7	6
Trade, finance and services	24	26	17	19	20	21	26	28

*Per cent of gainfully employed (aged 10 years and over) by occupation group.
Source: *Census of Canada, 1931*. All percentages are rounded to the nearest whole number except those under 0.5 per cent.

and in Alberta, was the working class able to assert itself with anything approaching general influence. In Winnipeg, working-class leaders were moderate and restrained in comparison to their B.C. counterparts, and were quite successful in putting forward labour's case, sending the first labour-oriented MP to Ottawa in 1900. But even moderation did not save Winnipeg's trade unionists from the same fate as the B.C. militants. Employers were just as implacable in their refusal to recognize a moderately led trade union as they were one led by militant syndicalists. As we have seen, the government in 1906 lent the same complete support against unions in Winnipeg as they did in the Nanaimo coal fields. In Alberta, the miners shared the militancy of their B.C. counterparts, and, in common with Manitoba and B.C., established an early independent socialist political presence. Strikes in Alberta's mines were regularly suppressed by police, and Alberta governments typically supported employers in their refusals to deal with the unions. In Saskatchewan, the working class was weakest and had no significant impact on the province's politics until the founding of the CCF in 1932.

The working class in Saskatchewan more completely faced the problems shared by all Prairie workers. The Prairie working class was very dependent on the prosperity of the Prairie farmer. Wage-work in virtually every sector — except perhaps industrial and construction work in Winnipeg and mine work in Alberta — was directly or indirectly related to servicing agriculture. Good times in agriculture meant jobs; hard times, lay-offs. Furthermore, unlike B.C., which was more or less polarized between workers and employers, Prairie politics were increasingly dominated by the farmers. Prairie workers, therefore, not only had to contend with traditional employer hostility to unions in the daily economic struggle, but also with the political necessity of winning their case among the grain growers. Furthermore, as small employers, grain growers, who relied on seasonal labour, and often some year-round labour as well, did not generally support ideas like universal minimum wages and reduced work days. Indeed, when such concessions were finally made, rural and small-town labour were excluded in the legislation.

Grain-grower organizations often complained of the high cost of labour in the same breath as they complained of high freights and low grain prices. As well, Prairie farmers were appalled and disturbed by the deep class conflict that was emerging, usually denouncing both sides, while presenting themselves as the great reconciliators between antagonistic capitalists and strike-prone workers. Furthermore, the working class' main weapon — the strike — provoked deep hostility among farmers. Strikes in transportation, grain handling, meat packing, flour milling, and so on, were seen as direct threats to the prosperity of the farmer. Strikes in all branches of industry were viewed as at least indirectly increasing the farmers' costs of goods as manufacturers were forced to pay higher wages. The grain growers were highly ambivalent, therefore, in their attitudes to the working class and its trade unions. While often sympathizing with the plight of the exploited worker, the grain grower could not unreservedly support general working-class demands.

Yet there was a significant minority opinion within the grain growers' organizations supporting thoroughgoing farmer-labour unity. Even the early Grange in Ontario had called for an alliance between the "toilers of the field" and the "toilers in the city." But this fine sentiment did not prevent the Grange from rejecting support for an 1886 TLC call for an eight-hour day by saying, "It would be impracticable on the farm, a waste of valuable time, and must necessarily lead to an increase in the price of the products of labour."[12] In Alberta, the Society of Equity, a radical agrarian group that helped to create the UFA in 1909, had long supported the need to unite farmer and worker in the same organization to fight the "Special Interests." Yet in the UFA they remained a minority if active opinion. Henry Wise Wood, who later became the dominant leader of the UFA and its major ideologue, explained farmer hostility to labour in 1907 by saying, "the farmer was an employer and a capitalist."[13] That view expressed the majority sentiment. Later the Non-Partisan League, which forced the UFA into direct politics, abandoned its advocacy of a coalition of farmers, workers, and returned veterans, and of an "open door" to labour to join the UFA, without too much fuss.

Trade unions and labour political parties on the Prairies therefore found themselves reduced to generally supporting the farmers' major demands in exchange for dubious and uncertain support on only a few of labour's demands. This was understandable. The interests of farmers and workers were quite different. Farmers were small capitalists who owned land and engaged in commodity production for a capitalist market. It was in their interests to have high prices, low freight rates, low input costs, as well as low wages and long hours for farm wage labour. Further, farmers were deeply concerned about the growth of unions among urban labour, fearing that higher wages for fewer hours of work would inevitably push up the costs of things they needed — consumer goods, machinery, fertilizer, and transportation. Farmers also had a deep affection for high prices for products of the farm — eggs, milk, wheat, beef, and hogs. Workers wanted cheap food, the cheaper the better. Further, workers wanted higher wages, legal limits on the daily hours of work, legal minimum wages, new social welfare benefits, union recognition, and the right to strike to win their demands. Consequently, the uneasiness of relations between farmers and workers was to be expected. Certainly, farmers and workers began to co-operate, but it was hesitant, sometimes hostile, always distant.

The tariff question was a case in point. On a national basis working-class opinion was deeply divided on the tariff. Central Canadian workers were generally pro-tariff since they believed that protection created industrial jobs. Prairie workers, who derived little direct benefit from the tariff in the form of jobs, tended to support the farmers' case for free trade. The tariff increased the Western worker's cost of living. Yet Prairie workers did not go the whole distance on the tariff that Prairie farmers went — for Prairie farmers the tariff became the center of their complaints, for Prairie workers it remained a significant but still minor grievance. Agrarian calls for fairer freight rates, better grain prices, and orderly marketing, all were supported by Prairie working-class organizations. In exchange they got very little — Prairie farmers remained leery of minimum wages, the eight-hour day, trade unions, and strikes. Western workers and farmers did unite on more general Western grievances — the control of natural resources, a bigger voice for the West in national affairs, complaints about the failure to diversify the Western economy, and so on.

But many of the workers' employers also echoed such complaints.

As well, Prairie workers and farmers agreed about the need to stop unrestricted immigration — again for different reasons. The workers saw immigrants used repeatedly as scabs to break strikes and knew from experience that the presence of immigrants could only push wage rates down. The farmers saw unrestricted immigration as putting severe strains on the land base and the local government infrastructure. Prairie workers and farmers also united on demands to dismantle the system of "Special Privilege." But each group meant something quite different. For the farmer, dismantling "Special Privilege" meant tariff abolition and a return to free trade, small capitalism. For the worker it meant trade union rights, an end to government intervention on the side of the employer in labour struggles, and, ultimately, for many, the achievement of socialism. As well, farmer and worker united on the need for the political reform of the party system to ensure a deeper, more responsive democracy, as well as on the need to begin the construction of the welfare state — the establishment of a "social wage" in the form of a minimum social, educational, health, and economic security net for all. But again, the trade unions and the labour parties pushed the idea of the welfare state more persistently and further, while for the agrarian organizations such reforms were incidental to getting rid of the hated tariff. As a result, efforts at farmer/labour unity generally foundered in attempts to bridge the great gaps that separated the immediate and long-term interests of both groups. There was, therefore, never a marriage, not even one of convenience, of the two groups; rather there were a series of temporary liaisons, usually leaving both groups dissatisfied.

Upsurge, Defeat, and Small Victories

The coming of World War I temporarily dampened the growing general agitation among Canadian workers, except in the West. Western Canadian trade union leaders, as well as labour and socialist political leaders, did not stampede to embrace the patriotic appeals for a united war effort. Some opposed the war on the grounds of international solidarity among workers; others on the grounds of principled pacifism; still others out of the pragmatic fear that the few gains made by labour might be stolen during a war crisis, screened by calls to patriotism. Many Western workers, much more ethnically diverse than those in Ontario and Atlantic Canada, were less willing to answer the calls to patriotism from the same groups who were willing to describe some of them as "alien scum."[14] For many among the non-British Western working class there was little eagerness for this British war.

Central Canadian trade unions were more divided on the issue, especially as the war-induced boom in industry saw the growth of many jobs at good wages. The war boom was less directly beneficial to the Western working class. Prairie workers shared in the general increase in agricultural prosperity, but they did not share in much of the industrial growth. B.C. workers hardly benefitted from the war boom at all. Unemployment in B.C. remained high, lay-offs remained commonplace, and many B.C. workers joined the line to enlist more out of desperation than patriotism. Indeed, during the war, many B.C. workers receiving lay-off or termination notices in their pay envelopes, also received the following note, "Your King and Country need you — we can spare you."[15]

As the war continued, and as the human carnage in the trenches of Europe mounted, it became clear that conscription would be necessary to fulfill Canada's military obligations. Western workers, especially those in the trade unions and the labour and socialist political parties, were deeply opposed to conscription, in common with Quebec. Western farmers were not enamoured of conscription, though less deeply hostile to it. In fact, Western labour and farm organizations had mounted a general criticism of war-profiteering, of incompetence in the administration of the war, and of the evil consequences of a party system that was unable even to meet a national crisis without conniving to exploit it in favour of the Special Interests. They had called for the conscription of wealth before the conscription of men.

This Western sentiment, which doubtless would have found reflection in independent farm and labour candidates in the coming federal election, was a large part of the reason for the formation of the Union government. The prospect of Liberals and Tories splitting the pro-conscription vote in English Canada, especially in the West, perhaps thereby allowing the election of a large number of independent farm and labour MPs in the West, as well as Laurier's determination to continue as Leader of an anti-conscription Opposition, even if it reduced his Liberal representation to Quebec, would make a war-time conscription election uncertain.

Determined to avoid such uncertainty, Prime Minister Borden asked Laurier to join a war-time coalition based on Borden's conscription policy. Laurier refused, and refused again when Borden tried to sweeten the deal by a promise not to proceed with conscription until after an election. Therefore the Union government was formed uniting the governing Tories and only the anglophone Liberal opposition, and the 1917 election was called. Just before calling the election, determined to leave nothing to chance, Borden had Parliament pass the War Time Elections Act. This Act disenfranchised all Canadians naturalized since 1902 and all war objectors, while giving the vote to adult females in the immediate families of men in the armed forces and to all men stationed overseas.

The outcome was inevitable — the Union government swept to power, decimating the opponents of the government's war policies, including conscription, in English Canada. Laurier won decisively in Quebec and clung to significant popular support in the rest of the country, thanks to a deep popular fear of conscription. Borden and the Union government swept the country in terms of seats, but the civilian vote had only given him a majority of 100,000 votes. The addition of the military vote increased this to 300,000. It was a decisive parliamentary victory, but still an uncertain popular one (much of the farm vote, for example, had been won from opposition to conscription by a last-minute Order in Council exempting farmers' sons).[16]

Despite Borden's win, Western labour leaders did not cease their opposition to conscription. There were demonstrations and riots. Many were fired from their jobs. Some went to prison for draft violations. One prominent B.C. labour leader was shot in the back by Dominion police in his efforts to evade the draft. As inflation shot up, strikes and trade union agitations continued unabated in an effort to stop the decline in real wages. Western delegates took resolutions to the

TLC convention calling for opposition to conscription, up to and including a general strike. They were defeated, denounced as strongly by other trade unionists as they were by overzealous patriots from coast to coast.

As the war ended, Western trade unionists found themselves on the defensive. Increasingly, with the victory of the Bolshevik Revolution in Russia in 1917, an event they cheered publicly, they faced not only the ongoing hostility of employers and governments, but they also confronted the accusation that they were proponents of a Bolshevik Revolution in Canada. The end of the war also brought depression, unemployment, and wage cuts. This situation was to the employers' advantage — and they pressed this advantage. But the trade unions refused to yield, and polarization and confrontation increased. In the last year of the war, 1918, there were 169 strikes, more than there had been in the three previous years.[17] Most of the big strikes occurred in the West. The Union government responded with regulations under the War Measures Act banning strikes and a number of left-wing organizations.

Trade unions, having won such sparse victories, had nothing to lose in pushing their case, even during the post-War depression. Employers, fresh from the war boom and the political victories over conscription, saw even less reason why unions ought to be taken seriously. Indeed, they argued, pointing to Russia, unions were the harbingers of socialist revolution. Therefore, employers redoubled their efforts to defeat the trade unions, deepening the absolute polarization between capital and labour. The economic conditions of the time would today have undercut unions. Then, they spurred unions on to greater efforts. Returned veterans found little work, leading to growing disillusionment. Trade unions had two choices: fight or surrender. They intensified the struggle. In the West, more radical leaders came to leadership, even in traditionally moderate unions. Such leaders at least had some kind of strategy for struggle. More and more of the traditional craft unions in the West voted for industrial unionism. With the war's end therefore, Western trade unions — the longstanding syndicalist as well as the traditionally moderate — became increasingly radical politically and increasingly militant industrially. Even Winnipeg, long the bastion of the moderates among Western workers, elected a more radical leadership to the local Labour Council.

These events culminated in the March 1919 Western Canada Labour Conference convened at Calgary. Almost every Western Canadian trade union was represented. A decision to secede from the TLC and to form a Western labour central, the One Big Union (OBU), was passed overwhelmingly. The conference endorsed industrial unionism, the tactics of the general and the sympathetic strike, as well as making a series of immediate demands to be met under threat of a June 1, 1919 general strike. Politically the conference endorsed socialism, calling for the abolition of capitalism, and applauded the Bolsheviks in Russia and the Spartacists in Germany.

The scene was obviously set for a serious confrontation between capital and labour, particularly in the West. Though the battle could have been fought out in any of the major cities, especially Vancouver, events determined that the confrontation occurred in Winnipeg.[18] The story of the Winnipeg General Strike has been well told. In early May, 1919, the metal and building trades went on strike for union recognition, the eight-hour day, and improved wages. The employers refused to bargain. The strikers asked the Winnipeg Labour Council for support, whereupon the Council held a general strike vote among all Winnipeg trade unions asking for a living wage, the eight-hour day and union recognition backed up by signed collective agreements. A strong majority voted to strike. The walkout started on May 15; 24,000 trade unionists went out on strike. Soon thousands of Winnipeg's non-union workers joined them. It became truly a general strike. Across the country tens of thousands of workers joined in sympathetic strikes — involving 80 strikes and over 88,000 workers, mostly in the West. This general support for the strike was solid, even startling, yet it was far short of the general strike of syndicalist dreams. Many workers were supporting the strike, but not enough. Soon thousands of veterans were on the march in support of the strike, over 10,000 on one occasion in Winnipeg. This active and growing support among veterans, who were, as a group, deeply divided by the strike, gave great cheer to the strikers. Among government officials, however, it created dread. If the veterans werc to go over to the strike, actively and en masse, many officials believed, the situation could become seriously out of control.

The federal government therefore was convinced they faced revolution and acted accordingly. RCMP, regular military and militia reinforcements were brought to Winnipeg, including at least one armoured car and over a score of machine-gun squads. The entire Winnipeg police force, with the exception of the officers and two constables, was dismissed because of sympathy for the strike. They were replaced by special constables (largely recruited from among Winnipeg's middle and upper classes, anti-strike veterans, and farmers) whose inexperience and zeal created confusion and unnecessary violence. Firings of strikers began to spread, especially among civil servants.

In Ottawa a series of legal measures were put in place to aid authorities in efforts to break the strike on the grounds that it was seditious, including an amendment to the Criminal Code to allow the deportation of foreign-born agitators, which was passed in less than twenty minutes (this law affected all who were not Canadian born, including those from the U.K.). Later, Section 98 was added to the Criminal Code defining "unlawful associations" as those that advocated violence as a means of economic or political change and imposing draconian prison sentences of up to twenty years for membership in such organizations. Attendance at a public meeting was considered evidence of membership. Section 133 of the code was repealed, erasing any guarantee of freedom of speech. On June 17 six of the most prominent strike leaders were arrested, as well as a number of other militants from various organizations, 11 men in all, and charged with sedition.

After the arrests the expected collapse of the strike did not occur. Indeed, protest and support increased in the West and began, ominously, to grow across the country. Now demands included the release of those arrested. Even violent police baton attacks on peaceful demonstrators had the effect of redoubling support for the strike. On June 21 a silent parade to protest the arrests and the police violence was called. The Riot Act was read and the parade of men, women, and children was attacked by RCMP and Specials on horseback, swinging baseball bats. When this brutality failed to disperse the demonstrators, the police drew their guns and began firing into the crowd without discrimination — two were killed, 30 injured, 100 arrested. Military rule was imposed on the city, as armed military patrols and machine-gun nests became commonplace on the streets. The strike was broken and as the defeated, but still defiant, workers went back to work they faced severe, wholesale economic reprisals. The workers had been taught that employers, backed up by the government, were prepared to use all the force necessary to break the strike. Further resistance would have led to yet more bloodshed.

This suppression of the strike in Winnipeg was buttressed by authorities with a series of night-time raids of offices of trade unions and ethnic associations, and of homes of trade union and socialist leaders. This occurred not only in Winnipeg; the authorities settled accounts all across the Dominion, breaking in doors, searching homes, taking records, files, books, papers, membership lists, and correspondence. These actions were justified by the authorities as necessary for the collection of evidence to be used at the sedition trials. But the vehemence with which they asserted their police state powers over trade unionists and left-wingers indicated a desire to intimidate and to avenge. Eight strike leaders were charged with seditious conspiracy. Seven of eight were found guilty: one was sentenced to two years, five to one year, one to six months, another was found not guilty. The message was clear: determined industrial action by the trade unions, especially if it became generalized, would be repressed by all means possible. Agitations for a living wage, for an eight-hour day, and for collective bargaining rights were declared to be seditious.

The OBU reached its peak in membership during and immediately following the strike, with some 50,000 members (there were only about 380,000 trade

unionists in all of Canada in 1919, out of a work force
of over two million).[19] Yet it was clear to all that the
one serious application of industrial syndicalism had
failed — the general and the sympathetic strike was
ineffective when confronted by severe and determined
state reprisals. And contrary to the federal government's claims at the Winnipeg show trials, the major
leaders of the OBU were not Bolsheviks and revolu-
tionists, since none had advocated meeting state violence with revolutionary violence, the only real
alternative to final surrender. Indeed, the leaders had,
throughout the strike, counselled moderation, peaceful demonstration, and orderly protest; in fact, when
the police attacks began the leaders had advised
against further demonstrations.

The labour movement, therefore, despite the
momentary strength of the OBU, in the aftermath of
the Winnipeg defeat, saw a re-assertion in the West of
moderate labourism and traditional, business unionism, replacing the radicalism of syndicalism. A concerted coalition of government officials, employers,
and moderate trade unionists very quickly isolated the
OBU. Unable to win any gains in the face of government harassment and employer refusals to bargain
with OBU-led unions, the OBU saw its membership
returned piecemeal to moderation as more conservative unions won recognition and contracts with surprising ease. As well, advocates of moderate socialist
politics made great gains in elections immediately following the strike. In 1920 in Manitoba Labour elected
11 MLAs, including three imprisoned strike leaders,
and in 1922, six Labour MLAs were returned. In
Winnipeg, Labour candidates won three seats on the
school board and three on the council. In 1921 in
Alberta Labour elected four MLAs and a Labour

member was appointed to the UFA cabinet. In B.C. Labour took three seats in 1920 and 1924. Federally, two strike leaders were elected in Winnipeg as MPs, one in 1921, joined by a colleague in 1925.

Hence, radical syndicalism, though itself defeated, had set the stage for some modest working-class victories. More moderate trade unions began slowly to win recognition and collective bargaining rights. More moderate labour political parties established themselves permanently in the politics of the country. These working-class organizations kept alive the reform sentiment to replace the earlier militancy, which continued to be husbanded on the sidelines of the working class by the declining OBU and the newly formed Communist Party. The repression of the Winnipeg General Strike, the police raids across the country, and the punitive show trials had defeated the insurgent Western working class as the boom of the 1920s replaced the post-war depression. The road to workers' rights through the militant tactics of syndicalism appeared to be permanently blocked. More modest approaches to union recognition, and the establishment of a moderate working-class political presence, seemed to be the only way out of the defeat after the confrontation.

As well, the strike and its aftermath enhanced the problems of building a serious alliance between the farmers and labour. Farm organizations were deeply disturbed by the confrontation at Winnipeg and its aftermath. Their hostility and suspicion of the working class and its main tools of struggle — the trade union, the strike, the socialist party — deepened. Although labour was given a seat in the 1921 UFA Cabinet, this gesture was not repeated in 1926 or 1930. In Manitoba, labour MLAs and UFM MLAs had great difficulty co-operating — which only increased after the UFM won government in 1922.

A year after the Winnipeg strike the UFM President said, "The seeds of Bolshevism... are like wild oats — they will only grow when all the conditions are favourable... If we are disposed to criticize the labourman... much of the criticism is just, in fairness we should remember that men and women have wrought and toiled under the worst possible conditions."[20] This reflected the organized farmers' deep ambivalence toward labour. A year later, in an effort to distance farmers from Labour's repeated calls for socialism, he said, "There is... a very distinct limit beyond which it is not wise to go in the direction of state control of industry and commerce."[21]

Federally, the basis for farmer/labour unity laid out for the Progressive party in the run-up to the 1921 federal election was a bitter disappointment for labour. All the manifesto could reluctantly bring itself to advocate was that a "spirit of co-operation" ought to guide negotiations between capital and labour. Unemployed veterans were further offended by a section of the platform that suggested that men be kept in the army until work could be found. And the *Farmers' Platform Handbook*, published by the *Grain Growers' Guide*, laid out a very self-interested basis for farmer support of workers' demands for better pay, "An underpaid worker is a detriment to the farmer for he is a potential customer who cannot buy."[22] On the big issues facing the working class the farmers remained silent. Indeed, where the farmers won power in the West, Alberta and Manitoba, provincial government policy of hostility to trade unions and strikes remained largely unchanged.

The rising of the Western working class was massively defeated. Radical ideas, revolutionary socialist politics, and militant industrial tactics had been largely discredited, if only because of fear of ruthless state repression. Moderation had triumphed, but in its moderate triumph the working class had been granted some apparent concessions, if only to further discredit radicalism and to innoculate the working class against its return. Trade unions, collective bargaining, and some social reforms slowly began to be gained. A moderate socialist political presence had been permanently established. Farmers and workers had learned more clearly what to expect from each other, resulting in less ambitious efforts at unity in the future.

Most significant of all, trade unions gradually came to be accepted as an inevitable fact of life in Canada; but the structural problems confronting the Western working class remained — dangerous work in uncertain industries at unsatisfactory wages. And the establishment of trade unions and collective bargaining rights remained an uphill struggle against resisting employers and unsympathetic governments. The defeat at Winnipeg forced the Western working class to accept a smaller share of the boom of the 1920s than they had appeared prepared to accept in 1919. Yet finally the beating and shooting of innocent marchers, and the imprisonment of strike leaders, had merely instructed the Western working class on the limits set on what they would be allowed to have. Such events did not stop them from yearning for a life better than the one employers and the authorities were willing to permit. The legacy of the Western upsurge and the events at Winnipeg became a permanent fixture in Canadian politics — haunting the employers with the worst to be feared; inspiring workers to contemplate what again might have to be done.

6
Devastation and Protest: The Depression in the West

No one expected the collapse on Wall Street in the fall of 1929 to begin a decade of economic hardship. Indeed, it was not until the Depression was two years old that people, citizens and experts alike, began to realize how serious the situation had become. No one was prepared for the bleak years of the 1930s, especially farmers and workers. The farmers' organizations had withered throughout the 1920s and were, therefore, ill prepared to lead a fight for economic security and justice. The trade unions, and labour-based social democratic parties, had declined seriously in membership and influence throughout the 1920s and were in no position to recommence a general offensive to fight the Depression. But then, as the 1920s came to a dramatic end in 1929, few believed there was any need to worry.

The Great Depression was a world-wide disaster. Canada, as a predominantly resource-exporting nation, was particularly hard hit. Between July 1929 and December 1932 the prices for Canada's 17 major exports fell 53 per cent, export prices for farm products fell a full 70 per cent, industrial production fell 48 per cent, and employment fell 33 per cent.[1] The national averge per-capita income fell 48 per cent.[2] It was an economic downturn of unprecedented proportions. Canada's world markets contracted and the prices for her principal exports fell rapidly.

But if the Great Depression was a disaster for Canada, for the Western provinces it was cruel calamity. It was especially so since it followed so quickly on the heels of a brief period of prosperity, which had begun to heal earlier wounds. And it was cruel because the incidence of the Depression was even more unevenly experienced in Canada than all previous depressions had been. The West, almost exclusively a producer of resources for export, felt the full force of the collapse. The declines in average provincial per-capita incomes between 1929 and 1933 were greatest in the four Western provinces: Saskatchewan, down 72 per cent; Alberta, down 61 per cent; Manitoba, down 49 per cent; B.C., down 47 per cent (Quebec and Ontario each experienced a 44 per cent decline). Prairie agriculture was the worst hit, suffering a 94 per cent decline in net money income from 1929 to 1933. The fisheries, crucial to B.C. and Atlantic Canada, were not far behind, suffering a 72 per cent drop in net money income. Most importantly, although the prices of all Canadian exports fell an average of 40 per cent from 1929-1933, resources from the West fell further, faster.[3]

Meanwhile, the net money incomes of those employed in the protected manufacturing industries fell 37 per cent, while those who earned interest income from bonds, life insurance, and farm mortgages actually increased their net incomes by 13 per cent. Although most groups experienced sharp income declines, some groups improved their relative positions because they experienced less sharp declines. Canada's farmers' share of the national income fell from 15 per cent in 1929 to 7 per cent in 1933, whereas the share of the national income won by wage and salary earners in the tariff-protected industries improved marginally (1929, 14 per cent; 1933, 15 per cent). As well, salaries and wages in the so-called "naturally" sheltered industries and occupations (transportation, communication, merchandising, government, education, banking, insurance, and the professions) markedly improved their relative positions: earning 29 per cent of the national income in 1929 and 35 per cent by 1933.[4]

In other words, the Depression struck hardest at farmers, farm workers, fishermen, lumbermen, and miners, less hard at those in protected central Canadian industry, still less hard at those in the middle-class professions, while actually initially benefitting finance capitalists. Clearly, the unemployed across the country, conservatively 25 per cent of the wage labour force, along with the Prairie farmer and farm worker, faced the brunt of the economic collapse. But even here there was a regional inequity as the collapse of the Western resource industries, the very heart of the Western economy, created a much higher level of Western unemployment. Certainly, no part of the country was unscarred, but the scars in the West went deeper than elsewhere.

The impact of the Depression was so much greater in the West as a result of the West's overdependence on those industries that were the most immediately and hardest hit — resource industries. Saskatchewan and Alberta suffered most due to their overdependence on wheat, the prices for which fell farther and faster. In 1925 almost 76 per cent of Alberta's net value of production came from agriculture, most of that from wheat (in 1926, 67 per cent of Alberta's field crop was in wheat). Saskatchewan was even more dependent on wheat. In 1925 almost 93 per cent of Saskatchewan's net value of production came from agriculture, mostly from the new gold, wheat (in 1926, 69 per cent of Saskatchewan's field crop was in wheat).[5] From 1920 to 1943 fully 70 per cent of the total income in Saskatchewan was earned directly from the sale of wheat.[6]

Manitoba, less dependent on agriculture, did not share the depth of the collapse in the other two Prairie provinces. But Manitoba was dependent on the Western market for its small manufacturing sector, and on the general regional commercial activity, which flowed through Winnipeg eastward. With the Depression in the rest of the West, "the economic support of nearly 40 per cent of Manitoba's population virtually collapsed," according to the Rowell-Sirois report.[7]

B.C.'s dependence on a greater variety of resources, and resource processing, merely ensured that the downturn was not as steep as on the Prairies. The export prices for B.C.'s main products were cut by almost 40 per cent from 1929 to 1933. The value of timber production fell by 62 per cent, mineral production by 59 per cent, and fish production by 63 per cent. The total value of production fell 55 per cent. Unemployment reached almost 28 per cent in 1931, the highest in the Dominion.[8]

Dependence on resource production meant calamity; near exclusive dependence on one resource meant complete collapse. The problem of indebtedness exacerbated the situation. The problem of debt was general. To finance its rapid expansion during the wheat and war booms, and then during the boom of the 1920s, Canada borrowed heavily abroad through the massive import of foreign capital. Much of this money had been borrowed at boom-time interest rates. With the Depression, servicing this debt became difficult: in

1932-33 fully one-third of Canada's total export receipts was required simply to service the debt. But the problem of debt was bigger in the West. The 1920s boom saw the virtual completion of the settlement process in the West. A large part of this expansion was financed through borrowing, often at high interest rates, which, when added to the cost of earlier expansions, created a large debt load. Again, Saskatchewan and Alberta, the most recently settled provinces, were the deepest in debt. Farmers went into debt to begin, expand, and develop their holdings. Workers went into debt to build homes. Provincial and local governments went into debt to finance the basic infrastructure required by a rapidly burgeoning population. Even during the height of the boom of the 1920s the West echoed with loud complaints about the gouging interest rates of the financiers. With the Depression the debt load became quite simply unsupportable. In 1932, debt interest charges took 29 per cent of the Alberta government's total expenditures, nearly equal to combined expenditures in education, public health, and welfare.[9] In 1937 it was estimated that all interest and debt charges in Saskatchewan took 52 per cent of provincial revenues.[10] In 1935-36, 42 per cent of the Manitoba government's expenditures were on interest charges.[11] As early as 1933 B.C.'s credit as a province, and of its municipalities, was declared exhausted.[12]

The debt load of individual Prairie farmers was staggering. For example, a conservative estimate of Saskatchewan farm debt in 1936 was $525 million. To meet the interest payments alone would have required 50 per cent of the value of the total 1935 crop — another 17 per cent would have been required to meet tax obligations.[13] Needless to say, these obligations could not be met and hundreds of farmers were forced to abandon their farms, or were driven out by foreclosure. Urban workers lost their homes. Whole towns and cities, indeed provinces, in the West teetered on the precipice of bankruptcy.

On the Prairies these problems were compounded by the drought, which became so severe and general in Saskatchewan that the average yield per acre of wheat fell to 8 bushels in 1936, then, in the worst drought year, to 2.5 bushels in 1937.[14] The topsoil of whole farms, indeed whole crop districts in areas that ought never to have been put to the plough, simply blew away. But often too much is made of the drought. Had the price structure been normal, the drought would have meant a few bad years for those areas hardest hit. The fact is that, throughout the Great Depression, the prices paid for wheat would not pay for the costs of production even for those farmers who continued to harvest crops. In Alberta, which did not suffer heavily from drought, fairly good crops from 1930 to 1935 could not find a price to make their planting worthwhile. For those also afflicted by drought, a heartbreaking situation was therefore made soul-destroying

The situation in the West became increasingly desperate as each year failed to bring the turn-around to prosperity promised repeatedly by incumbent government politicians. By 1937 fully two-thirds of the total rural population of Saskatchewan was on relief,[15] joined by more than 1 in 5 urban residents.[16] From 1930-37, nearly two-thirds of the total revenues of Saskatchewan's municipal and provincial governments were consumed for relief expenditures. Over 13 per cent of total 1930-37 provincial income was required for relief, representing almost four times the average national relief burden.[17] Saskatchewan's per-capita income fell from $478 in 1929 to $135 in 1933.[18] Things were somewhat better in Alberta where, in 1938, over 52,000 people (in a population of about 775,000) were on relief.[19] Alberta's per-capita income fell from $548 in 1929 to $212 in 1933. In B.C. the situation was as bad, perhaps worse. By March 1933 there were about 120,000 people on the relief rolls (out of a total population of about 700,000).[20]

This figure did not include the many transients who flocked to B.C. only to find themselves ineligible for the meagre handouts that passed for relief. B.C.'s per-capita income fell from $595 in 1929 to $240 in 1937. Manitoba, the senior Western province, combined the problems of the Prairie farmer with mass industrial unemployment in Winnipeg. Manitoba's per-capita income fell from $466 in 1929 to $240 in 1933. Despair, degradation, fear — such words cannot begin to communicate the loss of hope among a whole generation of Western Canadians.

Government Responses

The responses of the federal and provincial governments were appallingly inadequate. All of them — with the exception of the Manitoba Liberal-Progressive hybrid — were ultimately defeated as a result of their record of indifference and neglect. Levels of relief were designed to provide the thinnest possible margin of simple survival to people who often literally could not feed themselves. Access to relief was a difficult and degrading process. Governments were niggardly in the amounts of relief they paid. Recipients were initially told they would have to repay the government's generosity, particularly farmers obtaining agricultural relief to continue production. Often relief was cancelled in the summer months to force men to look for work at any wage. Relief recipients were frequently compelled to provide at least one day's work a week on public projects. Some were paid small wages by government to provide labour to farmers. Thousands of recent immigrants, who became public charges, were deported. Transients, searching for work, were refused relief when no work was found.

Two of the many letters sent to Prime Minister R.B. Bennett, one from Lambert, Saskatchewan and the other from Sayward, Vancouver Island, portray the desperation of many. The Lambert letter, from the wife of a labourer, written in 1934, complained of the inadequacy of relief:

> I am writing you regarding Relief. Will you please tell me if we can get Steady relief and how much we should be allowed per week we have three children . . . one boy is going to School. Some day's he can't go to school as we have no food in the house & I won't let him go on those day's . . . everytime I go up to ask the Mayor here in Lambert for any assistance he always Says he can't help us as the town is broke . . . there are times we live on potatoes for days. at a time & its lasting So long I don't see how much longer it can last . . . I am five months pregnant & I haven't even felt life yet in my baby . . .[21]

The Sayward letter, from an old-timer, part-time worker and part-time homesteader, written in 1935, raised similar concerns:

> Please pardon me for Writing you. but I am In Such a Circumstances That I Really dont Know What to do. When Will This Distress and Mental Agitation Amongst the People come to an End. & how Long Will

This Starvation Last. I am on The Relief & only Git 4
days Work on the Public Road ... That are not Sufficient for both of us to Live on ... Next Came My Land
Taxes ... If I dont Pay it This year. Then The Government of B.C. Will Have My 40 acres Cancelled. & I &
My Wife Will be on The bear Ground. is That Way The
Government Will Help the Poor Men ...[22]

Provincial and municipal governments, responsible
for relief but without the funds to meet the huge
demands put upon them, had to beg for federal support. In exchange for such support, provincial governments were forced to retrench even more deeply than
they already willingly had — further cutting services,
sacking more employees, rolling back wages and salaries in the public sector even more, raising the taxes few
could pay even higher. This cap-in-hand approach to
Ottawa only made the situation worse, as inadequate
government services became even more so. And the
political price of federal support had the effect of
deflecting the provinces from demanding more
government intervention and yet more generous support from Ottawa. Incumbent politicians, federal and
provincial, were unable to think of the Depression as
long-term and therefore satisfied themselves with
simply dealing with the situation as if it were merely a
temporary disaster requiring only patience, hope, and
just enough help to get through to the next year, which
was going to be better. Indeed, government politicians, businessmen, and experts repeatedly claimed
that prosperity was just around the corner — and each
additional year of Depression only served to mock the
people with this continuing chorus of optimism.

The initial response of Western Canadians to the
calamity was groping. They had been disarmed during
the previous decade. The farmers' offensive had been

defeated, divided, contained. Agrarian organizations were shadows of their former selves. The workers' revolt had been defeated at Winnipeg and in the subsequent wave of repression. The early promise of moderation in advancing the workers' cause had evaporated as trade unions during the 1920s declined amid the combination of prosperity and business unionism. Labour parties were unprepared for the disaster and, having abandoned militancy, found it difficult to cope with the enormity of the collapse. Unable to win further concessions during the years of prosperity, traditional farm and labour leaders initially abandoned any hope of winning concessions during the Depression. Bargaining and strikes became half-hearted affairs centered, not on advances, but on minimizing defeats as employers rolled back wages and laid off workers with impunity. Farm organizations reflected their impotence as their standard appeals and petitions were ignored by banks, mortgage companies, and municipalities foreclosing on defaulting farmers. The unemployed and the relief recipient did not even have these weak voices to speak for them.

The Communist Party (CP) filled this initial leadership vacuum through the Workers' Unity League (WUL) and the Farmers' Unity League (FUL). Although national in scope, these organizations had their biggest impact in the West. The WUL, a new militant trade union central, advocated aggressive trade union tactics to deal with the Depression. They proposed that efforts by employers to cut wages and to refuse to bargain with existing unions had to be met by strikes, tough picket lines, and even sit-ins, while they also launched a concerted organizing drive among unorganized workers, especially in industries of large-scale, low-paid employment. Although most successful among miners, lumber workers, and agricultural workers in the West, and the textile industry in Central Canada, the WUL also began to make inroads in the new mass industries (automobiles, steel, and rubber).

The WUL led a series of bitter strikes over wage-cuts and lay-offs, as well as over union recognition and collective bargaining rights. They also organized relief recipients and the unemployed, an activity which made government officials uneasy. Under WUL leadership, or inspired by their example, the unemployed held "hunger marches," organized sit-ins, established picket lines, led strikes on make-work projects, and even held "relief strikes," demanding only, with the utmost simplicity, "work and wages," or failing that, adequate and dignified relief.

The FUL similarly organized farmers to demand better relief, to picket, and often to prevent, mortgage or tax sales of the property of evicted farmers. Even more disturbing to the authorities, they mobilized farmers to physically prevent the eviction of defaulting fellow farmers. For a time it appeared that the mass militancy of the farmers and workers of the 1914-1920 period would be re-ignited by these organizations.

The response of governments to these events was not unlike that applied in Winnipeg in 1919. Concerned with the growing unrest, Prime Minister R.B. Bennett vowed to crush Communism under "the iron heel of ruthlessness."[23] This the federal government, and all provincial governments, proceeded to do with a zeal they could not mobilize to cope with the people's despair and deprivation. Eight of the CP's top leadership were arrested under Section 98 of the Criminal Code and imprisoned at Kingston Penitentiary. (Section 98, passed shortly after the Winnipeg General

Strike and used primarily against the Communist Party, made membership illegal in an organization advocating the use of force to change the existing system.) Suspected communists, strike leaders, and agitators among the unemployed were frequently arrested under Section 98, often to be released when the back of the strike or demonstration had been broken.

Concerned with the volatility of the situation, the federal government, at the urging of many provincial governments, established remote relief camps across the country for single unemployed men, under the authority of the military. Single unemployed men found themselves faced with the "choice" of starvation and homelessness in the city, or "voluntarily" entering such camps. The WUL organized the camps, leading strikes and sit-downs to protest the conditions and to demand improvements. By the time of the cancellation of the program in 1936 over 170,000 of Canada's single unemployed had had a taste of life in what the WUL dubbed "slave camps." Hunger marches were dismissed as "red" plots, picket lines of unhappy relief recipients as "red" agitators, the demands of the unemployed for work as "seditious conspiracy." Strikes, demonstrations, and picket lines were smashed by police armed with tear-gas and clubs, backed up by machine guns.

In a peaceful demonstration emanating from a bitter coal strike at Bienfait, Saskatchewan three miners were shot and killed in cold blood by the RCMP. Participants in a 1932 hunger march in Edmonton were beaten indiscriminately by baton-wielding RCMP officers. The famous 1935 On To Ottawa Trek of unemployed men from B.C. relief camps was

stopped at Regina in a bloody Dominion Day riot.
The principal leader of the 1938 sit-in at the Vancouver Post Office was beaten almost to death in a
savage dawn raid by police. The response of the
authorities was to act as if insurrection was imminent.
The hungry, the unemployed, the relief recipient, the
striking worker, the dispossessed farmer, if they dared
to organize and to protest, met clubs, tear-gas,
machine guns, and prison.

History records that, in Canada, during the initial
years of the Depression, the Communist Party (CP)
articulated the complaints of the afflicted and organized their resistance. It was the CP's finest hour. The
courage and perserverance of the CP militants, and
those who were inspired by them without embracing
their ideology, rekindled the fighting spirit of Canada's working class, setting the stage for the emergence
of militant industrial unionism in the 1940s. The example of the FUL also helped to inspire Western farmers
to confront the self-evident failure of a social and
economic system that had betrayed them. And though
the authorities were most deeply disturbed by the
activities of the CP, they experienced deep consternation at two more successful, less militant, movements
of mass protest that emerged in the West. Just as the
hunger marchers, these movements were labelled as
"communist" and "revolutionary." But unlike the
CP, these movements drove irresistibly to power in
two Western provinces, and threatened to spread
across the nation. The movements were rooted, once
again, in the farmers of Western Canada and, once
again, new principles of political economy and of
Confederation were advocated and won broad
support.[24]

The Founding of Social Credit and the CCF

The arrival of the Great Depression simply completed popular disenchantment with the UFA government, a process underway since the 1921 victory. The UFA government had systematically betrayed every important principle on which it had been elected, with the exception of its promises to provide "business-like" government and to decrease dependency on government among the people. These latter two principles came to dominate the regime as it pursued parliamentary and fiscal orthodoxy and elevated parsimoniousness in government spending to a veritable secular religion. Upon the 1921 victory, the UFA rank-and-file had expected immediate, dramatic results and annual conventions became a battleground between demands for action from the membership and the government's refusals to act. A particularly bitter quarrel emerged between those committed to monetary and credit reform to relieve the burden of public and private debt and the UFA Cabinet, determined to avoid any reckless innovations that might annoy investors and damage the credit standing of the province.

By the time the UFA won its second term in 1926, the will of the Cabinet had been imposed and the organization withered, becoming a loyal rubber stamp of the regime's views. With its easy 1930 victory, the government became even more remote, convinced of the correctness of its previous ten years of uninspired rule, unbothered by any thought that there might be more that could be done. Even the arrival of the Depression failed to change the regime's attitudes as it marched forward to complete defeat in 1935.

The UFA regime proved to be as neglectful as all

other governments of the day. In fairness the UFA did not do any less than other governments, but neither did it do any more. For this the farmers who elected it never forgave it. Relief was hard to get and insufficient, besides being degrading. Strikes and marches in Alberta met the same repression as elsewhere. Labour demonstrations were red-baited. Once the Premier even advised the unemployed on a Hunger March to be "moderate" and "prudent." The 1932 Speech from the Throne exhorted the population to embrace "the spirit of the pioneers and have determination, fortitude and courage to meet and overcome emergencies."[25] At the 1932 UFA Convention the Premier declared the government's Depression policy: "The only course ... to follow in these times is with all the courage we can command to look for the best, but prepare for the worst."[26] This was to be done without too much help from the government: the UFA regime, in common with all others, proceeded to cut services, lay off civil servants, roll back wages and salaries, and raise taxes. In fact the regime did exactly what it did from 1921-23 to deal with the earlier depression: severe retrenchment. The depression of the early 1920s gave way to prosperity; the Depression of the 1930s got worse each year and traditional policies of retrenchment merely contributed to a further deterioration of the situation.

The UFA rank and file became only slightly less angry with the government than the Alberta Federation of Labour (AFL). Two basic Depression remedies emerged and were hotly advocated by growing numbers of UFA members. One remedy involved massive monetary and credit reform, including calls for a debt moratorium, for a suspension of bank interest, for the recognition of new currencies like "wheat dollars," for the issuance of credit at cost by the government, as well as often including the more thorough-going Social Credit proposals of men like William Irvine, a Labour and then a UFA MP since 1921, who was totally committed to the whole Social Credit package. The other remedy, finally officially endorsed by the 1932 UFA Convention, the "Co-operative Commonwealth," was defined as "a community freed from the domination of irresponsible financial and economic power, in which all social means of production and distribution, including land are socially owned and controlled."[27]

The UFA organization voted to affiliate with the newly established national Co-operative Commonwealth Federation (CCF). The UFA government, however, largely ignored this fact, refusing to contemplate the implementation of CCF measures, while expressing deep dismay at the continuing Social Credit agitation in the ranks. Indeed, the government studiously ignored pursuing either set of remedies vigorously, contenting itself with continuing to govern in accord with its record. This was a serious error. People wanted and needed solutions. The federal government's long-standing strategy of repression of organizations advocating revolutionary change, encouraged people to look for less costly, more painless solutions to the crisis. Both the CCF and Social Credit promised such solutions — more or less painless methods of radical but peaceful social change. Of the two, Social Credit came to appear the more painless, at least in Alberta.

The new national CCF, founded in Calgary in 1932, was really a federation of existing farm organizations and Labour political parties.[28] The ground had been prepared for the emergence of the new party by the

work of a group of Fabianesque intellectuals, who
established the League for Social Reconstruction in
1931, and the famous Ginger Group among the rem-
nants of Progressive MPs who had survived the
upsurge of the 1920s, largely composed of four
Labour MPs and a handful of UFA MPs from
Alberta. The Western Conference of Labour Political
Parties, held in Calgary in 1932, had invited various
farm organizations to send representatives, and that
meeting created the Co-operative Commonwealth
Federation. The original groups included the UFA
and the Canadian and Dominion Labour parties from
Alberta; the Socialist Party of Canada from B.C.; the
United Farmers and the Independent and Co-
operative Labour parties from Saskatchewan; and the
Independent Labour party from Manitoba. Only one
trade union attended, the Canadian Brotherhood of
Railway Employees, which decided later not to
affiliate.

A year later, in Regina, a comprehensive national
program was adopted, the "Regina Manifesto" with
its concluding promise to eradicate capitalism. The
new party almost immediately obtained a political
presence in Ottawa through its handful of MPs, as well
as representation in some provincial legislatures where
affiliated Labour parties held seats. But most important of all, despite the Alberta UFA government's
hesitancy about acting on CCF principles, the affiliation of the UFA had brought into the party an organization currently in government. As the organization
matured, the policies of the new political federation
must inevitably come to be expressed in Alberta
government policy. But an event just a few months
after the founding of the CCF determined that the
UFA government had neither the leisure nor the time

to work out how it ought to govern now that it was an affiliate of the new national CCF.

In the autumn of 1932 the Social Credit movement in Alberta was launched by school teacher and part-time evangelist William Aberhart. This was not a particularly unusual event. Ideas of monetary and credit reform, the Social Credit system most prominent among them, already had a mass following thanks to the agitations of the organized farmers, and were rapidly becoming a popular panacea to the Depression crisis in Alberta. As hundreds of farmers were forced to appeal to the Debt Adjustment Board for some compromise to avoid foreclosure, many others experienced foreclosure. Yet agricultural production remained high, prices impossibly low. The result was that the fruits of the farmers' production were siphoned off to finance and re-finance debts acquired for expansion during earlier, more prosperous times. This "poverty in the midst of abundance," a Social Credit aphorism used to good effect by Aberhart, was increasingly seen as unjust, as the result of the "despotic sway of the money kings."

Aberhart was able to use a crude re-interpretation of Social Credit doctrine, which addressed the very real crisis of debt and depression, to march irresistibly to office. Almost overnight Aberhart was able successfully to challenge the UFA for the political leadership of Alberta's farmers. More, he also won the political support of Alberta's conscious working class from the Labour party. He even won significant elements of the urban and small-town middle class. By 1934 Social Credit ideas dominated Alberta's politics. In a 1934 Calgary by-election the CCF-Labour and the Communist candidates endorsed Social Credit ideas, while the successful Liberal expressed sympathy for the notion. The UFA was riddled with prominent supporters of Social Credit. Increasingly what distinguished Aberhart from all other Social Credit supporters and sympathizers was his insistence that a plan could be implemented in Alberta alone with existing provincial powers, a contention he held to with blind tenacity against all gainsayers. It was in this context that mass defections of the UFA rank-and-file to Aberhart's Social Credit League occurred.

Aberhart has been variously painted as a demagogue, an opportunist, and an unprincipled and ambitious power-seeker. All this is beside the point. Such contentions can be proved or disproved by selective evidence. And often we revile in those with whom we disagree precisely those qualities we admire in those with whom we agree (Aberhart was a demagogue and a bible-thumper; T.C. Douglas was a great orator and a preacher). Whatever Aberhart's motives may have been, the way in which he approached his agitation for Social Credit endeared him to Alberta's farmers. His was a non-partisan movement, against the old-line parties, to win Social Credit to benefit all the people (and, of course, free or cheaper credit was particularly attractive to the farmer). He was not a seeker of office but a seeker of Social Credit. He went to the UFA, at Convention and in the Legislature and at countless local meetings, to beg them to take up the cause. He asked the same of the Tories and the Liberals. He dragged his feet when his supporters pleaded for political action. In 1935 Aberhart himself was not a candidate, awaiting the call to be MLA and Premier when his victorious supporters clamoured for his leadership. The point is he was *seen* to be non-partisan, politically reluctant, and resistant to the siren call of high political office, all postures (if postures they were) which only enhanced his reputation among an electorate dominated by agrarian crusaders for 14 years.

Like the UFA of 1921, when Aberhart spoke of the problems of debt, depression, unemployment, despair, and degradation, he was reflecting the real concerns of the farmers and workers, aggressively, angrily. In contrast, the UFA government seemed to counsel passivity and patience due to constitutional constraints. In short, Aberhart articulated the grievances of the people and offered to lead a struggle for a better, more humane social and economic system. Above all else, he said something could de done, and done *now*.

In the run-up to the 1935 election Aberhart published his *Social Credit Manual*, in which he described his "wondrously simple plan."[29] His basic premise: "It is the duty of the State ... to organize its economic structure in such a way that no bona fide citizen ... shall be allowed to suffer for the lack of the basic necessities ... in the midst of plenty." So bad was the situation that this premise proved to be electrifying. Aberhart argued that the root of the trouble lay in the fact that people lacked purchasing power, that "wild-cat profiteering" was occurring, and the "flow of credit" had been retarded by high interest rates imposed by "the Fifty Big Shots of Canada." Social Credit was the answer. Basic dividends would be distributed to all, solving the purchasing power problem.[30] A price control system would be established, ending wild-cat profiteering. Credit would be socialized and made available at administrative cost, breaking the Fifty Big Shots' stranglehold on the economy.

Once Social Credit was in place, the most urgent

problems would be solved. Just Prices would be paid to producers and exacted from consumers. A minimum economic security would be assured by the basic dividend. All would have the opportunity and leisure to pursue self-development. Unemployment would end. Credit would be available at cost. Gradually debts would be paid off. Just Prices and Just Wages would, on the advice of experts, climb with productivity and abundance. Economic justice would be firmly, irrevocably established. This solution to the basic problems of deprivation, want, idleness, and insecurity would prove the solution of other vexatious problems as well. "Contentment and happiness will lead men and women from debauchery." The abuse of alcohol would decline if not cease altogether. Wasteful advertising would end. Women would be more independent with the result that "there would...be more wholesome marriages contracted, [women] would not need to marry for a meal ticket." Young people would get all the education they wanted. Taxation would inexorably decrease. Ceilings on incomes would be imposed, no one would be "allowed to have an income...greater than he himself and his loved ones can possibly enjoy, to the privation of his fellow citizens." "Crime would be reduced. There would be no need for theft."

Social Credit was, therefore, such a basic solution to the root problems of society that inevitably other problems, caused ultimately by neglect, deprivation, and insecurity would begin to disappear. This was heady stuff. This was the stuff of dreams in the dark days of the Depression. Above all else Aberhart was promising hope, hope now, not at some vague, future, more prosperous time.

Social Credit in Power

On August 22, 1935 the people in Alberta embraced Aberhart. The electorate, still 63 per cent rural and including residents on over 100,000 farms, poured out to the polls in an unprecedented 83 per cent turnout.[31] The UFA failed to win a seat. Labour was decimated. The Liberals won 5 seats, the Tories, 2. Social Credit won 56 seats with over 54 per cent of the popular vote, taking all but one rural seat and nearly sweeping the towns and major urban centres. The *Financial Post (FP)* described it as "a popular mandate for a complete transformation of the political and economic system." The problem was, the *FP* went on, "Alberta is only a province... with none of the powers that its new political leader will require... so instead of a social revolution Alberta faces only chaos."[32] Before the week was out Alberta's bond market collapsed. Yet this did not prevent the Alberta electorate from electing 15 Social Credit MPs (and 1 Liberal and 1 Tory) in the October, 1935 federal election, completing the decimation of the once-proud UFA.

The farmers and workers of Alberta seemed to agree that the "chaos" was caused by the Fifty Big Shots of finance capital, rather than by Aberhart. The financial crisis, it was hoped in orthodox circles, would deter the Social Credit government from any rash action. It did not. Aberhart's Social Credit regime embarked on a course of sustained constitutional defiance of the federal government, complemented by a frontal assault on finance capital. It resulted in a chain of events without parallel in Canadian politics, before or since.

The events began, in a serious way, in 1936 when the Alberta government defaulted when a 1916 issue of provincial bonds fell due by simply refusing to pay off those holding the bonds. This sent shock waves through the federal government and financial institutions, since default might prove an attractive option for other beleaguered provinces, not to say municipalities and school boards. This action was followed by a unilateral cut in interest rates on all of Alberta's public debt to one-half the previously agreed rate, with a floor of 2 per cent. Alberta refused to pay any more until a settlement was reached some years later. The calls from across the country for a re-negotiation of all public debt at lower rates of interest now became deafening.

The federal government and the financial community scrambled to oblige, setting in process negotiations that proved surprisingly generous, though Alberta refused to yield (other provinces did and took good advantage of the consequences of Alberta's initiative). The Alberta government proceeded to enact a series of Social Credit laws to establish the system in the province. These measures were first greeted with derision, then with horror. This thrust was supplemented by a more practical, and more serious, attack on finance capital, as the government began to pass debt adjustment legislation that made foreclosure for default virtually impossible.

As the confrontation deepened, the government passed laws to license banks and to force them to carry on business in accordance with Social Credit laws, issued its own currency, imposed punitive taxes on banks and all other corporate opponents, and even tried to squeeze fairness out of the province's daily press by drafting a law to force newspapers to print the government's side in an atmosphere that became increasingly hysterical.

The pro-business opponents of the Social Credit government became almost frenzied. At one point the *Financial Post* said,

> Alberta's brand of Social Credit is [a] thin disguise for Communism... there is underway in Alberta an effort at social revolution which may thrust Canada into a major... crisis... [It] is an unprecedented attack on private capital... akin to the confiscation of private property. It strikes at the very root of commerce, business and finance in a way which characterized the early stages of the Russian revolution.[33]

The Montreal *Gazette* echoed,

> [The Aberhart government]... has now run amok through a field of radical legislation that is without precedent in any country, civilized or savage. It has legalized theft. Having attempted to exploit the banks, to muzzle the press, and to tie the hands of the courts, and having been frustrated in these efforts, it has proceeded to the enactment of laws which are equally if not more vicious.[34]

Aberhart's government countered with mass rallies, radio broadcasts, and an endless stream of printed propaganda to keep the people on side. One Social Credit leaflet was so extreme that the Social Credit MLA and an employee of the government who drafted and authorized its release went to jail for criminal libel. While one side listed nine prominent Albertan enemies of the Social Credit government, the other said ominously,

> My child, you should NEVER say hard or unkind things about Bankers' Toadies. God made Bankers' Toadies, just as He made snakes, slugs, snails and other

creepy-crawly, treacherous and poisonous things.
NEVER, therefore, abuse them — just exterminate
them![35]

Naturally virtually every controversial piece of legislation was challenged in the courts. And frequently
when the government lost, the legislation was re-
drafted and re-passed. This was especially true for the
debt adjustment laws, since as long as the law in
question was before the courts, foreclosure could not
occur. Therefore, no sooner was this or that aspect of
Aberhart's debt laws found *ultra vires*, then the
Alberta legislature re-enacted it in a cat-and-mouse
game that went on for years. The laws in question
unilaterally cut interest rates, declared a moratorium
on debt collection, imposed a general reduction in
debts, prevented foreclosure for debt, and tried to
transform banks into little more than community-
controlled credit clearing houses.

Of course the laws were struck down. Eleven provincial statutes were disallowed by the federal Cabinet,
while the Albertan Lieutenant-Governor refused to
sign three duly passed bills into law. Countless others
were taken to court in a series of legal battles, all of
which the Social Credit government lost. The whole
package of Social Credit laws was finally declared
ultra vires by the Supreme Court in 1938. Three years
later the Court struck down Aberhart's elaborate debt
adjustment legislative edifice. A further unsuccessful
appeal to the Privy Council only delayed the inevitable
a further two years. Out of this near-complete constitutional defeat, Aberhart snatched political victory.
The will of the people of Alberta was being subverted
by the Fifty Big Shots, he declared, supported in a
most sinister way by the federal government and the

courts. This declaration was widely believed in Alberta, largely because it appeared indeed to be the case.

While most attention was focussed on the fight over credit and debt, the Social Credit government was proving a sensitive regime during the Depression. Past indebtedness of farmers to the government for relief was gradually and regularly forgiven. Relief was made more generous and easier to get. The government, by putting a limit on how much it would pay on the public debt, freed up funds for other, more needed services. The most progressive, pro-labour trade union act in the Dominion was passed. Legislation on co-operatives was revamped in accord with farmer suggestions. Modernization and reform of the educational system was begun. Aspects of health care were "socialized." And on most day-to-day matters the government proved as competent as its predecessor. Such measures deepened support for the government. Furthermore, although the government failed to establish Social Credit or to distribute dividends, it had tried to do so only, Aberhart argued, to be blocked and blocked again by the superior powers of the federal government. And the government's debt adjustment legislation struggle was proving enormously helpful to farmers and workers, many of whom faced foreclosure. Emergency relief from foreclosure was provided as the court battles raged.

Even in those cases where foreclosure could be pursued, financial institutions hesitated to pursue such an option vigorously because of the political atmosphere. And, then, finally, when even Aberhart's debt laws were struck down, some discovered to their general rejoicing that the statute of limitations on debt collection had passed, making their debts virtually uncollectable. Despite his defeat in the courts Aberhart had provided, when the whole thing was over, five or six years of debt protection through the worst Depression years. Afterwards, doubtless softened up by the battle, banks and other financial institutions were reasonably generous in working out voluntary debt adjustments with victims of the Depression. (They claimed they would have been just as generous before the battle, but we will never know, and neither Aberhart nor the people of Alberta at the time were prepared to sit back and find out.)

In the run-up to the 1940 election, and despite the arrival of World War II, things continued to boil in Alberta. Aberhart's opponents were determined to defeat him, pulling out all the stops. Liberals and Conservatives formed a coalition and when they weren't accusing Aberhart of being a Nazi they were accusing him of being Communistic. The provincial and national daily press continued their shrill attacks on the Social Credit "Frankenstein," as the *Financial Post* once described the controversial regime. But Aberhart continued to stand firm, as the Throne Speech before the election made clear:

> We are determined to provide food, clothing and shelter for the people to the limit of our financial ability, and we will continue our unrelenting fight for monetary reform and social security with the determination to relieve unemployment and banish poverty from Alberta.... No person should be allowed to lose his farm or home....[36]

Aberhart and his colleagues pointed to the five year record without apology. He even turned the attack on him for failing to give the promised dividends against his detractors when he said:

> I can stand all the abuse heaped upon me when men whose farms I have saved by my debt legislation grip my hands in thanks... Never mind the dividends, let them go. After getting 95 per cent, are you going to pluck me on that?[37]

One telling Social Credit election slogan was, "Keep Aberhart In and Keep the Sheriff Out."[38] Although Aberhart lost a lot of his urban middle-class support, and even some working-class strength, the farmers kept the faith as Social Credit won 36 of 57 seats with 43 per cent of the vote. The *Financial Post* complained that the "most sinister aspect of the result is the Social Credit success in undermining the simple fundamentals of business morality." [39] The farmers and workers who elected Aberhart had clearly confirmed their rejection of "business morality" not so much in favour of Social Credit as in favour of a new economic morality which would free them from fear, deprivation, and degradation. Most important of all, for the farmers, Aberhart had exhibited remarkable ingenuity in using the limited powers of a province to help them keep their farms.

The CCF in Saskatchewan

While the arrival of the Depression in Alberta divided and then destroyed the organized farmer government there, in Saskatchewan the calamity finally drove the organized farmers into politics. Saskatchewan's farmers' decade of resistance to going political crumbled almost overnight as the Depression began. A decade of confusion, division, followed by reorganization and consolidation ensured that the farm movement was amply equipped to deal with the disaster when it struck. Unlike the organized farmers in Ontario, Manitoba, and Alberta, the Saskatchewan

Grain Growers Association (SGGA) had not earlier gone directly into provincial politics. Agrarian-dominated but formally separate political organizations had been established for the work of the federal and provincial wings of the Progressive party. The SGGA, divided on the issue of going into politics, containing strong pro-liberal elements, left the Liberal regime in the province, in power since 1905, intact.

The SGGA's indecision, moderation, and notorious cosiness with the Liberal party had offended many more militant agrarian activists, resulting in the establishment of the Farmers Union of Canada (FUC) in 1922. The aggressive FUC, adopting a farmer version of the One Big Union's constitution, called for a "class struggle" to advance the interests of "the great Agricultural Class."[40] It strongly opposed the party system and was totally hostile to involvement in electoral politics. The organization struck out aggressively at capitalism, especially finance capitalism, often borrowing Social Credit ideas freely. Radical debt protection and compulsory debt adjustment to the advantage of the debtor-farmer, as well as socialized credit at cost, were demanded.[41] In 1923 Clifford Sifton denounced the FUC as "an out and out radical deadbeat organization, appealing directly to the impecunious and those who are so loaded with debt that they do not ever expect to get out of debt."[42]

What pushed the FUC onto center stage in spite of its strong rhetoric was the marketing issue. Farmers had been enamoured of orderly marketing for their grain ever since the success of the Wheat Board during the war. The failure to establish a post-war compulsory wheat marketing board, as well as the SGGA's hand-wringing on the marketing issue, created a leadership vacuum that the FUC filled with the contract, wheat pool plan. Farmers were asked to commit themselves for five years to market their wheat co-operatively. The idea caught fire and even the more staid SGGA joined the FUC in the resulting Wheat Pool campaign. By 1926, 45,000 Saskatchewan farmers had signed contracts, encompassing 73 per cent of seeded acreage. Because of this success, the FUC became enormously influential and pushed agrarian opinion leftward on all manner of issues. As well, the success of the joint FUC/SGGA Wheat Pool campaign convinced the organizations to amalgamate into the United Farmers of Canada (Saskatchewan Section). The FUC gave up its class struggle constitutional rhetoric in exchange, as it turned out, for domination of a united organization of all organized farmers.

The United Farmers proved to be more like the Farmers' Union than like the SGGA, and former Farmers' Union militants ultimately won control of the new organization when in 1929, George Hara Williams, a former Farmers' Union organizer, won the presidency. Williams brought a more militant, class struggle, and a broader political and economic, orientation to the new United Farmers of Canada (Saskatchewan Section). No longer content to act simply as a pressure group, though still strictly non-partisan politically, and still absolutely opposed to direct political action, the new organization took radical political stands on a whole range of issues. Underlying every position paper and every proposed reform was a central commitment to the principle of co-operation applied to the social structure as a whole as the road to a much improved social system. Final success in redressing the grievances of the farmer, and of the people, was seen as ultimately dependent on a successful reconstruction of the social system, especially its economic foundation, according to the co-operative principles so long advocated by the organized farmers. In retrospect, everything the United Farmers did, particularly after Williams' victory in 1929, seemed a preparation for plunging directly into politics. With a membership fluctuating between 20,000 and 30,000, with an increasingly well-developed and clear program, with a president who had earlier been fired from the Farmers' Union for his efforts to steer it toward political action, the United Farmers could not have long remained a mere pressure group going cap in hand to discredited politicians. The Depression merely sped up a decision that was inevitable.

The United Farmers' decision to go political was further abetted by a decade of increasingly abysmal politics in the province. The earlier failure of the SGGA to go political at the height of the agrarian upsurge had left those opposed to the party system somewhat at sea. A separate provincial Progressive party organization had been set up and contested some seats in provincial elections during the 1920s, regularly winning a handful of seats. However, the provincial Progressives failed to capture the political leadership of Saskatchewan's farmers since the party proved unable to reflect the farmers' growing radicalization. Apparently oblivious to events around them, the Progressives remained moderate, incapable of taking relevant or distinctive positions on most important issues.[43]

In desperation a large bloc of Saskatchewan's electorate, won over to the critique of the party system, had started voting independent. Consequently the political situation in Saskatchewan became an unpredictable morass of confusion and contention during the

1920s. Although the Liberal party stayed in power, it did so only by shrill partisanship and judicious patronage, dropping all pretense of being a farmers' party. The Opposition, composed of a confused conglomeration of Tories, Progressives, and Independents, was united only by an overriding passion to oust the Liberals. And as the economy improved in the 1920s the issues on which the Opposition assailed the government became increasingly confused. Since all political groupings rhetorically supported the general demands of the agrarian crusade, clear political distinctions could not be drawn on agrarian issues. Increasingly, therefore, the issues that came to dominate public debate became religious and racial.

The Opposition, under the leadership of the Tories, was aided by a new and dramatic extra-parliamentary force: the Ku Klux Klan (KKK).[44] The Klan emerged as a frontal attack on Catholics, continental European immigrants (especially Eastern European), Jews, Orientals, the French language, indeed, upon any forces that tended to erode true morality, patriotism, British institutions, and the Anglo-Saxon "race." Such groups were attacked in language that can only be described as violent, abusive, and potentially dangerous. The KKK received enormous support: the Grand Wizard was a prominent Tory; Anderson, the Tory leader and 1929 Premier, helped the KKK organize Saskatoon by providing membership lists; many Protestant clergymen joined; members of all political parties joined the KKK, but the Tories led the field with the Progressives close behind. At its height the KKK had between 20,000 and 30,000 members. In other words, the KKK appealed to the sentiments of a wide section of the population. The KKK was decisive in electing aldermen to city councils, had a big effect on who became mayor in the larger centers, and, in the 1929 election, aided in unseating the Liberal government.

In fact, in the 1929 election the Tories and the Progressives tended to win in those areas where the Klan was best organized. The KKK episode brought into sharp relief the political bankruptcy of the provincial Progressives. Unable and unwilling to gain the blessing of radicalizing elements among the farmers, confused about what kind of alternative to offer, uncertain about what issues to push, the Progressives degenerated to the point where they submerged themselves in a parliamentary alliance with the Tories and damaged themselves by benefitting from the KKK agitation. Desperate in a search for issues upon which to defeat the Liberals, the Progressives joined the Tories in a determined exposure of Liberal patronage. Yet this same desperation led them to pander to the Klan campaign of racial and religious intolerance, which painted the Liberal government as puppets of the Pope, diluters of pure Anglo-Saxon blood through unrestricted immigration, and therefore unfit to govern a British society.

In 1929 the newly resuscitated Tories won 24 seats, the Progressives 5, and the Independents 6. The Liberals took 28 seats. There was no doubt that there was active co-operation between the Tories and the Progressives: their platforms were very similar and only 12 of 63 fights were three-way. Very quickly the Tories and the Progressives, with the support of the Independents, formed a coalition and replaced the Liberals as government. They called themselves the "Co-operative Government."[45] But the farmers of Saskatchewan felt that a Tory government by any other name was still a Tory government.

The Tory-led coalition government of 1929-34 was a defeated government when it took office in September, 1929. Less than two months later the Depression collapse began. The government's response was typical of the day — retrenchment, higher taxes, wage rollbacks, staff cuts, and reduced services. For this they were bitterly attacked. On other issues the government behaved like a ping-pong ball, now trying to appease business interests, now trying to appease the farmers. The government's behaviour on two crucial issues exemplifies this: the compulsory pool and debt adjustment. The 1929 crop had been good and the Wheat Pool, expecting good prices, had made an initial serious overpayment to its members. As a result the Pool was almost bankrupted. One result of this crisis was a strong farmer agitation for a legislated 100 per cent compulsory wheat pool. The government acquiesced, passing the legislation and thus offending business interests.

Yet while passing the law the government washed its hands of it, failing to stand behind the law as it was inevitably challenged in the courts, thus offending rather than appeasing the farmers. The law was finally declared *ultra vires* and the government, in its attempt to get the best of both worlds ended up getting the worst of both. In the case of debt adjustment the government began to respond to demands for debt protection and adjustment from the farmers with a weak and unsatisfactory law and was gradually pressured, as the years of Depression went by, to make the law stronger and more interventionist on the side of the debtor. The resulting law finally offended business interests because it went too far down the road of intervention, and offended farmers by not going far enough. Clearly, most agreed, the government would have to go. For the organized farmers, however, there was no alternative.

It is therefore understandable that the 1931 United Farmers convention decided to enter politics almost unanimously and virtually without debate. A series of resolutions was passed laying the basis for political action, and the convention committed itself to seek an alliance with labour. Negotiations were successful, and a joint convention of the United Farmers and the Independent Labour Party (ILP) founded the Farmer-Labour party (FLP) in 1932 and affiliated with the national CCF. This formal fusion should not cloak the fact that the new FLP was essentially a farmers' party — there was no doubt that the UFC(SS), with 27,000 members, was the senior partner in the fusion. The ILP never had more than 500 members. And although the United Farmers continued to function as a farm organization, the new FLP political structure resulted from a tremendous overlap of United Farmer leadership and membership. Clearly the farmers of Saskatchewan had learned from earlier mistakes by founding a party that was committed to "broadening out" to include workers, teachers, small businessmen, and professionals, as well as farmers. But farmers remained in the dominant group in the alliance and the backbone of the new movement.

The progressive elements among Saskatchewan's organized farmers, long frustrated by a lack of unity on the question of political action, had finally won the opportunity to stop behaving primarily as a pressure group to defend the interests of farmers and instead to put on display their vision of a new society. The Depression provided the justification for the need of a new society and the new political party provided the vehicle, now more or less free of the constraints of the older agrarian organizations.

The "ultimate objective" of the new party was bluntly stated:

> the present economic crisis is due to inherent unsoundness of the capitalistic system, which is based on private ownership of resources, and capitalistic control of production... We recognize that social ownership and co-operative production for use is the only sound economic system.[46]

In order to achieve this objective, the public ownership of all natural resources was proposed. Agricultural land would become publicly owned under a voluntary perpetual "use-lease" system by which the land would continue at the productive disposal of the farmer, who was also assured of the right to pass the farm on to his heirs. In the meantime, foreclosure would be prevented. Compulsory co-operative marketing of agricultural commodities would be established. Social security and public insurance of all kinds would be put in place. Work at decent wages was promised. Federally the first order of business was the socialization of currency and credit.

Such ideas were finally formulated into a 15-point program. The first three points were key: "a planned system of social economy"; "socialization of the banking, credit and financial system" and "the social ownership... of utilities and natural resources"; and "security of tenure... by perpetual 'use hold' on home and lands... when requested by... present owner or dispossessed owner... The prevention of immediate foreclosures by an exchange of provincial non-interest bearing bonds." The other points promised social security, socialized health, educational reform, workers' rights, and so on. But the centerpiece of the program was the economic planks, on which the new party would rise or fall: planning, public credit, publicly owned resources and utilities, and protection of farm and home from foreclosure.

Socialist rhetoric notwithstanding, this was not socialism. This was a program designed primarily to defend the people of the province, and most particularly the farmers, from the ravages of the Depression. Its implementation would take key economic sectors out of the private sphere, and generate larger public revenues, but it would most significantly keep the small property-owners on their land with their rights to individual commodity production unimpeded.

This was key: the program would protect the small agrarian capitalists from losing their farms through debt protection and public ownership of farmland, while ensuring that all their other rights as small capitalists — production for a market for profit; entrepreneurial freedom; guaranteed control of the land, including the right to pass it on to their heirs — would remain intact. The program clearly would dramatically tip the scale of the relationship under law between finance capital and the farmer in the latter's favour. The fact that the program promised to save the wage worker's home and to provide work and wages to the unemployed does not in any way lessen the qualitatively greater benefits the program would bring to the farmer.

The new party was immediately attacked by the politicians of the old parties and the press. The Minister of Public Works called the FLP a "union of socialists, communists, and men of all shades of radicalism."[47] The press carried on an uninterrupted campaign against socialism and radicalism, increasingly focussed on the FLP. The efforts of the old parties and the press to label the new party communist were legion and unrelenting. Ironically, almost simultaneously the Communist Party, through the FUL's newspaper, *The Furrow*, mounted a vigorous left-wing attack on the FLP. The FLP responded to such attacks with a program of ceaseless agitation and education.

The most savagely attacked FLP policy was the public ownership of farmland and the use-lease system of tenure. The simple defense that the proposed program was purely voluntary, and that no one would be forced to enter the program, did not placate hysterical critics, who likened the policy to forced state expropriation. G.H. Williams' repeated assurances that "the basis of the CCF land policy was a recognition of the family farm as the fundamental unit,"[48] and that the use-lease proposal was merely a way to prevent confiscation by financial interests, had not dented the widely held belief that the FLP wanted to collectivize agriculture. Both the Tories and Liberals had good reason to nurture and broadcast such distortions of the FLP program: the Liberals, because they recognized the FLP as the real challenger to their return to power; the Tories, because the FLP had already destroyed the future of their coalition by winning much of the Progressive and Independent electoral base.

In the 1934 election the Liberal party pulled out all stops, promising everything to everybody: work and wages; adequate relief; debt protection; moves to state medicine. Indeed, they stole much of the FLP's thunder, rhetorically at least. The Tory government was a non-starter; few took it seriously. Both Tories and Liberals accused the FLP of being communistic, of wanting to confiscate farms and businesses, putting the FLP on the defensive. The FLP election policy therefore was more directed against "the financial interests" than against capitalism in general, promising true "economic freedom" if elected. The results were disappointing for the FLP, winning only 5 seats with 24 per cent of the vote, compared to the Liberals' 50 seats with 48 per cent. The Tories and Independents won no seats. All 5 FLP seats were rural, clustered in better-off agricultural areas. In fact the FLP did best in the prosperous rural areas, worst in the poorest areas. Most disappointing, the FLP failed to win a single urban seat, trailing both the Liberals and Tories in urban popular vote. Clearly the FLP emerged as the Official Opposition and the major challenger to Liberal domination among the more economically advanced farmers. Among the poor farmers the FLP ran a poor third behind the Liberals and Tories.[49] This should not be surprising: the FLP was primarily the creation of the organized farmers with deep roots among the "middle sort" of farmer, the better-off though not rich, the ones with a viable stake to defend and extend, those with sufficient self-confidence to fight to improve their position in the economic system.

The election of the Liberal party brought no change — the Depression continued and worsened. The next political test of the provincial CCF (the FLP name was dropped after the 1934 election) occurred in the October, 1935 federal election. Alberta's massive endorsation of the Social Credit Depression remedy had rekindled the attractiveness of Social Credit doctrine, long a central part of the beliefs of the organized farm movement in Saskatchewan. Things went so well that the Social Credit party in Saskatchewan ran in 20 federal seats, winning two rural seats, and outpolling the CCF in eight other rural seats, with 18 per cent of the popular vote. The CCF also won two rural seats with 21 per cent of the vote — but both had been won with Social Credit co-operation. In Weyburn the victorious T.C. Douglas was a joint CCF-Social Credit candidate and, in Rosetown-Biggar, M.J. Coldwell received the unsolicited blessing of the local Socreds. Of the four seats with significant urban components, the CCF was outpolled by the Socreds in two. The CCF was badly shaken. Clearly the advanced farmers of Saskatchewan were seriously split between CCF and Social Credit Depression remedies. Had the two reform movements co-operated, at least 11, and perhaps more, instead of four seats, would have been wrestled from the old parties.

This double political crisis — the 1934 failure and the Social Credit challenge — was met by a wide-ranging debate in the CCF regarding program changes and co-operation with other reform groups, most notably Social Credit. Although those committed to retaining the organizational integrity of the CCF by refusing formal co-operation with other groups won the debate, it was not certain that, on the hustings, the CCF could retain its leadership of the reform-minded among the farmers. The Social Credit party had made much of the CCF "use-lease" land proposal and general commitment to public ownership, while the CCF pointed to the futility of focussing solely on financial reform as the way out of the Depression. Aberhart's failure to deliver Social Credit in Alberta helped the Saskatchewan CCF immeasurably as the 1938 election approached. At the same time, the CCF modified its platform significantly while, as Official Opposition, dominating reform politics on a day-to-day basis.

The 1936 convention of the Saskatchewan CCF replaced the old FLP program with a nine-point platform. Gone were ringing declarations about socialism and eradicating capitalism. In their place were calls for the co-operative commonwealth and attacks on trusts, monopolies, and big business. Gone was the use-lease land program, in fact, gone were any overly complex policies. In their place was a simple direct, moderate, pragmatic platform: "security to farmers on the farms and to urban dwellers in their homes," "drastic reduction of debt," "socialized health services" "public works with wages at trade union rates and... adequate relief," "equal educational opportunity," "increased social services," "the national issue and control of currency and credit," "a Growers' National Marketing Board... to... fix... a price which will return... the average cost of production plus a decent standard of living," and "the maintenance of Peace and... extension of... Democratic rights."[50]

The decisions to moderate the platform and to retain the CCF's organizational integrity, were supplemented by a rather confused campaign against Social Credit ideas. On the one hand, the CCF attacked the soundness of Social Credit doctrine and emphasized provincial constitutional constraints. On the other hand, the CCF began more and more to emphasize those policy areas — such as foreclosure prevention, debt reduction, and socialized credit — that were close in content to Social Credit policy. As a result, the exchanges between Social Credit advocates and CCF advocates became sharper and sharper.

The 1934 program and manifesto of the CCF had made much of its policies on finance and credit. It had called for the socialization of credit; it had promised to "protect the farmer from foreclosure or eviction"; it had promised debt relief "by reduction of existing debts"; it had promised a "publicly owned rural credit system"; it had promised to protect the homes of workers from foreclosure and to provide work to all on "socially useful public works . . . financed by public credit."[51] Such themes continued to occupy center stage in CCF policy declarations, as did rhetoric about purchasing power, the money power, and the slavery of debt and interest. Increasingly, the CCF, to set itself apart from the Socreds, also pointed to those policy areas that complemented such guarantees from the cruel ravages of finance capital: social ownership through co-operative and public enterprise; orderly marketing; the construction of a comprehensive public health and welfare system. Yet the promise of security of tenure — of farmers on their farms and the workers in their homes — continued to be the central feature of the CCF agitation as the Depression deepened and threatened even this small but tangible evidence of economic security. Again and again, the CCF promised security of tenure, real debt adjustment, adequate welfare, and work and wages as the basis of its total program.

The 1938 election, following on the heels of the worst year of Depression and drought, was shaped by an invasion of Social Credit. Aberhart, facing total opposition from the federal government, the courts, and business interests, recognized the need to win Social Credit by winning the country, province by province if need be. Saskatchewan was the obvious place to start, especially since the Social Credit party had done well there on short notice in the 1935 federal election. Social Credit organizers streamed into the province from Alberta. CCF efforts to arrange an informal "saw-off" were rebuffed by Aberhart —

Social Credit was out to win the province for the cause. Other reform groups were active as well, further muddying the waters. Independent Labour, the Unity movement, which advocated united action by all reform groups, and the CP all ran some candidates. The CCF therefore fought for sheer political survival rather than facing the problem of winning against what ought to have been a thoroughly discredited and vulnerable government. The CCF decision to run in only 31 of 52 seats was a public admission that they could not hope to form a government. The problem was simply to survive the Social Credit onslaught by concentrating on areas of known strength.

The Liberal party also saw Social Credit as the major threat in 1938. This was not surprising. Aberhart had swept Alberta provincially and federally, decimating all political parties. Aberhart's legislative program was the talk of the country and the nightmare of the business community. The prospect of the Social Credit party, now entrenched in Alberta, adding Saskatchewan to its victories was appalling to Ottawa, the old parties, and business interests. Such a success would transform the movement overnight from a dangerous effort at experimentation in Alberta, to a potentially disastrous national force. As a result the Liberal party virtually ignored the CCF and, again promising nearly everything to everyone, opted for an hysterical anti-Social Credit campaign. One Liberal pamphlet proclaimed, "Communism is the Threat, Do you want Alberta's Stalin regulating your daily life?"[52] Aberhart's broken promises were detailed, his "misuse of public funds" lamented, his "futile debt legislation" ridiculed. Aberhart was accused of establishing a "dictatorship" in Alberta, "in active cooperation with the Communist party and other subversive forces." If Aberhart won, "Saskatchewan's industrial development will be sacrificed to pay ... dividends in Alberta." Aberhart and other Alberta Socred notables plunged into the campaign, with Aberhart regularly outdrawing the Premier at rallies throughout the province.

The CCF was caught in the squeeze and had to fight hard just to keep its program on public view. The crisis was so serious that the CCF did not even attempt a break-through in urban areas, focussing its efforts on keeping its farm base. The CCF tried to make the Liberal record the issue — to no avail. Attention was rivetted on the Social Credit invasion. Therefore, the CCF joined in the attack on Social Credit, dubbing it "the last illusion of capitalism."[53] The Social Credit invasion would "split the reform vote" and keep the Liberals in power. The CCF claimed that "Social Credit has failed to give the things it promised in Alberta" and "those things it has done were CCF platform, not Social Credit platform."[54] While thus rebuking Social Credit, however, much of the CCF campaign mixed co-operative commonwealth and Social Credit rhetoric to good effect, promising to do virtually everything to save the farmer and worker from finance capital that Aberhart was doing, and to do it more effectively.

> The CCF is determined that Humanity will come first ... and will ... use this power to protect the people ... and will keep on using it against the imposition of usury, until the powers of entrenched finance give a square deal to the Farmers and Home Owners of this province.[55]

Aberhart could hardly have said it any better.

The 1938 results were a further disappointment for the CCF. The failure to run in urban centers made the CCF claim to be a farmer-labour coalition more myth than fact. The CCF won ten seats with 19 per cent of the vote, while the Social Credit party won two seats with 16 per cent (one of these seats was won for Social Credit by the 1934-35 President of the United Farmers). Two Unity candidates won seats and their votes together with the other reform currents reached almost eight per cent. The 1934 decimation of the Tories was re-confirmed with no seats, while the Liberals took 38 seats with 46 per cent of the vote.

The CCF had defeated the Social Credit threat, holding its base among the province's reformist farmers and retaining its position as Official Opposition. It was a bitter-sweet success, for had the various reform currents, especially the CCF and Social Credit, united, the Liberal government would have been defeated. Interestingly the 1934 pattern of support for the CCF was repeated in 1938 — the CCF did best among the more prosperous farmers.[56] All ten CCF MLAs were successful farmers and CCF support was effectively concentrated, as the leader put it, "in that portion where crops have been harvested,"[57] no insignificant fact in the worst Depression year. Indeed, the CCF claimed that Liberal threats that federally supported relief payments would end if the Liberals were not returned had been used to frighten less secure farmers.

Although the arrival of World War II and the end of the drought slowly began to drag the province out of Depression, the social and economic burden of the Depression legacy lingered on: debt remained, instability remained, indeed, all the basic structural problems that had brought the CCF into existence remained. Despite constant attacks on its loyalty and silly efforts simultaneously to equate the CCF to Communism and Hitlerism, the CCF continued to flourish in Saskatchewan. A good test of the CCF's growing support was provided in the March, 1940 federal election. Liberals again accused the CCF of being communists, Nazis, and disloyal pacifists. The tactic failed — the CCF won five of Saskatchewan's 21 seats with nearly 29 per cent of the vote. This election also announced the end of the Social Credit upsurge in Saskatchewan — no seats with just over three per cent of the vote. The support pattern continued. The CCF won no urban seats. In rural areas the story was different. Four of the five rural seats won by the CCF were won with more than 50 per cent of the vote, including one seat in which Social Credit took over eight per cent. Three of the victories were two-way fights with the Liberals. In the seven rural seats the CCF failed to win, CCF candidates came a strong second. Election victories in Saskatchewan were still decided on the farm in 1940, and the federal results made clear that provincial power for the CCF only awaited the next provincial election.

Both the CCF and Social Credit movements saw themselves as more than merely agrarian, sectional movements. Although they had their greatest successes in the West, hardest hit by the Depression, both movements believed that they had uncovered new principles of political economy that ought to be applied nationally. Indeed, the CCF in Saskatchewan always maintained that the achievement of the co-operative commonwealth required federal power. The Alberta Social Credit movement, after failing to implement its ideas provincially, reluctantly agreed on the need for federal power after the federal cabinet and the courts repeatedly slammed the door on Alberta initiatives. Therefore both movements sallied forth to win the whole Dominion to their ideas. The CCF had considerably more success since, from the outset, a national movement was envisaged and a significant group of Labour and Progressive MPs supported the new party. As well, almost every provincial section of organized farmers affiliated with the CCF, giving the new party a good organizational toehold across the country. The Alberta Social Credit movement had less luck, forced to build a national organization outward from Alberta with no significant indigenous core to incorporate in other provinces, and often facing resistance from more orthodox Social Crediters.

The CCF believed it had made the biggest breakthrough when the Alberta UFA affiliated with the national group. As we've seen, this was a short-lived triumph. In Manitoba, the new provincial CCF was able to win seven seats with 12 per cent of the vote in the 1936 election, yet failed finally to become a serious contender for provincial power until the 1960s. In Alberta the CCF was gradually extinguished after the UFA's massive defeat in 1935. The CCF tried to make a breakthrough in Atlantic Canada with little luck. In Quebec the party was humbled from the beginning. In Ontario the CCF won one seat with seven per cent of the vote in 1934, only to be rolled back in the 1937 contest. Federally, in 1935, the CCF won all seven seats and most of its nearly nine per cent of the national vote in the West. And in 1940 the pattern was similar — seven of eight seats were won in the West, as was the bulk of its national popular vote. In the West the party did well, though not as well as many had hoped. In 1935, the CCF won 19 per cent of the federal vote in Manitoba (two seats); in Saskatchewan 21 per cent (two seats); in Alberta, 13 per cent; in B.C., 34 per cent (three seats). In 1940, the party again took 19 per cent in Manitoba (one seat); 29 per cent in Saskatchewan (five seats); 13 per cent in Alberta; and 28 per cent in B.C. (one seat). And the situation worsened as the Depression dragged to an end. In 1935, only 43 per cent of the CCF's national vote was won in the West. By 1940 this figure reached 78 per cent. Clearly, the CCF failed to win the nation to its vision of the co-operative commonwealth.

Yet the CCF did come close to winning B.C.[58] In fact, second to Alberta, the greatest hopes were held by the new party for early success in B.C., particularly after the 1933 election when the new B.C. section of the CCF won seven seats with an astonishing 32 per cent of the vote and became the Official Opposition. This result was astonishing first of all because the 1928 Labour vote in B.C. had collapsed to just under five per cent and only one MLA had been elected. The trade unions and labour parties in B.C., in common with the rest of the West, indeed of the Dominion, were in disarray, apparently on the threshold of extinction when the Depression struck.

The economic downturn revived the Independent Labour Party which, as it grew, changed its name to the older Socialist Party of Canada, and attended the 1932 Calgary meeting. The new party grew with incredible rapidity. The 1933 electoral result was astonishing too because of the disputes that had marked the founding of the provincial CCF in B.C. The Socialist Party tended to be more radical in its approach to socialism, many of its members were intellectual adherents of Marxism. A variety of more moderate groups — a whole series of independent CCF clubs (which amalgamated into the Associated CCF Clubs of B.C.), the more softly socialist League for Social Reconstruction, the Reconstruction party — clamoured for affiliation to the CCF. After much controversy and debate, a founding convention including the Socialist Party, the CCF Clubs, and the Reconstructionists was held. The policies adopted tended in the more radical direction of the Socialist Party, which remained the dominant influence in the B.C. wing of the party. Almost overnight, therefore, the B.C. CCF organized itself, settled old battles by uniting warring factions, established a platform and ran in a general election, which returned it as Official Opposition with almost a third of the popular vote. The party seemed on the road to victory.

However, an unprecedented campaign of vilification, red-baiting and scare-mongering by the press, combined with the new 1933 Liberal government's efforts to help the victims of the Depression, broke the party's momentum. A re-emergence of even more divisive internal squabbling took an additional toll. The CCF's vote fell to 29 per cent in 1937, returning the same number of MLAs, but losing Opposition status to the Tories. The subsequent revival of the party at the beginning of World War II, when in 1941 the CCF won more votes than either the Liberals or the Tories, and permanently became the Official Opposition, convinced the two old parties to form a coalition to keep the CCF out of office. The coalition was successful and, when it was near collapse, Tory back-bencher W.A.C. Bennett formed it anew in the

1952 election under the Social Credit banner. The tactic of uniting the so-called free enterprise vote to keep the CCF out of power remained effective in the province until the early 1970s. In fact the B.C. CCF (and later NDP), throughout the 1940s, 1950s, and 1960s, seemed destined to remain in perpetual opposition, victory often just slightly beyond its grasp.

The Social Credit party did not go anywhere in its efforts to organize beyond Alberta. Certainly they dominated federal and provincial politics in Alberta, but failed to convince other Canadians. The Socreds had their best results in Saskatchewan until the CCF finally beat them back. Except for the two seats won in Saskatchewan in 1935, the Social Credit party went nowhere in the other provinces in federal elections. Results in provincial elections were just as bad. In 1937, B.C. gave Social Credit just over one per cent of the vote. In Manitoba, Social Credit picked up five seats in 1936 with nine per cent of the vote, but collapsed thereafter. Outside the West, the story was worse. In the 1935 federal election, all Social Credit votes were cast in the West, 67 per cent of those in Alberta. In 1940, 91 per cent of Social Credit votes were cast in the West, 75 per cent of those in Alberta.

By the beginning of World War II, and as the Depression began to end, it appeared that these new movements with their outlandish ideas had been effectively bottled up in the West. Their challenge had been met and rolled back, their influence, it appeared, largely confined to their Western roots. Canada was not about to establish either a Social Credit system or the Co-operative Commonwealth. The farmers and workers of the Prairies had presented two new visions of a new basis for the national economy. The visions were defeated and rejected by the rest of the country, just as the vision of the Progressives of the 1920s had been. This time, however, the two new movements did not disintegrate. Rather they began to consolidate their Western power bases and to continue to demand concessions to deal with the grievances of the farmers and workers they represented. The Depression ended, painfully slowly in the West, but the agitations did not.

7
Concession and Compromise: The War and After, 1940-1960

While Canadians outside the West may have rejected the doctrines of social credit and the co-operative commonwealth, they increasingly agreed with many of the complaints of the two movements. The burden of public and private debt was unbearable. Unregulated capitalism in crisis created widespread human suffering. State repression was not the best way to deal with the demands of the unemployed, the striking worker, or the evicted farmer. The absence of adequate systems of relief in times of economic crisis took an appalling toll not only in material suffering but in degradation and humiliation. Governments had an obligation to intervene in times of crisis to help those who, through no fault of their own, could not help themselves. Increasingly all politicians were compelled to accept these as truisms and to begin to develop policies to deal with the crisis. Liberal and Tory alike, in or out of power, began to accept and advocate selected aspects of the basic social security programs of both the CCF and the Social Credit. As they did, Canada, in common with all capitalist nations, slowly began to construct the modern welfare state.

Furthermore, the unevenness in the effects of the Depression revealed even more starkly that the economic crisis was also a crisis of Confederation. It was clearly a crisis partly resulting from the economic tasks assigned to the various regions. The West, a region overwhelmingly dependent on the extraction and export of resources, was obviously highly vulnerable. At the same time, Central Canada, the designated region of industrial concentration, though still devastated, enjoyed a more secure and resilient economic base even in Depression times. But it was also a more general political crisis emanating from the division of powers between federal and provincial governments.

The economic crisis therefore revealed the basic constitutional crisis that has beset Canadian politics ever since. The economic crisis simply brought the constitutional crisis to a head in a way which could not be avoided.

Events were making it clear that a country that tolerated such grave regional economic inequities was in danger of disintegration in times of deep crisis. Furthermore, a federal political system that based its unity on the brutal assertion of the superior powers of the federal government could not long survive.

The disallowances and reservations of the Alberta Social Credit measures were only the latest examples of an unbridled use of federal power to keep the provinces in line. From 1867 to 1946, 122 provincial statutes were disallowed by the federal cabinet: 86 of these, or 77 per cent, were statutes passed by the four Western provinces. During the same time, there were 69 reservations by provincial lieutenant-governors, and 36 of these, or 52 per cent, were bills passed by Western legislatures.[1] Such an approach to governing a federal system could not long survive in the 20th century.

Indeed, due to the extremity of the situation, separatist sentiment had again emerged in the West just as it had during the railway agitations in Manitoba in the 1880s and during the agitations leading up to the 1885 Saskatchewan Rebellion. The famous "Wilkie Charter" in Saskatchewan, a document circulated among agrarian activists in the early 1930s that figured large in the early formulation of the policies of the United Farmers as it went political, had threatened secession. And the legislative program of Aberhart was separatist in all but name. Clearly, the estrangement of the West was deepening — one of the few measures we have of how deep this estrangement went was a poll conducted in 1938 by the Regina *Leader Post* that found 42 per cent in favour of secession, 47 per cent against and 11 per cent undecided.[2] Separatist sentiments could only grow in the absence of some accommodation.

The United Farmers in Saskatchewan had presented a vision of a more just system of political economy and of Confederation in the following terms:

> We desire to build up in Canada, a well-rounded Dominion, where the best of feeling prevails between class and class, province and province, and believe that this can only be done by treating fairly all classes and parts of the country, and eliminating all special privileges to any class or section.[3]

The Social Credit government in Alberta put it less eloquently in 1938:

> Successful confederation cannot continue when benefits and burdens of national policies are unequally distributed. The benefits of policies instituted for the

general good should not in practice be restricted to particular groups or areas. Where national policy, deliberately or by force of circumstances, impinges unequally on various groups or areas, there should be some corresponding compensation.[4]

There ought to be, according to Social Credit, at the very least, "a nation-wide minimum standard of living." Such ideas were not completely novel, but the depth of the economic crisis, and its increasingly ominous political accompaniments, made it clear that the issues at the heart of the crisis — regional economic inequality and the federal-provincial distribution of powers — would have to be addressed. A failure to do so could fracture the nation, or worse, from the point of view of the establishment, lead to the more basic and radical restructuring proposed by the new Western movements.

The old-line parties, especially the Liberal party after its return to federal power in 1935, began to search for an accommodation significantly short of the simplistic and outrageous financial utopia of social credit or the more dangerously radical and popular notions of the co-operative commonwealth. The Rowell-Sirois Royal Commission on Dominion-Provincial Relations was established in 1937 with a wide mandate to look into the crisis, reporting in 1940. The Report documented the depth of the economic crisis and the accompanying crisis of Confederation. Apart from the regional inequities structured into Confederation, the report also confirmed the incapacity of existing federal-provincial arrangements to cope with the situation.

The British North America (BNA) Act had been drafted to establish a strong central government to play the key role in nation building. Therefore the federal government had been granted the major economic powers, as well as unrestricted taxation powers. Provincial governments were placed in a very subordinate position, concerned mainly with "generally all matters of a merely local or private nature in the provinces," according to the Act. Consequently, the provinces' economic powers, in the context of the 19th century, were weak, and the tax fields left to them small and restricted. But the provinces were given strong social powers: education, health and social welfare. In the 19th century, such areas were not central, there was little government involvement in such activities. As well, the federal government, by 1869, was committed to providing annual grants or subsidies to supplement weak provincial revenues. In the 20th century the social powers of the provinces took on a new importance as the population began to demand more public programming and spending in health, education, and welfare.

The provinces, despite having the responsibility for these areas of growing expenditure, did not have the taxing powers to finance them. The Depression therefore brought what was already a growing crisis onto the center of the political stage, as the Rowell-Sirois Commission recommended a series of reforms to deal with the problem. The Commission recommended a re-distribution of some important powers, a clarification of taxation areas, as well as a coherent program of federal grants to provinces to ensure a basic minimum, common level of social services in each province. Opposition from the provinces vetoed the Commission's specific proposals, but, politicially, the report had vindicated the complaints, especially those from the West.

The War

The coming of World War II began to pull the country out of Depression. National unity for the war effort initially appeared to deflect people's attention from the political and economic agitations of the previous decade. The 1940 election results revealed that the CCF and Social Credit challenges had been locked up in the West with little growth in support. Increased responsiveness by governments of the old parties, as well as the growing public recognition of the need for some reform of Confederation, seemed to augur a return to political stability, despite Aberhart's re-election in 1940.

They did not. The turn to a degree of prosperity, the view that WWII was a battle of world progressive forces against those of fascism and reaction, actually raised expectations and intensified demands for change. The 1941 B.C. election had returned the CCF to official Opposition status with over 33 per cent of the vote.[5] The 1941 Manitoba election had seen the CCF increase its vote to over 17 per cent. The 1941 Nova Scotia election had seen the CCF win three seats with 7 per cent of the vote. In February, 1942 a local CCF candidate defeated federal Conservative leader Arthur Meighen in a by-election in Ontario. And a 1943 Gallup Poll showed that CCF support had tripled since 1940 — to over 25 per cent.[6] The growth of the party seemed irresistible. The declaration of the Canadian Congress of Labour that the CCF was viewed as the political arm of labour continued the momentum.

Most dramatic of all, because it suggested that the CCF was breaking out of the West, the 1943 Ontario election saw the CCF win 34 seats with 32 per cent of the vote (only four seats fewer than the victorious Tories). And in 1944 the CCF swept to power in Saskatchewan, winning 47 of 52 seats with over 53 per cent of the vote. While Social Credit had been securely blockaded in Alberta, the CCF seemed on the verge of a national breakthrough. The 1945 federal election, therefore, took on great significance.

The CCF failed to make the expected breakthrough. Although winning 28 seats with 16 per cent of the vote, the only seat won east of Manitoba was in Nova Scotia. The dramatic showing in the 1943 Ontario election did not spill over into the federal election — indeed, a provincial election in Ontario one week before the 1945 federal vote had reduced the CCF to eight seats and 22 per cent. In the 1945 federal vote the CCF was humbled in Ontario. In the West the story was different. The CCF swept 18 of Saskatchewan's 21 seats with 44 per cent; five Manitoba seats with 32 per cent; and four B.C. seats with 29 per cent. Even in Alberta, though winning no seats, the CCF got a respectable 18 per cent of the vote. Therefore, 27 of 28 seats and more than 55 per cent of all CCF votes were won in the West. This was an improvement over 1940, but hardly sufficient to claim a national breakthrough. For Social Credit the situation was worse: all 13 seats won were won in Alberta, as were 53 per cent of all votes. In the West as a whole, Social Credit won fully 68 per cent of its national vote (which had fallen to four per cent).

Yet the CCF and Social Credit had obviously had a significant impact during their first ten years on the political stage. Thanks to their agitations, and the ongoing political threat they posed, Tories and Liberals increasingly joined them in the advocacy of the welfare state, and the Liberals began to embrace a watered-down version of the CCF's call for economic intervention and planning by governments. The CCF's surge in the 1940s had decisively pushed the Liberals in this direction.[7] Prime Minister Mackenzie King called upon the basic resiliency that had earlier allowed him to win the support of the Progressives for his minority government in 1925 by implementing old age pensions. Early in the war, the federal Liberal government negotiated the transfer of responsibility for unemployment insurance to federal jurisdiction and, in 1944, established a federal family allowance scheme. Recommendations prepared by senior Ottawa civil servants urged the establishment of a federally funded and administered comprehensive social insurance program, including health insurance, family allowances, unemployment insurance, and workers' compensation. This would have required a massive transfer of provincial powers to Ottawa and provincial consent was therefore unlikely. As well, the federal government was urged by some advisors to declare its commitment to government economic planning to encourage full employment. A federal department of Health and Welfare was established. The principle of additional federal transfer payments to provinces in urgent need was approved, providing fiscal security to provinces faced with serious economic difficulty.

Therefore the federal government, in preparation for the 1945 election, and haunted by the CCF, had responded to the great public fear of another post-war depression by putting in place a modest start on a social insurance scheme, while adopting the rhetoric of government initiatives to guarantee near-full employment. Although the federal government did not move on the other features of a general social security program it convened a conference with the provinces to discuss the issue and appeared to be moving, albeit slowly, in the direction advocated by the CCF. Simultaneously, convinced they were on the upswing, CCF national strategists had moderated the party's policies sufficiently that, in fact, much of the rhetoric of the CCF and of the federal Liberal government was indistinguishable on many questions. Clearly a corner had been turned in Canadian politics — all major parties, at least rhetorically, now conceded that it was the responsibility of governments to ensure a basic social and economic security to all. This principle, and its articulation, had been central to the CCF and Social Credit successes in the West. But this moral victory was small consolation: the two movements remained stymied West of the Great Lakes, merely a decreasingly ominous presence to keep the old parties on their toes.

Provincial Consolidation: Social Credit in Alberta

The failure to break out of Alberta combined with the repeated failures to establish social credit and radical debt protection, turned the Social Credit government increasingly inward. The government continued its gradual improvement of the social welfare, health, and educational systems that had characterized it during the Depression. The government held fast to its refusal to settle with the financial interests holding Alberta's public debt, insisting on a low adjustment and declining to pay more than the low rate of interest fixed by Aberhart. Supports and aid to farmers continued the process of agricultural diversification. But the inspiration was gone, save for conspiratorial speeches and pamphlets warning of the "hidden hand of Finance which rules the world."[8] With the death of Aberhart in 1943, even this continuing agitation against the tentacles of finance capital disappeared.

Ernest Manning, the new premier, after some further expansion of the welfare state and a promise of "Social and Economic Security and freedom for all,"[9] sought his own mandate on August 8, 1944, less than two months after the Saskatchewan CCF victory. The main enemy of the 1944 Social Credit campaign was no longer the "Fifty Big Shots" of finance capital, as it had been in 1935 and 1940. This time it was a fight against "socialism" and "bureaucratic regimenta-tion"[10] embodied in the CCF, "this pinkism,"[11] "these Socialistic soap-box orators."[12] Certainly Manning promised to continue to fight for financial reform, but given the last nine years of struggle such reform await-ed federal power, an increasingly unlikely prospect for the Social Credit party. And, it was clear, after the June 1944 victory in Saskatchewan, that the CCF was the only serious contender to replace the Social Credit government. As a result the Social Credit party pulled out all stops to beat the CCF, especially since the CCF was accusing the Manning regime of having sold out to the capitalists. The CCF argued that the election of the CCF was the next logical step in the progressive movement's evolution in Alberta, noting that the Social Credit government had accomplished a good deal but the CCF would "take up where Social Credit left off, and continue more speedily."[13]

Manning swept the province, winning 51 of 57 seats with 52 per cent of the vote (the CCF won two seats with 25 per cent). The press, which had never had a good thing to say about Aberhart, cheered Manning's victory. As the *Financial Post* said, "the monetary reformists ... have proved harmless in their efforts to achieve their monetary policies, but at the same time have given nine years of good government."[14] The Edmonton *Journal* praised Manning for "the decisive rejection of the CCF, which was desirable above everything else."[15] Upon victory, Manning settled the outstanding issue of Alberta's public debt by offering a new 33-year bond to debenture holders. Alberta thus returned to the fold as a safe investment for finance capital.

Manning, with unseemly haste, took the advice offered to Aberhart in 1936, to become, as the *Financial Post* had so delicately put it to Aberhart, "a socially minded conservative of deep human sympathies."[16] As well, Manning heeded the combined threat and promise, spurned by Aberhart, when he was promised that millions in oil capital were "poised to enter promising fields" in the province "if Premier Aberhart swings away from the left."[17] Manning swung very speedily. The sudden transformation of the Alberta Social Credit government from the champion of the common people of the province against finance capital and its corporate and federal government allies into a pro-business, anti-socialist provincial management team was disturbing to some. In fact, Alf Hooke, a long-time Social Credit cabinet minister under both Aberhart and Manning, said in his 1971 memoirs that under Manning "politics in Alberta took a strange turn, with the result that people even today are confused."[18]

Manning presided over a government that increasingly became an orthodox, "socially aware" conservative government, with little reflection of the earlier confrontation with finance capital, though it was not above standing up for Alberta against the federal government. Indeed, Manning later advocated a political realignment that would have fused the Social

Credit party with the Tories. By 1970, after his retirement, Manning had become a director of the Canadian Imperial Bank of Commerce — an ironic turn of events for the party that had decried "Bankers' Toadies." The Alberta agrarian populist crusade for a new Canada, for a new National Policy and a reconstructed political economy, ended with Manning's victory in 1944. His ascension to power marked an end of the use of provincial government power in Alberta as an instrument for political mobilization and confrontation in order to fight for structural political and economic reform. Manning's anti-socialist, frequently hysterical, rhetoric led Alberta away from any meaningful state intervention in the economy and permanently placed the Alberta electorate on the right wing of Canadian politics.

Yet Social Credit still had a province to govern and the party wanted to continue governing it. A reasonably sensitive approach to social welfare, health, and education was not, in itself, enough. The government required increasing revenues to deliver its version of good government. Furthermore, economic diversification was crucial in order to decrease the province's deep dependence on agriculture, particularly wheat. In the 1935 election, the Social Credit party had assumed that the establishment of its financial utopia would automatically lead to rapid diversification. "Why not have machines in Alberta, save all freight and expense, letting us manufacture the finished article in Alberta, giving our producers a Just Price for their raw materials?" they asked.[19]

Social credit and dividends were therefore only the first steps in the dawning of a new and abundant industrial order that would see new industries mushroom — woolen and leather goods factories, brick factories, pulp and paper mills, food processing plants — followed by a mass immigration of skilled and useful people. Alberta's new industrial order would be a magnet "to draw the inventors, the manufacturers, and the people who follow them, and [the] standard of living will be lifted to higher planes."[20] Although, obviously, this did not happen as Aberhart's dreams were struck down, still something had to be done to encourage economic diversification.

Unwilling to use the provincial government directly in the economy as initiator, organizer and entrepreneur, Social Credit relied upon attracting private capital investment to create new economic activity. The provincial government was active, through aid and supports, to facilitate and encourage agricultural diversification. As well, the government proceeded to modernize the province's infrastructure to attract new investment. But the most dramatic event was the 1947 Leduc oil strike, which transformed Alberta from an agricultural province with some oil and natural gas to an oil province with some agriculture.

Although the Alberta government was extremely generous to the oil industry, taking only quite modest royalties and allowing virtually unregulated development and expansion, the new revenues still proved vast enough to silence serious opposition. This, then, was the extent of Alberta's economic diversification — to the basic economic foundation of a diversifying agriculture was added the boom in oil and natural gas development. The resulting prosperity seemed endless enough that the population was largely content to believe their Social Credit leaders' claims that Alberta had solved her problems. The Social Credit government became virtually unassailable, as election after election returned comfortable majorities until the regime's defeat in 1971 by the Tories.

Provincial Consolidation: The CCF in Saskatchewan

The 1944 "CCF Program for Saskatchewan"[21] was the most detailed manifesto yet presented to the electorate, revealing the nature of the coalition built from 1938 to 1944 among progressive farmers, urban workers, and progressive elements of the professions, especially teachers. The first section of the program, and clearly the new CCF government's first priority, was the "provision of security," "farm security," and "urban security." "Farm security" took pride of place in this most agricultural of Canadian provinces.

A CCF government would "stop foreclosure and eviction from the farm home"; prevent the seizure for debt of sufficient of the crop to provide for the livelihood of the farm family; and "force loan and mortgage companies to reduce debts" and "prevent accumulation of new debt." More, a CCF government would "encourage the development of the cooperative movement" with a view to replacing capitalism "by community ownership." As well, a CCF government would deal abruptly with the institution most hated by progressive farmers: the government would "press for the closing of the Winnipeg Grain Exchange." Finally, the CCF would pressure Ottawa to obtain "parity prices for agricultural products." (Parity prices simply meant that the price farmers received would fairly reflect the costs of production and a reasonable profit for their labour and skill.)

Clearly the CCF program crystallized the major

demands of the organized farm movement, developed over decades of agitation. Gone were such proposals as "use-lease," instead, the CCF stood four-square for protected individual private ownership of farm land and denounced the Liberal government because of the lamentable increase in the percentage of rented lands in the province.

The CCF's 1944 "urban security" package was in marked contrast to its simple "work and wages" labour programs of 1934 and 1938. To bring about security for urban workers, the CCF promised fairer laws to permit the development of trade unions and to make collective bargaining compulsory for employers organized by a trade union. Higher minimum wages, the 44-hour week and stricter enforcement of such laws were promised, as was a more adequate system of workers' compensation.

By far the greatest portion of the manifesto had to do with social services and educational reform — an attractive package of general social security measures. Commitments were made to socialized health services, increased old age pensions, pensions for "all who are unable to care for themselves," increased mother's allowances, improved child protection, and so on — the list seemed almost endless. A massive reform of the educational system was proposed: larger school units to provide a bigger tax base to finance improved services: improved teacher earnings; provincial government grants in aid to school units to speed up the construction of modern facilities; free textbooks.

It was the final section of the manifesto that stirred the most controversy — "planning, public ownership and finance." In an effort to explain where a CCF government would get the revenues to pay for its ambitious program, the party was exceedingly blunt.

> The lion's share of the wealth of the province has been
> stolen from the people who produced it. This must
> cease.... The CCF maintains that our natural resour-
> ces must henceforth be developed in the public interest
> and for public benefit. They cannot continue to be
> exploited in a hit-and-miss manner. The CCF stands
> for the planned development of the economic life of the
> province and the social ownership of natural
> resources.[22]

It was this commitment to public ownership and planning on which the CCF's enemies focussed in efforts to
smear the party as communistic. The proposed CCF
measures to raise revenues for its programs were just
as deeply upsetting to business interests. A CCF
government would: "refuse to pay the high interest
rates currently levied to service the provincial debt"
thus freeing "a large sum of money" for other expenditures; establish a Fuel and Petroleum Board to market
wholesale petroleum products; expand the electrical
system, generating more revenue; establish government marketing boards for the distribution of "staple
commodities, say food or machinery"; and develop
resources under public ownership. All these measures,
the CCF argued, as well as "the elimination of graft ...
in the public service" and more aggressive demands on
Ottawa, could provide more than enough funds to
carry out the CCF program. CCF critics pointed out
that such measures would not simply generate more
government revenue, but would make the government
the principal economic actor in the province.

The program was repeated throughout the election
in long and short versions, in versions especially for

farmers, others designed for workers, still others for housewives, for teachers — no group was ignored as the CCF carried its general message in the 1944 election. And as a final touch, the CCF issued a pamphlet listing all its candidates and their occupations in an effort to show that its coalition represented a cross-section of the province. The 52 candidates included 29 farmers, eight teachers, seven industrial workers, three professionals, three merchants, and two housewives.[23] The professionals were a doctor, a lawyer, and a preacher (T.C. Douglas). Clearly, if one goes by candidates nominated, a rather crucial indicator of the vital middle leadership, the party was a farmers' party that had successfully developed alliances with other key sectors of the population: workers, teachers, small merchants, some professionals. And the 1944 victory reflected this coalition; the CCF won 47 seats with 53 per cent of the vote. A somewhat more detailed breakdown is significant: the CCF won over 58 per cent of the rural vote while its urban wins in working-class areas were even more decisive. The CCF heavily won the farmers and the working class, while the Liberals took the majority of the urban and small-town middle classes.[24] No matter how one examines the results, the CCF had won a convincing mandate to carry out its detailed and controversial program.

In the heady years of 1944-48 the CCF moved aggressively to implement its program. The promises made to the farmers were implemented quickly and thoroughly (although the crop failure clause of the Farm Security Act, which freed farmers from mortgage payments during years of crop failure, was later ruled *ultra vires*). Marketing boards were to be set up if over 50 per cent of the farm producers voted in favour. (Marketing boards act on the same principle as the

Canadian Wheat Board: all producers market through the Board and earn the full final price obtained in the marketplace, less a fair cost of administration.)

Massive relief debts incurred by farmers during the Depression were written off. Aggressive government support of farmer efforts to re-fund outstanding debt was provided. Rural Saskatchewan was modernized as the CCF strove to deliver the amenities of urban life to the farm. Programs of support and aid to agriculture encouraged farmers to modernize and diversify to lessen the great dependence on the monoculture of wheat. Almost as quickly, the promises made to the workers were delivered: the most pro-labour Trade Union Act in Canada, higher minimum wages, paid annual vacations, the 44-hour week, a more generous workers' compensation system. For the general benefit of farmer and worker, dramatic steps were taken toward the construction of a comprehensive system of social security in health, education, and welfare. An economic planning agency was set up. Crown corporations in insurance, power, fur marketing, timber, cardboard box production, fish filleting, wood products, leather products, bricks, and bus transportation were established.

With the exception of insurance, power, bus transportation, and telephones (which had long been largely publicly owned), the public enterprises were all modest operations. But they did indicate, initially, a certain seriousness in the government's determination to strive to diversify the province's economy by means of publicly owned industries closely linked to Saskatchewan's natural products. In 1946 Premier Douglas outlined the CCF's vision of growing economic diversification:

First, it is to process... by means of private industry, public enterprise or co-operative development, our agricultural and other primary products... to turn our wool into clothing, our leather into shoes... to process the by-products of the farm, and... the forest... and so on. In other words, instead of being exporters of base primary products, wherever we can, to carry those primary products one stage farther along the course of economic development, with small factories in various communities turning these primary products into more saleable commodities. [This will] provide employment for the people... on these prairies. I do not think that the people... are prepared, for ever and a day, to be hewers of wood and drawers of water.... [Then] we should use those industries... to produce revenue to give our people a certain measure of social security....[25]

The vision that motivated the CCF program, and the government's initial moves, was clear. The Co-operative Commonwealth was viewed as a society founded firmly in the family farm. The provincial government, within the constitutional limits (federal power was essential for the full construction of the Commonwealth), would use its powers to defend and extend small agricultural production and its socio-economic basis, the productive enterprise of the working farmer. However, the social ownership of selected areas of the economy was essential. Social ownership was conceived by the CCF in various forms: co-operative ownership, municipal public ownership, provincial public ownership, and federal public ownership. The CCF also, with some twists and convolutions, insisted that the private ownership of farms by family farmers was a form of social ownership since the land was disbursed, not monopolized or concentrated. The provincial government would use its powers and resources to support, encourage, and even to subsidize, co-operative ventures of all kinds.

Further, the government would enter into the ownership of utilities, insurance, and natural resources: the first two were seen as essential public services that would be unwisely left to private planning for private advantage; the last was seen as the people's birthright. As well, due to Saskatchewan's economic vulnerability, the government would proceed to do some of those things the private sector refused to do: it would embark on a modest industrialization program, linked directly to the natural products of the province, in order to widen the province's economic base. Wage workers, with the exception of farm wage-labour, would be accorded an unfettered right of combination and collective bargaining, buttressed by strong labour standards and a higher minimum wage. But it would remain wage-labour and traditional relations of production would obtain in the public as well as the private spheres. Finally, health, education, and welfare services would be improved, expanded, and gradually extended into new areas of public good. This was the vision of 1944-48.

But in the run-up to the 1948 election the CCF government had already begun to abandon its commitment to develop natural resources under public ownership. Indeed, the hysterical red-baiting attacks by the Liberal Opposition, and the growing Cold War mood, also convinced the government to back off from its program of modest industrialization under public ownership. More and more the government pointed proudly to the advances made by the Crown corporations in power, telephones, insurance, and transportation, less and less at the more controversial public industries in blankets, shoes, boxes, fur, fish, and clay. These latter enterprises were not doing too well, as they found the capitalist marketplace largely closed to them. Convinced by the growing mood of anti-communism, as well as its own belief that a provincial government did not possess the capital and the expertise essential to a full-scale and rapid development of the province's natural resources, the CCF government increasingly opened the door to private investors to develop the new resource growth industries. By the pre-election budget speech in 1948 the CCF government had made it flatly clear that it did not intend to pursue public ownership in natural resource development. That task would be left to private capital under the watchful eye of the government.

The general decline in support for the national and Ontario CCF found its reflection in Saskatchewan. As the old parties pursued their policy of a judicious adoption of aspects of the core CCF program, combined with an anti-CCF campaign of vilification and smear in the context of the growing Cold War mood, the CCF, even in its Saskatchewan bastion, faced a decline in support. Indeed, the 1948 provincial election results revealed some significant erosion of CCF support. The erosion might have been even more serious had the Saskatchewan Liberals learned to be more moderate than they proved to be — in 1948, the Liberal party failed to articulate its alternative version of the social welfare state, contenting itself with a near-hysterical red-baiting campaign against the CCF. The government was re-elected with 31 of 52 seats and about 48 per cent of the vote, reflecting a loss of over five per cent in popular vote and 16 seats. The biggest loss came in rural areas, which returned 19 Liberals and 24 CCFers. The CCF urban, working-class support remained solid, but there was a serious erosion and had the CCF faced a united free-enterprise alternative, in the context of the red-baiting that took place, the government might well have been defeated. The federal election a year later confirmed that erosion. A drop of less than four per cent in the popular vote reduced the CCF from 18 federal seats in the province to just five seats in 1949. Nationally, the CCF's total number of seats fell from 28 to 13, its popular vote to just over 13 per cent. Again, the CCF was corralled in the West — 11 of 13 seats and almost 53 per cent of all the votes polled by the CCF. Clearly, the federal results confirmed the need to take stock.

Although the *Financial Post* believed that the 1948 results revealed that the "socialists" had been "unmasked" and that the "virtual defeat" suggested that the electorate saw the CCF as "a narrow socialistic class party,"[26] the CCF government saw it differently. The government believed that the results confirmed the correctness of the policy of a continuing moderate consolidation of its basic 1944-48 program. No dramatic new initiatives were contemplated. The legislative program of the government, as well as its annual budgets, from 1949 onward reflected this fact. There were no new experiments in public enterprise and the government continued to place its emphasis upon the crown corporations in power, telephones, insurance, and transportation. There were no new adventures in publicly owned industrial plants and those that existed were increasingly put on the rear shelf of public display, and most were finally allowed to die more or less natural deaths. Resource development — especially of the new mineral riches — was to be carried out by private capital.

After considerable internal party debate, as well as careful and moderate analyses of the possibilities of a public ownership strategy of resource development, the government had irrevocably decided to go with private development. This decision was motivated partly by an uncertainty about whether the government of a small province could mobilize sufficient capital and expertise, as well as develop secure international markets, to ensure the success of large-scale public resource development. As well, the decision was motivated by deep political doubts about whether the growing political conservatism in Canada would accept serious public ownership beyond basic essential services. The commitment to public ownership of resource development was, therefore, unceremoniously dropped, not to be picked up again until the initiatives of the NDP government in the 1970s.

Advances in welfare, health, and education were slowed down to allow increasing balanced economic growth. As well, the CCF continued its aggressive advocacy of government programs to aid and further agricultural development and the establishment of co-operative enterprises. Largely gone were ringing declarations about the ultimate establishment of the co-operative commonwealth, gone were denunciations of capitalism as a system. In their place was the rhetoric and practice of a sound, Western-oriented, business-like administration, careful management of the province's affairs, a commitment to social security, a dedication to obtaining a decent share of resource profits through taxation and royalty schemes, and a clear intention to provide all essential aid necessary for agricultural prosperity and stability.

This moderation and consolidation paid off in handsome electoral dividends as the CCF government easily retained power throughout the 1950s, a remarkable feat that boggled the minds of the Liberal Opposition, completely confounded by the fact that Saskatchewan's farmers continued to elect those "reds" and "socialists." Only in 1960 did the CCF make a dramatic move to extend the welfare state by campaigning for re-election on a promise to implement a universal medicare system. Easily re-elected, the CCF moved to implement the program, the first in Canada, against the wishes of the medical profession, supported by the province's despairing right-wing forces. The resulting doctors' strike of 1962, and the incredible right-wing political agitations that accompanied it, finally united the CCF's political foes sufficiently that in 1964 the 20-year-old regime was defeated by the long-suffering Liberal Opposition.

The Quieting of the West

The moderation and consolidation of the CCF and Social Credit regimes and their undeniable success in providing good government, contributed to a quieting of the agitation in the West. Clearly denied the chance to apply their remedies nationally, both the CCF and Social Credit governments retreated to provincial strategies, focussing on establishing all-class political coalitions by providing solid, competent, reasonably sensitive, and business-like government. Both movements had begun by advocating an aggressive restructuring of capitalism, and of Confederation, in favour of the common people — most particularly, in favour of the Prairie farmers they represented. Thwarted in such efforts by a failure to win national power, and by the evolution of a less harsh welfare-state capitalism, the two movements more and more focused on becoming competent provincial administrations defending their people in battles with the federal government in the growing morass of federal-provincial gamesmanship.

This consolidation of the two movements in Alberta and Saskatchewan was accompanied by relatively poor results in the other two Western provinces. In Manitoba, the Liberal-Progressive government continued to survive by moving sufficiently on basic reforms. The CCF, but for a strong showing in 1945 (34 per cent of the vote), retained its third-party status, a fate that seemed sealed when the more "progressive" Tories gained office in 1958. The Manitoba Social Credit party failed to gain any credibility at all.

In B.C., the CCF continued to be electorally outflanked by the free enterprise coalition. A near CCF win in 1952, when the old Tory-Liberal coalition collapsed and was replaced by W.A.C. Bennett's Social Credit party, was not repeated. In 1952 the CCF gained the most votes of any party and missed forming a minority government by just one seat (the CCF won 18 seats; Social Credit, 19 seats; Tories, four seats; Liberals, six seats). Bennett's minority government of 1952 was returned with a solid majority in 1953 when sufficient additional Tory and Liberal voters finally agreed that Bennett alone could save the province from socialism.

Social Credit had done very poorly in the province previously, for example, only winning just over one per cent of the vote in 1949. But Bennett's party, the control of which he wrested from orthodox Social Crediters, had nothing to do with Social Credit doctrine, except for the odd bit of florid populist rhetoric that Bennett indulged in from time to time. The party had most to do with making Bennett premier. Bennett's more favoured rhetoric was anti-socialist and

anti-communist, and the need to unite the free enterprisers against the socialist hordes. But this extremely
reactionary rhetoric did not deter Bennett from pursuing the construction of a reasonably generous system
of social security in the province, if only to steal at least
some of the CCF's thunder. As well, Bennett picked
up a lot of the federal bashing, anti-Central Canada
rhetoric that had characterized the earlier Alberta
Social Credit and the Saskatchewan CCF. As a result,
the movements, especially the CCF, were denied decisive success anywhere but in their original fortresses.

The two movements were therefore not just locked
up in the West — they remained locked up in Alberta
and Saskatchewan, unable even to win the hearts and
minds of sufficient people in the other two Western
provinces to join either crusade. This failure helped
speed up the process of moderation of the movements.
In the case of the CCF, the process was sped up by a
conviction that the old socialist remedies for harsh
times had to be modified to meet the new situation. In
the case of Social Credit in Alberta, the process was
sped up by the government's conviction that fortress
Alberta required careful tending as the sole province
with a genuine Social Credit government, indeed, the
sole province with a genuine and significant Social
Credit party.

The federal government helped subdue the expression of grievance through a series of significant concessions, gradually, often reluctantly, but inexorably. In
recognition of the growing expense of programs in
areas of provincial jurisdiction, the federal government conceded the need to generously supplement
provincial revenues. As well, the federal government
completely took over particularly expensive areas of
social security. Unemployment insurance, old age pen-

sions, family allowances, and, later, a general pension plan, all became federal responsibilities. Major cost-shared programs in hospital insurance, post-secondary education, and medicare committed the federal government to massive injections of revenue into programs established and administered by provincial governments. Regular federal equalization payments to needy provinces established a guaranteed minimum provincial revenue base. New tax fields were opened to the provinces and vacated by the federal government; other lucrative tax areas were increasingly shared between the two levels of government.

Federal support and aid to agriculture helped the West, as did the continuation of the Canadian Wheat Board and the Crow statutory rate. John Diefenbaker's federal regime proved especially sensitive to the West. Price supports for a whole range of agricultural products were established. Massive amounts of federal funds were contributed to the modernization and diversification of Prairie agriculture and rural society. Economic development grants to areas targeted as needy were put in place to try to deal with the problems of regional disparity and the need for general economic diversification, especially in areas dependent on natural resource exports. Increasingly the voices of the Western provinces were simply four voices among nine and then ten clamouring for more and more from the federal government — more tax powers, more shared-cost programs, more direct federal spending.

The election of the Diefenbaker government in 1957, and his sweep in 1958, rooted partly in his flamboyant populist rhetoric, had deeply undermined the two Western movements. Diefenbaker, the first truly Western prime minister, seemed to promise that he would redress Western grievances by action in Ottawa. His "northern vision" foresaw an era of growth and prosperity which would not only diversity the Western economy but elevate the West to its proper place of influence in the nation. His rhetoric, denouncing the corruption, arrogance, and indifference of the federal Liberal government as well as its smug corporate backers, electrified the West. In 1958 the West had rewarded its man electorally with all 14 seats and 57 per cent of the vote in Manitoba; 16 of 17 seats and 51 per cent in Saskatchewan; all 17 seats and 60 per cent in Alberta; and 18 of 22 seats and 49 per cent in B.C. In Alberta, the Social Credit party was wiped out as a federal presence — for the first time since 1935 Social Credit ideas would not be heard in the House of Commons. The Saskatchewan CCF's federal wing did not fare much better, winning only one seat. The CCF nationally was reduced to eight seats and just under ten per cent of the vote — and, again, five of eight seats and 52 per cent of the total vote was won in the West. As a result the CCF, as a national force, came close to being extinguished, even its major remaining role as the Western voice of reform threatened by Diefenbaker's populist rhetoric.

Poised on the threshold of national extinction as the 1960s began, the CCF and Social Credit movements were victims of their own successes. As the latest expressions of Western grievance, an expression that began with the first Riel Rebellion, the movements contributed significantly to winning the great concessions that helped shape the Canada we know today. Indeed, the Western agitation had a long legacy of concessions to which it could lay some claim of authorship: the establishment of the province of Manitoba; more adequate federal political representation; an end to the CPR monopoly clause; some freight rate relief; the regulation of the grain trade; public involvement in the storage and handling of grain; some selective tariff relief; direct federal agricultural assistance for a whole range of programs; debt adjustment; regular and guaranteed federal equalization payments; the Bank of Canada; the Canadian Wheat Board; the Farm Credit Corporation; and so on.

The greatest general gain, for which authorship must be shared with victims of the Depression all across the Dominion, was the growing federal financial commitment to the construction of a welfare state through programs to ensure a minimum level of well-being for all Canadians regardless of place of residence in the country. There is no doubt that the fundamental character of capitalism had been softened. Furthermore, the growing federal commitment to the notion of "co-operative federalism" altered the practice of federal-provincial relations by conceding more and more ground to the provinces.

But, in fact, though muted, the West's structural grievances remained. This was reflected in the continuing strength of the CCF and Social Credit movements in the politics of the four Western provinces in spite of the Diefenbaker sweep. The grievances remained because the basic structure of Confederation and the West's political and economic place in that structure continued fundamentally unaltered. Cap-in-hand petitions to Ottawa, even proud outbursts, brought modifications, but modifications on the terms and at the pleasure of the federal government. What the federal government could give, the federal government could take away — and the federal government frequently had its own ideas of what it should give, ideas often at variance with provincial governments. Though the federal government neglected to use them, the over-riding federal powers of disallowance and reservation remained at the disposal of Ottawa, to be used should a provincial government get out of hand again.

Economically, the West remained a hewer of wood and drawer of water — a source of diversifying natural resources for export. Certainly, the list of resources to be exploited for export grew, but the fundamental vulnerability of the West's resource-based economy remained. Despite all the significant concessions made to the West, no concessions were made to what Vernon Fowke called the political and economic terms of "national integration."[27] The structure of Confederation and the economic role of the West in the national economy remained as in place as it had been when Clifford Sifton called for the exploitation of "the wealth of the field, of the forest and of the mine ... in vast quantities." The concessions muted and quieted the agitations. But the basic grievances remained, festering below the surface of the decorous federal-provincial conferences.

8
Of Resources and Constitutions: The Rising of the New West

As the Western provinces moved into the 1960s they found themselves still structurally destined to remain most importantly producers of primary resources for export. Certainly diversification had occurred, but it had occurred in the resource sector and, of course, in common with all other advanced capitalist societies, in the growing service and construction sectors. Agriculture had been greatly diversified on the Prairies as new cash crops and expanded livestock production were added to the backbone of wheat and other grains. But there had been costs associated with this modernization: there were far fewer farms, farm land had concentrated, and the rural Prairie social structure was in steep decline, as more and more people left the land to take jobs in the growing towns and cities.

As well, farmers as a class had been deeply divided — the days of a single agrarian organization speaking with one voice for the majority of farmers in a province were irrevocably over. New farm organizations emerged to reflect the special interests of different commodity groups — stockmen, cow-calf producers, rapeseed producers. Even the wheat growers were increasingly divided between conservative and progressive wings. Conservative groups, like the Cattlemen's Association and the Palliser Wheat Growers, tended to advocate the return to pure, competitive free enterprise in the marketplace, while more progressive groups, like the Cow-Calf Association and the Saskatchewan Farmers' Union (later joining in founding the National Farmers' Union), fought to retain and extend the reforms won for agriculture over the years like marketing boards, the Canadian Wheat Board, the Crow Rate, federal price supports, and so on.

Land concentration had resulted in the growth of a class of very large, very rich grain or cattle barons who looked to new non-agricultural investment opportunities. Farmers with small- and medium-sized farms were increasingly insecure, and for thousands survival became possible only through off-farm wage work, often for both farmer and spouse. The overwhelming direction of government aid to agriculture seemed to speed up the process of modernization and concentration — smaller farmers discovered that rather than keeping them on the land, such programs seemed more designed to hasten their exit from farming. Government agencies and their programs were increasingly committed to the idea of the economically viable farm unit — and farmers whose farms were considered to be too small were encouraged to exit from farming so their farmland could be used to increase the size of other units.

In the absence of general economic diversification, the Western provinces found themselves forced to take the only road left to them — an opening of their provinces to virtually unrestricted resource development. Indeed, the provinces were forced to compete with each other for scarce investment by offering increasingly favourable terms to largely foreign capital eager to open the new West. Tax incentives, low royalty schemes, few environmental regulations, government guaranteed loans — the incentives offered to lure such new investment seemed endless as the provinces competed in a desperate gamble to maximize development.

It became the era of the resource mega-project, of rapid and uncontrolled development, based on the premise that such activity would inevitably have spin-off benefits for the economy as a whole. The argument was that the province would not only benefit from the jobs, temporary and permanent, in the development itself, and in the generation of revenues through taxes and royalties, but in the multiplier effects as economic activity to service such projects would create jobs for workers and economic opportunities for entrepreneurs. This doctrine became increasingly fiercely held as the few industrial jobs located in the West, especially in the Prairie West — in railway shops, in meat packing, in flour milling — began to disappear as these industries modernized and centralized.

Even Manitoba, the Ontario of the West, with its well-diversified economy rooted in agriculture, forest, and mineral resources, and a strong manufacturing sector, could not escape the pressure. Manitoba's manufacturing sector was, and remains, rooted in the dual tasks of food processing and of servicing the limited Western market. Unable to break into national or international markets with new manufacturing activity, the province joined the scramble to diversify by opening its virtually undeveloped north to forestry and mining development on terms favourable to private capital. The biggest debacle in this effort resulted in the disappearance of about $40 million in public funds. In 1966 the Tory government announced the Churchill Forest Industries project at The Pas, a com-

munity about 760 kilometres northwest of Winnipeg.[1]
The project, organized by a Swiss company, was to
consist of a $100 million unified complex involving
pulp, paper, and lumber mills. Great promises were
made: 2,000 new jobs directly; another 2,000 indirect
jobs; good opportunities for employment for native
people; the beginning of an industrial turn in Manitoba. Ultimately the provincial government put up $92
million, the federal government, $15 million, as almost
daily the costs of the project spiralled. There were to be
no pollution controls. Timber concessions of a size
equal to the area of Portugal were to be granted. The
Pas forgave most of its local taxes. The owners and
investors, whose identity initially was kept secret, were
able to develop the project without investing a cent, in
fact, they were able to walk away with a great deal of
public funds. The project collapsed and was scaled
down: less than 1,000 jobs were created, public money
had disappeared in a complex maze of interlocking
foreign companies, and the government was finally
forced to take the project into receivership and to
begin to seek legal remedies. The whole thing turned
out to be a disaster and a rip-off — for which the
taxpayers of Manitoba paid.

The Saskatchewan CCF's open-door policy to
investors in new resource development in oil and
potash, and later in uranium, was extended even more
aggressively by the 1964 Liberal regime. Potash mine
after potash mine was allowed to come on stream in
efforts to increase production to the limit. Further oil
exploration and production were encouraged as the
Liberals expanded on the CCF's policy of following
Alberta's lead in oil development policies. Efforts
were made to encourage pulp production, again
through generous incentives to foreign capital.

The pulp decision proved to be among the more politically costly for the Saskatchewan Liberal government. Desperate to diversify the province's economy, and thereby to show the superiority of free enterprise over socialism, the provincial Liberal government entered into an agreement with an American-based firm, Parsons and Whittemore, to construct two pulp mills in the province — one at Prince Albert, about 220 kilometres north of Saskatoon, and one farther north, at Meadow Lake.[2] The province agreed to assume virtually all the risks by guaranteeing almost $160 million in loans, for a 30 per cent equity in the mills. As well, the government agreed to build a gas pipeline, a bridge, and a new road, as well as 320 kilometres of roads every ten years in the Prince Albert district to facilitate the harvesting of wood. Again, no serious pollution controls were put in place. Although the project went forward, the deal caused a political furor that helped defeat the Liberal government in 1971.

In Alberta, the Social Credit government continued its virtual "hands-off" approach to oil and natural gas development. The doctrine was simple: let the industry do it, and have its way, and Alberta would prosper through royalties and spinoffs. The low royalty revenues gained were, it was believed, offset by the maximization of exploration and production activities and, of course, the resulting general stimulus to those servicing the industry. The Alberta government continued to approach oil and gas production as if they were limitless sources of wealth. In fact, oil and gas development was and remained Alberta's mega-project, the star to which all else was tied.

B.C. was the master of the resource mega-project strategy. Martin Robin's two-volume political history of the province, *The Rush for Spoils* and *Pillars of Profit*, both subtitled *The Company Province*, records the massive give-aways that occurred in B.C. from the beginning.³ The government was, in its early days, seen simply as the mechanism for providing the right to exploit resources, and for building the infrastructure necessary to do so. Mineral and timber rights on a vast scale were given to entrepreneurs without the slightest concern for adequate returns to the public treasury. In addition to granting these concessions, the B.C. government concentrated on providing access, publicly funded, to the resources: roads, bridges, port facilities, railways. The Bennett government of 1952 simply raised this basic economic strategy to an art form with a massive program of highway and bridge construction and resource give-aways.

Such give-aways, low tax and royalty schemes, a virtual absence of government regulation, continued to be the approach of the government as it strove to maximize economic spinoffs by maximizing resource production — which, of course, meant to let the entrepreneurs have their head. Bennett, in the 1960s, added to his name as a road and bridge builder that of a dam builder as he harnassed B.C.'s great rivers for cheap hydro-electric power. The basic strategy of the government remained simple: give away the resources; build the infrastructure to allow their exploitation; and watch the province grow.

As a result, the basic vulnerability of the West's resource economy continued. A collapse in grain prices would devastate the Prairies. A collapse in potash prices would hurt Saskatchewan deeply. A collapse in lumber prices would be disastrous for B.C. And, for Manitoba, a downturn in any of the Western provinces would create difficulty for its manufacturing sector. Clearly the Western economies were no longer as vulnerable as they had been in the Great Depression. Each had a more diversified resource base, and, it was hoped, a collapse in one sector would be offset by continuing strength in other sectors. Should agricultural prices decline, Saskatchewan could fall back on potash, oil, uranium, and a range of other minor resources being developed; Alberta had its oil; and Manitoba had its manufacturing base, as well as growing forestry and mining developments in the north. B.C., however, despite high levels of prosperity, remained extremely vulnerable to events in the forestry and related industries.

The Re-emergence of Unrest in the 1970s

As the 1960s came to a close, a series of events indicated that people in the West were increasingly uneasy with this economic strategy. Simply stated, the strategy was just not working. Workers were not enjoying growing employment opportunities. Local business groups found that there were not the expected golden investment opportunities in spin-offs from large resource developments. The new environmentalist lobby was exposing the terrible implications arising from such uncontrolled and unregulated growth. Conservationists were increasingly listened to as they warned that resources, non-renewable as well as the theoretically renewable (like forestry), were being seriously depleted and resource exhaustion was on the relatively near historical horizon. This latter concern was particularly strong in Alberta, as the end of sweet, conventional oil reserves was predicted to be surprisingly imminent, and in B.C. where the forests and the fishery were being ravaged at a pace that could not possibly be sustained. Even the Prairie soil was being mined for the wheat economy to such an extent that serious soil problems would be confronted in a generation or two.

During the 1960s the relationship between Ottawa and the Western provinces began to harden again. The eternal federal search for a way to patriate, and provide for the amendment of, the constitution, including some kind of charter of rights (especially language rights), intensified. Ottawa, faced with the Quiet Revolution and the disconcerting evidence of the Report of the Royal Commission on Bilingualism and Biculturalism, which vindicated Quebec's complaints, was determined to deal with Quebec's grievances, at least partly, through constitutional change. The other nine provinces, including the four in the West, were mainly concerned about a way to protect existing provincial powers from future erosion through an unacceptable amending formula. Simultaneously, the federal government, especially under Pearson, moved quickly on a number of generous concessions, not only to Quebec, but to all provinces: shared cost agreements on medicare, post-secondary education, social welfare, as well as a federal pension plan.

The Western provinces were not overly active in the constitutional process in the sense of pushing for enhanced provincial powers, but they were eager for further federal economic concessions. W.A.C. Bennett took a cavalier attitude to federal-provincial meetings, often dismissing them as irrelevant to B.C. Ernest Manning was committed to the traditional view out of the Depression, that more should be squeezed out of Ottawa. Meanwhile, Premier Thatcher of Saskatchewan, eager to put some distance between himself and the Ottawa Liberals, contented himself with vague fed-bashing in the absence of a coherent alternative approach to federal-provincial relations. Premiers Roblin and then Weir of Manitoba shared the views of Manning — the federal government ought to be putting up more money for the programs the provinces were forced to put in place.

There was, therefore, no new Western initiative on constitutional reform, except for a determination to safeguard existing provincial powers. There was a lot of Western concern about favouritism to Quebec, but this was eased somewhat by federal largesse in other areas. Further, the Western provinces had nothing new to say about a national economic strategy — they were largely content to go with the foreign investment, expanded resource extraction, mega-project strategy and only demanded that Ottawa, through measures like the Department of Regional Economic Expansion, further support this thrust by sweetening provincial give-aways to such investors with federal grants as well. In the event, the near agreement on the constitution at Victoria in 1971 went the way of the earlier 1964 Fulton-Favreau proposal — Quebec vetoed it.

In general, then, the Western provinces during the 1960s were not overly worried about the constitution. What they wanted from Ottawa was more financial concessions and they appeared prepared to go along with Ottawa to satisfy Quebec as long as it didn't cost anything. There was almost a certain contentment, despite the raised voices demanding concessions from Ottawa from time to time, because the West was prosperous and the programs from Ottawa, though never quite enough, were buttressing that prosperity. The West, especially B.C., even shared a bit of Central Canada's enthusiasm for Trudeau in 1968. The Western provinces seemed to be saying, let's keep Quebec happy; yes, let's have a just society; but, more importantly, let's keep the economic boom going and let's continue to pump more federal money into the public infrastructure. The carping voices of left-wing critics, trade unionists, environmentalists, and noisy students were minor discordant notes in what was, or appeared to be, a booming symphony of prosperity and growth. But this didn't last — the boom of the 1960s staggered and then fell.

The relatively high level of Western prosperity was replaced by a general recession, as incomes began to contract and unemployment rose. In 1968-72, B.C.'s average per-capita income fell to the lowest point, relative to the national average, in over 17 years, and unemployment began a steady climb in 1966.[4] Alberta's average per-capita income, having reached the national average in the late 1960s, stalled and fell slightly in relative terms in the early 1970s. Manitoba continued to limp along at about the same level of prosperity. A severe recession in agriculture in the late 1960s and early 1970s plagued the Prairie economy. Saskatchewan was particularly hard-hit as its 1969 and 1970 average per-capita incomes, relative to the national average, fell to the lowest ebb since the 1959-61 recession. A collapse of the potash market further deepened Saskatchewan's difficulty and contributed to deep doubts about the wisdom of all-out development of resources as the road to diversification and prosperity.

Aggressive agrarian agitations re-emerged on the Prairies, led by the National Farmers' Union, complaining that federal and provincial policies were destroying agriculture. The 1969 Federal Task Force on Agriculture report particularly incensed Prairie farmers by advocating a deliberate policy of massive acceleration of land concentration as marginal farmers were forced to leave agriculture. In fact, the Task Force Report advocated programs to bring about the ultimate exit of about two in three of Canada's farmers.[5] This enraged Westerners. The federal Lower Inventory For Tomorrow (LIFT) program, designed to discourage wheat production to overcome a world oversupply and low prices, was assailed as the Lower Income For Tomorrow program (the farmers turned out to be correct — those who participated in LIFT found themselves without a surplus of wheat to sell when demand and prices went up). Such developments contributed to some rapid and astonishing political upsets in the Western provinces.

In 1969 the Manitoba NDP, led by Ed Schreyer, went from third-party status to government. A large part of this upset can be attributed to the NDP's critique of the Tory government's resource give-away approach to development, particularly growing public uneasiness over the Churchill Forest Industries megaproject. In 1971 the Saskatchewan NDP, led by Allan Blakeney, swept the province. Again, significant in the campaign had been an NDP critique of the Liberal approach to resources and agriculture, and, again, scandals around some of the government's largesse to foreign capital played a role in its defeat. In 1971 the newly revitalized Alberta Tories, under Peter Lougheed, won office. His drive to power had almost exclusively focussed on the Social Credit failure to use the oil and gas boom either to capture sufficient revenues from these depleting resources, or to use the boom as a base to create significant economic diversification. In 1972 Dave Barrett led the B.C. NDP to a surprise victory after nearly 40 years as Official Opposition. The B.C. NDP victory, although mostly due to divisions among free enterprisers (Liberals and Tories joined the fray against the Socreds), was also rooted significantly in the NDP's ongoing critique of the B.C. government's irresponsible approach to resource development.

Without exception, although there were clear differences between the Alberta Tories and the three NDP governments, the new regimes promised a bigger role for provincial governments in planning and pacing resource development, as well as aggressive new tax and royalty schedules to increase returns to public treasuries. Although the NDP regimes, especially those of Blakeney and Barrett, promised a significant public role in resource development through crown corporations, the Lougheed Tory government in Alberta proved also to be surprisingly interventionist.

The Blakeney, Barrett, and Schreyer victories reflected most clearly a defeat of the local business elite, which had tied its star to the mega-project, trickle-down strategy for economic enhancement. As well, the argument that the old strategy was ill-serving the West in its efforts to carve out a decent economic niche in Confederation proved compelling. The Lougheed victory amounted to a defeat of the farmer-rooted Social Credit by a growing and more aggressive urban business elite, convinced that provincial powers could be used much more effectively both to maximize economic opportunities for local businessmen and to steer and stimulate economic diversification through capturing a bigger share of the oil and gas wealth for provincial use.

The common denominator aiding the election of the four regimes was dissatisfaction with the resource strategy of the 1950s and 1960s. Everyone in the West wanted economic diversification, new development, jobs, and prosperity — but they began to question the price. Clearly, resource development by external, largely foreign, capital was not doing the job. Tremendous give-aways; concessions on taxes, pollution controls, and conservation rules; faith in the magical expertise of international capital — all had not paid off. Quite simply the provinces were being ripped off, and the rip-off was less acceptable because the promise of general prosperity had not been realized. In different ways, the electorates of each of the Western provinces had said clearly: there had to be a better way. Surely the Western provinces could control resource development so that Westerners would retain more benefits. Surely sensible pollution controls and reasonable conservation measures would be a long-term boon to both businessmen and the public.

The election of the four regimes marked a new era in the West's struggle for a place in the sun in Confederation and in the national economy. The older agitations had won the West significant concessions, but had not overcome the basic structural problems. Content with the victories in Saskatchewan and Alberta, the traditional movements on the Prairies, largely reflecting agrarian interests, had rested on their laurels. Indeed, they had won much and done much, but the problems persisted while the concessions simply softened the reality. The Social Credit and CCF governments had initially proven to be surprisingly aggressive in their use of provincial powers to defend the farmer, their basic constituency, but had failed to recognize that these same powers could serve the interests of the province further. Just as the great social powers conferred on the provinces by the BNA Act had allowed the movements, upon victory, to push for the construction of the welfare state in the era of the Great Depression, the provinces' control of natural resources could be used to push for a better economic deal for the West. This power was all the more vital in the modern era both because of the growing range and diversified richness of the West's resources, and because of a continuing national dependence on the export of resources as the foundation of the national economy.

This realization of the growing potential power of the West because of its resource riches was magnified by an increasing sense of Western alienation from the federal government. The defeat and degradation of Diefenbaker, the failure of the CCF/NDP to make a national breakthrough, and the Pearson government's growing pre-occupation with Quebec all tended to increase a Western sense of political distance from Ottawa. The brief hope contained in Trudeau's election in 1968 was quickly replaced in the West by an ever-growing alienation from and hostility to the federal Liberal government.

Trudeau's pre-occupation with Quebec separatism, his clumsy policy initiatives in the West, like LIFT and the Federal Task Force on Agriculture, and his lack of sympathy for Western concerns about resource development, began a process of Western political estrangement that saw the Western Liberal party, federally and provincially, virtually annihilated in a decade. Indeed, the once-proud Liberal party in the West, which in 1969 could boast 27 MPs, 56 MLAs, and the control of the Saskatchewan provincial government, had been reduced, by 1979, to three MPs, and one MLA.[6] Trudeau's conviction that a large part of the Quebec problem, indeed of the growing crisis of Confederation, had to do with an excessively weak federal government and his consequent commitment to strengthen it, ensured a further confrontation with the

West. The West was happy enough to see Trudeau flex federal muscles against the Québécois, such as during the 1970 October crisis, but did not appreciate a similar flexing against the West on the issue of resources.

Two contradictory forces ensured a deep confrontation: the growing sense of power in the West and a determination to use provincial powers aggressively to maximize provincial benefits from resource development; and a growing conviction on the part of the Trudeau regime that federal power, atrophied by lack of use during the Diefenbaker and Pearson years, had to be re-asserted. Ottawa found itself fighting a constitutional battle on two fronts: to the East, the Quebec separatists, who won provincial power in 1976; to the West, the growing assertion of provincial powers over natural resources.

The Western Resource Boom

In the early 1970s the recession plaguing the West began to turn around. Agricultural prices improved steadily, lifting the industry out of its temporary trough. Potash prices began to rise, leading to great hopes for the industry in Saskatchewan. A boom in international demand and prices for uranium spurred significant developments in Saskatchewan. But overshadowing everything else was the phenomenal increase in the world price for oil. Western industrial capitalist nations had become deeply dependent on cheap oil from the Middle East; indeed, they had become nearly exclusively dependent on oil for their energy supplies. Cheap oil was the secret of a mass auto market, of a view that central heating for all in detached homes was a right, and, most significantly, of a competitive edge in the markets for manufactured goods. An endless supply of cheap oil had become a basic necessity for the economic prosperity of Western Europe and North America.

Canada was doing very well out of oil. Exports of Western oil and natural gas to American markets had mushroomed as Alberta and Saskatchewan scrambled to reap the benefits of the U.S.'s insatiable need for energy. Although Canada was forced to import oil to fulfill demand in eastern Canada, the massive exports from the West made the country a net earner as exports offset the costs of imports.

In the early 1970s the picture began to change. Oil-supplying countries had organized themselves into a cartel, the Organization of Petroleum Exporting Countries (OPEC), determined to reap a greater share of revenue from oil for the producing countries. Sporadic pressures to increase the world price of oil continued until 1973, when OPEC began a series of unilateral moves which doubled, then tripled, and then quadrupled world oil prices. The major oil companies joined the crusade for higher prices by drastic revisions downwards of their estimate of recoverable, conventional oil and gas reserves in North America, especially Alberta, suggesting that oil exhaustion was disturbingly imminent.

The "oil crisis" was upon us, creating a bonanza for the oil-producing countries and for the major international oil companies. The crisis was a disaster for the oil-consuming countries. The industrial sectors of the advanced countries, deeply dependent on cheap oil, found themselves in a crunch. The costs of home heating and auto fuel deeply cut into the disposable incomes of families, while oil-price-related spiralling inflation and interest rates further contracted incomes. Third World oil-consuming countries were dealt a staggering blow in their efforts to modernize and develop. And in Canada, the oil crisis created a further Confederation crisis.

The Western energy provinces — led by Alberta, more or less supported by Saskatchewan and B.C. — moved aggressively to capture the windfall profits associated with the oil price rise (which also stimulated a rise in the price for natural gas, as consumers and industries rushed to convert from oil).[7] The federal government moved aggressively as well. Ottawa imposed an oil price freeze in the fall of 1973, slapped on a federal oil export tax to capture increased revenues, and decided to deny resource companies the right to deduct provincial royalty charges before computing federal taxes. These moves markedly diminished the extent to which the energy provinces could capture the windfall. They were supplemented by a 1974 law granting Ottawa the power to fix oil prices. Further, Ottawa threatened to impose a federal tax on natural gas exports and resisted dramatic increases in natural gas prices in Canada.

Alberta and Saskatchewan moved quickly as well, revising their royalty schedules upward and, in the case of Saskatchewan, taking into public ownership all non-crown oil and gas rights and imposing a surcharge on oil production (the surcharge was later ruled *ultra vires*). Alberta similarly moved to establish technical public ownership rights over its oil, though hesitating to go as far as Saskatchewan, through a marketing commission mechanism and by declaring that the royalty share of oil going through the marketing commission was publicly owned.

These legislative moves, as well as a host of other technical enactments and amendments, were designed to buttress provincial control over all aspects of oil and gas development — production, marketing, and pricing. By asserting their ownership rights over oil and gas after they were out of the ground, the provinces were, they believed, less likely to be seen to be interfering with trade and commerce, an area of clear federal jurisdiction. These moves were supplemented by aggressive new royalty and taxation schemes to increase the share of the oil and gas wealth collected by the province. By 1975, an impasse was reached with both levels of government sharing the wealth in the context of hostility and confrontation.

This atmosphere of contention was increased by the Saskatchewan NDP government's 1975 decision to nationalize a significant portion of the potash industry. This decision was taken as a result of the industry's efforts to resist the government's taxation policies (which had dramatically increased potash revenues flowing into provincial coffers), the government's general efforts to plan and pace the development and expansion of the industry, and the government's desire to participate on an ownership basis in future potash expansion.

The potash industry, largely supported by the federal government, consistently challenged the constitutional right of the province to take the potash measures it was determined to take, taking the province to court repeatedly. The outcome of such challenges was sufficiently uncertain to convince the province to nationalize a portion of the industry — ultimately about 50 per cent. As the challenges dragged through the courts, the potash experience simply confirmed the oil experience — the provinces had only very imperfect and uncertain authority over natural resources. Furthermore, it was clear that the federal government, through its superior taxation powers and its control over trade and commerce, could easily frustrate every provincial move. As well, federal disallowance and reservation powers could ultimately be used in any serious showdown, nor was there anything preventing the federal government from invoking the "general advantage" clause of the constitution by declaring the oil industry to be in the vital national interest and therefore subject exclusively to federal control.

As the 1970s continued, both Blakeney and Lougheed won two renewed and convincing mandates from their electorates by declaring their intention to continue to fight for provincial control of resources against the arrogant intrusions of the federal government. In 1979 Saskatchewan's Premier Blakeney clearly articulated a general view of the Western resource rich provinces, a view more or less shared across the West:

> Now, we feel, resource development potential... finally offers us a chance to diversify our economic base. But, like any farmer, we're a bit cautious. Saskatchewan isn't called Next Year Country for nothing. Being intimately aware of what happens in a high-risk, single resource economy [wheat], we ask ourselves the question: how can we manage this promised development of other resources [oil, potash, uranium], each of them individually just as risky, so that we move closer to our number one goal: economic stability?
>
> The best way to minimize the risks inherent in a primary resource economy, we feel, is to utilize our short-term wealth in order to create long-term benefits. By taking the substantial revenue from our rapidly depleting oil reserves, for instance, and investing it in potash which, at current rates of production, has a life of several thousand years. Perhaps a more enduring method of achieving this kind of stability... is to use part of our short-term wealth to initiate and support a

vigorous manufacturing sector in this province. We may have to export some of our primary resources, but we do not want to export all the jobs with them.[8]

Premier Lougheed outlined a similar approach:

I believe it [Alberta's approach to development] means building on strengths such as our energy potential . . . to be self-reliant, getting away from the idea that there are so few "have" provinces and so many "have not" provinces. Processing our resources up stream to the extent that we can do so to spread job opportunities. . . .[9]

For his part, such arguments notwithstanding, Trudeau made it clear that he had no intention of letting the Western provinces hold the nation to ransom over energy pricing.

The West had a strong case. Resources were clearly an area of exclusive provincial jurisdiction. Yet when the BNA Act was drafted, its authors had in mind such resources as timber and land, as well as the apparently insignificant mining sector. Resources were seen as incidental to the great effort of nation building and the construction of an east-west economy where the wealth to be made most importantly lay in commerce and manufacturing. Furthermore, the resource control concession was essential to win the quasi-independent British colonies in North America to agree to Confederation. Finally, superior federal powers were ample and the federal government in the 19th century had exhibited no hesitation in using them.

As the new resource wealth of the West was developed, since most of it was for export, federal powers over trade and commerce had easily contained the situation. However, Western provinces' efforts in the

1970s to extend their control over resources involved new aggressive departures. No longer simply content to sell the rights to exploit resources to investors, and then to collect royalties as the resources were extracted and exported, the provinces were now trying to control the whole process — production, marketing, and pricing. The federal government, faced with losing all say in resource development, felt obliged to defend its prerogatives from the provinces, particularly in oil and natural gas.

The West's unanimity on the question of resources was surprising. The Tory Lougheed regime, the Blakeney NDP regime, the Barrett NDP regime (replaced in 1975 by the Bennett the Younger Social Credit regime) and the Schreyer NDP regime (replaced in 1977 by the right-wing Tory Lyon regime), all agreed on the need to enhance provincial control of resources, including the provinces' rights to determine the development of resources and to derive the lion's share of the benefits from such development. They all agreed that the West's resource boom was an historic opportunity for the region to use this new wealth as a basis for economic diversification, as well as a revenue source.

At this point the unanimity broke down. The NDP regimes, representing political coalitions of progressive farmers, workers, and elements of the middle class, argued that the provincial government must not only establish firm control on the direction, development, and revenue flows in resource development, but also use public ownership to capture additional profits, jobs, and increase decision-making authority. Public ownership would not just win additional revenues, but would ensure that as many jobs as possible were retained in the province.

The Lougheed Tory regime (supported by Bennett

in B.C. and Lyon in Manitoba) rejected such socialistic talk, while agreeing that an interventionist government could capture large shares of revenue to be judiciously used as loans to the private sector to help diversify the economy. Further, the government could use its powers to encourage the participation of local businessmen in economic activity associated with the boom. Lougheed, whose province's boom rested on a rapidly depleting resource, went furthest down this road, establishing a Heritage Fund out of the revenue windfall to aid provincial diversification. Blakeney's NDP regime followed suit with its own more modest Heritage Fund, though much of its disbursement of funds went to support the further development of public participation in potash, oil, and uranium, as well as a range of other public industrial investments. Despite these obvious differences in ideology and strategy, the Western provinces were one on the issue of provincial control of resources and were united in their determination to push provincial powers in the area to the maximum limit.

For its part, the federal government also had a strong case. The oil crisis had driven up the price for oil to the point where Central and Atlantic Canada were in deep trouble. Forced to pay burgeoning world prices for much of Canada's needs in the east, the federal government tried to soften the impact on these areas through enforcing a low domestic price for oil. The difference between the world price paid and the administered domestic price had to be made up, the federal government argued, at least partly by the greatly expanded revenues being earned for Western exports of oil and natural gas. By 1975, Canada was in a serious deficit position in the oil trade — its imports of oil at world prices outpaced the revenues from exports of Western oil. The resulting dislocation and inflation would be a disaster for the national economy. Furthermore, the rise in oil prices had worsened the growing crisis in Central Canadian industry, which required, to help it out of decline, cheaper than world price energy sources in order to sustain a competitive edge. Therefore, the federal government argued that it was in the interest of the national economy, in this case the industrial heartland of the nation, to establish energy policies to protect Canada's manufacturing sector. It was, the federal government argued, in the national interest to shelter Central and Atlantic Canadian consumers and industries from the full negative weight of world oil prices.

The Western provinces largely agreed with such arguments in principle. The debate centered on how much of the bonanza the West ought to give up in the national interest. The West argued that it was not fair that it should again be exclusively called upon to bear the full cost of Canadian nationhood. The wheat boom in the West had set the stage for the realization of the idea of a viable and successful east-west economy cementing the Dominion. The West had largely paid, through land grants, mineral rights, and a period of monopoly, for the railway that first bound Canada together. The West's captive market had helped make Central Canada's industries successful. Now, once again, Canada was calling on the West to give up the energy resource boom to help salvage the viability of the nation. Many in the West felt that too much had been asked in the past, and too much was being asked again. As Premier Blakeney put it:

> As a provincial government, we intend vigorously to protect what is constitutionally ours — in particular the

revenue from our natural resources — but we understand that in order to reap the benefits of Confederation, we must be willing to give a little. . . . And in recent years, that is just what Saskatchewan has done. For the good of all Canadians, we — and Alberta — have accepted substantially less than the world price for our oil. We have, therefore, deflected the blow of rising oil prices from the rest of Canada. And that deflection has cost us dearly [$283 million in 1979 alone, or $300 per capita, in Saskatchewan]. You will find few Western separatists in Saskatchewan.

You *will* find people who believe that for too long Saskatchewan has not had its fair share of the benefits, those who are tired of the West being considered a hinterland for the industrial triangle of the St. Lawrence valley.[10]

Out of the negotiations, the federal and provincial governments agreed on a policy of a gradual move of oil prices upwards, though the federal government refused in principle a commitment to a rapid move toward world prices. Further a complex formula for federal-provincial-industry revenue sharing was negotiated. There was also an agreement providing for federal-provincial-industry involvement in the development of unconventional oil — the tar sands and heavy oil upgraders. (Heavy oil upgraders transform thick, gummy heavy oil into a lighter synthetic crude, which can then be refined.) The compromise was almost completely unsatisfactory to the West, which continued to insist that the region was being asked to surrender too much of the boom to aid the nation. Acrimony and bitterness increased.

It was in this context that Joe Clark's Tories won the May, 1979 federal election. The West delivered to Joe Clark, the second Western Prime Minister. Liking his decentralized vision of Confederation as a "community of communities," the West gave him 57 of 77 seats.[11] Atlantic Canada was less enthusiastic, yet still gave him 18 of 32 seats. The key to victory however was Ontario, where the Tories won 57 of 95 seats. Although a minority government (136 Tory, 114 Liberal, 26 NDP, six Créditistes), the West was significantly represented in a federal government for the first time since John Diefenbaker. And very quickly the West got some major concessions in the proposed budget presented by the Tories in late 1979 — a $4 a barrel increase in oil prices in 1980 (representing what Trudeau was only willing to concede over two years), followed by equally dramatic increases in subsequent years. This would have been a bonanza for the West, especially Alberta. This energy decision was received with deep concern in Ontario, a province that, above everything else, wanted cheap energy.

The demands of Tory Alberta and Tory Ontario were just too contradictory for the Clark government. Atlantic Canada was concerned, too, though Newfoundland's Peckford was happy because Clark had agreed to Newfoundland's claim for substantial control of off-shore resources. The concern in Ontario might have abated with time, but time was something that Prime Minister Clark did not have. A series of other unpopular measures in the budget, combined with Clark's serious political miscalculations (he was determined to govern as if he had a majority!), brought about the defeat of the government in the House of Commons over the budget on December 13, 1979.[12] The government had lasted less than seven months. The ensuing election, and its aftermath, sparked the most serious confrontation between the West and Ottawa in this century.

Confrontation with Ottawa

Joe Clark's 1979 defeat occurred when the crisis of Confederation had reached a watershed. The hopes of the West for obtaining major concessions from Ottawa on resources were dashed. And the hopes of Newfoundland to obtain federal recognition of provincial control of off-shore resources were similarly undercut. The contradictory demands of Canada's regions had reached a point where conciliation and compromise seemed out of reach. Quebec had elected a separatist government, which was moving confidently toward a referendum on sovereignty association. Atlantic Canada wanted a strong central government in order to ensure a continuation of equalization payments and of federal support of the region's weak revenue base. Yet Newfoundland also wanted significant provincial control of the fishery and off-shore resources. The West wanted confirmation, and a firming up, of provincial control over natural resources, as well as concessions to allow the Western provinces to increase their share of the resource boom. Yet the West also wanted continuation of federal participation in shared-cost programs. Ontario wanted a strong federal government to assert and impose a new national economic strategy to help industry out of its deepening stagnation.

The West was seriously isolated, since all other regions wanted lower energy prices than the West wanted. The rest of Canada generally supported federal initiatives to regulate energy prices and to capture a share of the boom from Western energy exports to help off-set the spiralling costs of energy in the consuming provinces. The West's complaints received less and less sympathy in the rest of Canada. Earlier Western complaints, especially during the 1920s and 1930s, had received significant support in Central Canada, most notably Ontario. But these earlier complaints were presented by movements of farmers and workers advocating a new and more just vision of what Canada could and should be. The Western complaints of 1979-80 were presented by provincial governments, and resource entrepreneurs, demanding more revenue — a demand that would inevitably increase the cost of living for consumers as well as exacerbate the industrial stagnation of Central and Atlantic Canada. No new vision of a more just Canada was offered by the West. Understandably, many Central and Atlantic Canadians saw the demands of the West as motivated by greed and sectionalism.

Hostility to the claims of the West was exaggerated by the deepening recession in Central Canada at a time when the West's resource-powered economy was booming. The facts seemed to confirm this. Alberta became the national income leader in 1979, replacing Ontario. Wages in the West became better than those in Central Canadian industry. Alberta and Saskatchewan boasted near-full employment while Ontario, Quebec, and the Atlantic provinces were facing dramatically rising unemployment. While most provincial governments and the federal government were facing budget deficits and cutbacks, Alberta and Saskatchewan were buttressed by the resource revenues filling their Heritage Funds.

An exaggerated view of the booming West was purveyed by the Central and Atlantic Canadian press and politicians, rendering the West's complaints unconvincing to most Canadians. The headlines, while based on fact, created an image of a rich, arrogant, and selfish West. "Alberta pay nation's best, figures show," yelled a page one headline in the *Globe and Mail*.[13] Another, on the first page of the *Financial Post*, proclaimed: "Only Alberta stays ahead."[14] Another announced, "Alberta's provincial taxes about half those facing Ontario."[15] Another asserted: "Growing oil wealth spawns a Bay Street West."[16] Ontario's historic economic lead had never received as much breathless attention as Alberta's lead of only two or three years. Alberta, and the West as a whole, became the bad boys of Confederation, needing a sharp rebuke.

The hard facts of the continuing vulnerability and instability of the West's economy were forgotten in the temporary boom. At the height of the boom, in Alberta, the biggest single portion of investment capital still went into oil and gas. Most of the province's budget, over 55 per cent in 1980, was derived from taxes and royalties on natural resources, most importantly oil and gas. Despite the boom, about 44 per cent of Alberta's gross domestic product (GDP) was derived from minerals, another eight per cent from agriculture.[17] Hence over half of Alberta's annual GDP was based on minerals (mainly oil and natural gas) and agriculture. Alberta's efforts at diversification had only made a few gains in the petro-chemical industry, some in food processing, and some in non-conventional oil projects. Agriculture and oil remained Alberta's main sectors of real wealth production. Alberta's per capita income from 1950 to 1980 had reached or exceeded the national average in 18 years, and had never reached Ontario's until 1979, when the boom had pushed Alberta into the position of national income leader.[18]

In Saskatchewan the situation was similar. Saskatchewan's economy was deeply dependent on its major resources: wheat and other agricultural products, oil and natural gas, potash, and uranium. Although not as dependent as Alberta on a single mineral sector, Saskatchewan remained a resource economy. About 51 per cent of the province's GDP in 1980 was still generated in agriculture and minerals. And agriculture remained Saskatchewan's biggest economic sector, accounting annually for between 40 and 50 per cent of total value produced, while mining was the next biggest sector. In the years 1950 to 1980, Saskatchewan's per capita income exceeded the national average in only four years, never matching Ontario's. Indeed, Saskatchewan's per-capita income continued to fluctuate wildly from year to year, largely reflecting booms and busts in the wheat economy.

Despite its apparent wealth, B.C. had always been plagued by a fragile economy. Always considered a rich province in Confederation due to a strong industrial base, which comprised about 39 per cent of GDP in 1980, and a very active resource sector, 13 per cent of GDP in 1980, B.C. had been haunted by uncertainty. B.C.'s industrial production was mostly related to the forestry industry — in fact, the forestry industry remained the biggest single sector in the province — and rose and fell dramatically with world (especially American) market conditions. And although B.C.'s per-capita income from 1950 to 1980 consistently surpassed national averages, it exceeded Ontario's in only 12 of those years.

In 1980 Manitoba had the most diversified Western economy. Only 22 per cent of the province's GDP was derived from agriculture and minerals, while a healthy 35 per cent was earned in industrial production. Yet Manitoba's manufacturing sector continued to be largely related to processing the West's natural products, and in servicing the limited Western market, rendering the province highly dependent on general levels of Western prosperity. In the 1950 to 1980 period, Manitoba's per-capita income exceeded the national average only during two years, and had remained chronically behind that of Ontario.

But such a complicated assessment of the nature of the Western economy was drowned by all the boom talk that swept Canada. The West's continuing complaints were not taken seriously, particularly in the context of the deepening recession plaguing Central and Atlantic Canada. Indeed, the West was seen as selfish and unreasonable.

It was therefore not surprising that Trudeau was re-elected with a majority government in the February, 1980 election. There is no doubt that the victory can be largely attributed to Trudeau's promise to Central and Atlantic Canadians that he would keep the lid on the West's demands for increased oil prices and that he would continue to frustrate Western efforts to gain unimpeded jurisdiction over resources, especially energy resources. The Liberals won 19 of 32 seats in Atlantic Canada, 74 of 75 seats in Quebec, and 52 of 95 seats in Ontario.[19] In the West the Liberals were decimated, winning only two seats in Manitoba. Clearly what had won the election for Trudeau was the shift in Ontario, largely as a result of his energy promises and with the clear support of the premier of Ontario, a province increasingly desperate for cheap energy. Trudeau had promised to slow down the rise in the price of oil and natural gas to continue federal moves to share significantly in the revenue windfall generated by Western exports. For this, the Ontario electorate rewarded him.

The impasse between the West and Ottawa therefore deepened. Alberta refused to accept a new oil price agreement anywhere short of that promised by the Clark government and warned that a federal export tax on natural gas, the price of which was rising rapidly in the U.S., would be viewed as little short of aggression. In preparation for a drawn-out struggle, Alberta enacted legislation giving the Cabinet the power to determine levels of crude oil production (if they couldn't get the price they wanted, they could stop selling oil).

In October, 1980 the federal government brought down its budget, which included the National Energy Program (NEP).[20] This program unilaterally imposed federal authority over energy resources and established new price and revenue sharing regimes in the absence of consent from the West. The price regime involved a complex calculation of a "blended" price determined by the world price and the domestic price. Prices for domestic oil were to go up $2 a year per barrel from 1981 to '83; $4.50 in 1984 and '85; and $7 per year thereafter. However, the domestic price would never be allowed to go above 85 per cent of the world price in order to ease the burden on Canadian industries and consumers.

The new price regime was not the issue — it did, after all, go a long way in meeting the West's demands for significant increases. The revenue-sharing regime, however, provoked deep anger in the West. Traditionally oil and gas revenues had been distributed as follows: 45 per cent to the province; 45 per cent to the industry; ten per cent to the federal government. By 1979 this had changed to: 49 per cent to the province; 39 per cent to the industry; 12 per cent to the federal government. The NEP revenue formula for 1983 changed this drastically: 41 per cent to the province;

31.6 per cent to the industry; 27.5 per cent to the federal government. NEP also established policies, mainly incentives, to encourage the Canadianization of the oil and gas industry (the goal was 50 per cent by 1990), as well as to push non-conventional developments and frontier exploration in order to reach energy self-sufficiency. A greatly expanded federal government role directly in energy development, through Petro-Can, was also promised.

The complicated formula for determining generous federal incentives in order to encourage frontier exploration, besides encouraging Canadianization, also determined that the focus of exploration would shift to areas controlled by the federal government — in the north and off the east coast. Some aspects of NEP were clearly in the public interest — like the bigger public role in the oil and gas industry and the effort to carve a Canadian-controlled industry out of what had hitherto been the near private, monopolistic preserve of the foreign-owned major oil multinationals. In the West these good points were lost in the anger over the federal effort unilaterally to determine the shape of the industry and to grab a huge share of the wealth being produced. Indeed, the view in Alberta, shared with more or less intensity by Saskatchewan and B.C., was that this was nothing more than a naked federal effort to take over control of energy resources and to appropriate an increasing, and unjust, federal share of the revenue. As Premier Lougheed declared, "They'd like to siphon off western resource money that will be gone in a few years."[21] Lougheed expressed a view of Ottawa's approach to the West, a view increasingly shared in the West generally: "Let's make sure the West is suitably subservient and we continue to get cheap food and cheap oil and the tax revenue flows."[22]

This confrontation over energy resource policy was deepened by Trudeau's declared intention, with the support of only Ontario and New Brunswick, to proceed with the patriation and significant amendment of Canada's constitution.[23] Western provincial governments viewed this determination as a blatant attempt to increase the power of the federal government at the expense of provincial powers. The federal government, it was felt widely in the West, was determined to get through naked power what it couldn't get through negotiation — control of Western resources and a growing share of the wealth realized from these resources. Even Premier Blakeney, usually circumspect and careful, became exceedingly blunt during a spring, 1980 tour of Central Canada:

> For Western Canadians the reasons for the push towards constitutional reform are not difficult to understand. Ever since Alberta and Saskatchewan became provinces in 1905, people on the prairies have been struggling against the dominant forces in Confederation — the political, business and financial interests in Central Canada — for a say in national policy, for a fair share of the economic and social benefits of this country. We in Saskatchewan thought that resource wealth would finally help us achieve our place in the sun. But as prices of western resources began to rise, and substantial revenues began to accrue to our provincial treasuries, the federal government stepped in. With price controls; an export tax on oil; a unilateral decision to declare provincial royalties non-deductible for income tax purposes. And the Supreme Court of Canada, in the CIGOL and Central Canada potash cases, began to interpret "indirect taxation" and the federal trade and commerce power in ways that threatened to

> undermine provincial power to manage and tax resources.
>
> Those developments have led us to demand constitutional changes that will confirm and strengthen provincial powers over resources.[24]

Overall, the view widely held in the West was that these two federal initiatives — the NEP and the unilateral patriation of the constitution — were nothing less than another concerted effort to make the Ontario perspective on Confederation the "national" perspective through the use of Ontario's considerable political and economic strength. Ontario had won the election for Trudeau, now he was rewarding that province. In return, Ontario's support of unilateral patriation of the constitution was vital to provide Trudeau what little credibility his initiative had.

Western anger and alienation grew incredibly. Suddenly Western separatism, a long-husbanded dream of a tiny minority of Westerners, became nearly respectable. Meeting halls across the West filled to capacity as the formerly isolated voices of Western separatism found eager listeners. Long cherished as a dream by elements among the traditional agrarian movement, Western separatism found receptive audiences among what commentators variously dubbed "blue-chip separatists"[25] and "the silk stocking crowd."[26] Oilmen, professionals, executives, entrepreneurs, academics, as well as farmers, were reported to be swelling Western separatist ranks. Separatist organizations — Western Federation (West-Fed), Western Canada Concept, United West, Unionest — were growing across the West and making exaggerated membership claims. During the early spring of 1980 the separatists gained their first elected members of a Legislative Assembly in the West when two Saskatchewan Tory MLAs left the party and founded the Unionest party, committed to Western separation and annexation to the United States. As events unfolded dramatically, the various separatist organizations began to discuss unification.

The debate became more and more heated. Tory Opposition Leader Joe Clark made a series of speeches across the nation in which he argued that Prime Minister Trudeau and his policies were driving Westerners to consider separatism. During a speech at a Calgary dinner Ernest Manning (now a senator) warned of violence should Western separatism become a serious threat. Lougheed expressed the fear of a loss of control of the separatist mood should Ottawa rebuke the West any further. The respected and non-partisan Canada West Foundation suggested that separatist sentiment could explode in the West if the polarization continued and worsened. Blakeney expressed a fear of a separatist surge in 1981. Even Quebec's Premier René Lévesque joined the debate, accusing Ottawa of having "ravaged Alberta's resources."[27] Trudeau provided much grist for the Western separatist mill with his explicitly contemptuous dismissal of the movement, warning the West not to use separatism to blackmail the federal government.

The publication of a series of public opinion polls documenting the growth of Western separatist sentiment further deepened the debate. The *Financial Post* reported a secret Alberta government poll that found over 20 per cent support for separatism among Albertans.[28] A joint Edmonton *Journal*-Calgary *Herald* poll found 23 per cent support for separation in Alberta.[29] In Saskatchewan, a poll conducted for the CBC in summer 1980 found that ten per cent would vote for a separatist party if one appeared on the hustings.[30] A poll conducted by Edmonton publisher Mel Hurtig found 14 per cent pro-separatist sentiment in Alberta,[31] and a similar figure was reported by a later CBC poll in the West as a whole.[32]

Needless to say, 1980-81 will go down in history as years of Western anger of unprecedented depth. The crisis, in fact, deepened. In February, 1981 Lougheed warned Albertans to "prepare to suffer and bleed"[33] in the battle with Ottawa. The four Western premiers met and began to revive traditional grievances regarding the tariff and freight rates. B.C.'s Premier Bennett claimed that the West contributed, between 1973 and 1980, almost 45 per cent of Canada's total economic growth, while Ontario, 25 per cent larger in population, contributed only 28 per cent in the same period. [34] He alleged a massive and unjust transfer of wealth from the West to Central Canada. On March 1, 1981 Alberta cut the flow of oil eastward by five per cent, or 60,000 barrels a day, an unthinkable act just a year before. In April, an Alberta cabinet minister accused Ottawa of "bare-faced aggression" against Alberta.[35] Ontario worsened the situation by an arrogant proposal for a national sharing of resource revenues.[36] In May, Lougheed accused Trudeau, "mandarins" in the federal civil service, and the eastern-based media of orchestrating a "conspiracy" against the West to end its boom.[37] One June 1, 1981, Alberta cut the flow of oil eastward by a further five per cent.

Western support for Confederation was at an all-time low. A Gallup Poll conducted in early 1981 found that 25 per cent of people in the Prairie provinces, and 20 per cent of the people of B.C. believed that Canada would break up.[38] A poll conducted by the Canada West Foundation in the spring of 1981 obtained some rather ominous results.[39] No less than 36 per cent of

Westerners agreed that "Western Canadians get so few benefits from being part of Canada that they might as well go it on their own." Forty-nine per cent of Albertans agreed. Fully 84 per cent of Westerners agreed that "the West usually gets ignored in national politics because the political parties depend upon Quebec and Ontario for most of their vote," and 61 per cent agreed that "Western Canada has sufficient resources and industry to survive on its own." Such results were the cause of deep foreboding since they indicated a growing, general disaffection among Westerners.

This general disaffection was fertile ground for the firm 10 per cent separatist sentiment in the West as a whole (17 per cent in Alberta). The depth of alienation and accompanying political crisis is well illustrated by two events that occurred in Saskatchewan during that period. In January 1981 the biggest rally ever held in the small city of Weyburn took place, sponsored by the separatist organization, West-Fed. Anywhere from 900 to 1400 people attended, depending on whose count you believe.[40] In May, 1981, in Yorkton, another small Saskatchewan city, a pro-federalist group, annoyed at the growing separatist agitation in the region, organized a meeting in support of Canadian unity. They were modest in their expectations. Only 200 chairs were put out. Nine people came.[41] Needless to say optimism about the viability of Confederation was rare indeed in the West.

Uncertain Victories

The same day (June 1, 1981) that Lougheed staged in his second five per cent cut in the flow of oil eastward, Trudeau finally made a significantly conciliatory speech at Fredericton, New Brunswick. In that speech,

Trudeau said he foresaw "improved regional representation as the next issue for constitutional reform" recognizing "a common perception that legitimate regional representatives do not exercise enough influence in the Canadian parliament and therefore in the national Government."[42] Gestures of conciliation recurred from both sides largely because the impasse was creating an impossible situation for both Trudeau and the Western premiers. Constitutional opinion was divided, but many experts argued that Trudeau could not hope to gain the patriation and significant amendment of the constitution with the consent of only two of ten provinces. There was no consensus in appeal court decisions in Quebec, Newfoundland, and Manitoba. The Supreme Court confused the issue further by ruling that "substantial" provincial consent was required for such moves by convention but not by law. Therefore Trudeau could act legally in a unilateral fashion, but such action would be conventionally improper. In order to obtain patriation and amendment without more deeply dividing the nation, Trudeau clearly needed to win some of the eight dissenting provinces over. It would be a seriously divisive outcome if all the provinces of one region, like the West, continued in opposition.

The Western premiers, especially Lougheed and Blakeney, were deeply worried about the developing separatist sentiment. Clearly a continued impasse could only encourage this trend. Lougheed's decision to turn down the flow of oil eastward had led him to the precipice: if he continued the shut-down Ottawa would eventually assert federal power to stop him, perhaps completely taking over regulation of the energy sector, justified on the grounds of defending the national interest from Lougheed's sabotage. Such an event would lose what gains Alberta had made and obviously provide an incredible stimulus to separatist sentiment. Lougheed needed a way out or he risked disaster. Therefore the needs of Lougheed and Trudeau came together, setting the stage for a compromise on both oil-and-gas policy and the constitution, a compromise out of which both sides could claim victory. By yielding a bit on oil and gas prices and revenues, and on resources in general, Trudeau could hope to woo the Western provinces to his constitutional package. By yielding a bit on oil and gas prices and revenues, Lougheed could hope to extricate himself from an increasingly dangerous political stance.

In September, 1981 Ottawa and Alberta announced a new energy-pricing agreement to be in place until 1986. Alberta agreed to accept a slightly modified NEP in principle and to accept the principle that the domestic oil price would never rise beyond 75 per cent of world prices. Finally, Alberta agreed to the maintenance of a low domestic price for natural gas. In exchange Alberta obtained substantial price hikes for oil — more than double the increases earlier agreed to by Ottawa. Additionally, Ottawa promised not to impose an export tax on natural gas going into the lucrative American market. A revenue sharing agreement was also approved: 30.2 per cent to the province; 25.5 per cent to Ottawa; 44.2 per cent to the industry. The proposed price hikes had increased the revenue pie considerably — to a projected $212 billion by 1986. Lougheed and Trudeau toasted the agreement as a victory for both sides — an intelligent compromise that judiciously balanced the interests of Alberta and of the nation.

In early November, 1981 a First Ministers' Conference reached agreement on the constitution with the blessing of all provinces except Quebec. The Western provinces made some significant gains in wringing concessions from Trudeau. The amending formula — constitutional amendments require the agreement of the House of Commons and at least seven of ten provincial legislatures representing more than half of the population of Canada — gave the West an effective veto. If all four Western provinces were united against an amendment, the amendment would not pass. Additionally, equalization payments and special programs to overcome regional disparities were written into the constitution. Thus the principle of sufficient revenue from the federal government being made available to provinces to maintain a minimum level of services and well-being became a constitutional right. Finally, the new constitution granted the provinces clearer jurisdiction in natural resources, including exploration, development, production, and interprovincial trade. Furthermore, the provinces' resource taxing powers have been made unlimited ("any mode of taxation").

These were clear victories for the West, constitutionally redressing for the first time some of the most basic political grievances of the region. These concessions did little to change the basic economic structure of the West's place in the national economy, but they did give the West, potentially, some of the political powers necessary to extract the maximum benefit from its resource strength. Trudeau had his constitution. The West had its resources. Now the Western regimes could get back to work using the resource-powered boom to encourage diversification, work that had been interrupted by the battle with Ottawa.

It was not to be. The Western boom began to collapse in 1982. The NEP's effects had already cut conventional oil and gas exploration activities in Saskatchewan and Alberta by more than half. The reasons for these cuts were complex. The revenue sharing proposal resulted, the industry declared, in a loss of cash flow of at least $2 billion in the first year of the NEP, thus reducing the funds available for conventional exploration.[43] The NEP itself, because of the generous subsidies and write-offs available, attracted exploration funds to frontier and off-shore exploration. The NEP's Canadianization incentives encouraged a rash of take-overs, or buy-ins, of foreign firms by Canadian interests, further reducing the cash available for exploration (this accounted for $5.1 billion in 1981 alone). The continuing uncertainty of the situation, as well, encouraged many in the industry to engage in a kind of "capital strike," to force further concessions from Ottawa and the provinces.

President Reagan, while attacking Canada's NEP, opened up U.S. exploration areas on generous terms to drillers who had been active in the Canadian oil patch. Wells drilled in Saskatchewan fell from 1498 in 1980 to 807 in 1981. By August of 1982 only 147 of the 465 oil rigs once active in the West were drilling.[44] With the new year the recession that had plagued the rest of Canada finally caught up with the West. World oil prices began to fall, and continued to fall. The combined effects of conservation and high prices had deeply cut into consumer demand for oil and gas, and this, together with maximum production from new sources (North Sea oil particularly), resulted in a glut on world oil markets. The 1981 OPEC price stalled at $34(US) and spot prices, which in 1980-81 had reached as much as $40(US), began to fall. By 1983 the OPEC price was $29(US) and the average spot price was $26(US).[45] Potash, uranium, and grain prices all softened. Western unemployment figures rose dramatically.

Alberta and Saskatchewan had enjoyed near-full employment during the boom, and had often complained of a shortage of skilled labour. Alberta's unemployment figures more than doubled between October, 1981 and October, 1982 (40,000 to 97,000). By March 1983 Alberta's unemployment figure had reached 146,000 — almost four times the number in 1981, representing 11 per cent of the labour force. Similarly, Saskatchewan's number of unemployed doubled in the same period, from 18,000 in 1981, to 28,000 in 1982 to 37,000 in 1983, reaching almost seven per cent of the labour force. Unemployment insurance comission payments in Alberta went up 89 per cent from January to May 1982. While such unemployment figures were less than the national average, they were dramatic because they came about so quickly. One year, Alberta and Saskatchewan had very little unemployment, the next year they suddenly faced double the number of unemployed.[46]

The boom was over. Saskatchewan, two years before the economic leader of the nation in terms of growth, plunged to the predicted lowest growth rate in the country in 1983.[47] And the Conference Board predicted that Alberta, the envy of Central Canada during the boom, would enjoy virtually no growth in 1983.[48] In 1983, for the first time in history, all four Western provincial governments simultaneously faced serious deficits.[49] Contrary to general perception the boom had never been general in the West. B.C. had already long faced unemployment levels higher than the national average — indeed higher than anywhere but Quebec or Atlantic Canada — due to a collapse in the lumber industry. In fact, in August 1982, B.C. had set a record of sorts — the unemployment rate reached 13.8 per cent, the highest since 1946.[50] The revenues from B.C.'s small oil-and-gas industry had simply helped prevent a bad situation from becoming worse. Manitoba had not directly shared in the boom at all — the province had experienced the national recession from the beginning. Manitoba's oil-and-gas and potash industries remained fond hopes as the province encouraged exploration, begging any capital, foreign or otherwise, to get to work. The fact was that the so-called "boom" had been limited to Saskatchewan and Alberta. But in 1982 even that limited, narrow Western boom began to fizzle, as world prices for the provinces' resources began to fall. Alberta's share of $212 billion in oil and gas revenues became a piece of paper.

The massive investment coalitions to develop the tar sands and heavy oil fell like houses of cards.[51] Oil from the tar sands in Alberta could no longer be as profitably produced. Syncrude, a tar sands project started in 1978, producing about 100,000 barrels per day, shelved a $2 billion expansion plan. The smaller Suncor, established in 1967, abandoned a more modest expansion. The Alsands consortium (Shell, Petro-Canada, Amoco, Hudson's Bay, Gulf, and Dome), involved in a tar sands project slated to cost over $13 billion, abandoned the project, claiming that they might proceed in the indefinite future with a scaled-down version. Imperial Oil's $11 billion Cold Lake project was stalled, to be picked up again on a much more modest scale in 1983 to produce mainly asphalt for the U.S. market. Studies for a new tar sands project by a Petro-Canada and Nova partnership stopped. The proposed $35 billion Alaska highway gas pipeline was forgotten.[52] The proposal of a consortium

(Husky, Gulf, Shell, Petro-Canada, and Saskoil) to develop a $1 billion heavy oil upgrader in Saskatchewan was abandoned.[53]

The West had lost again. First, large pieces of the boom were stolen by the federal government. Then, the boom was stolen by world market conditions. The West's great victories, at least temporarily, seemed hollow and meaningless. And even Ottawa began to hurt, as expected oil and gas revenues from the NEP agreement fell by a full two-thirds and the costs of frontier exploration incentives became enormous[54] — in 1982, the total bill for all exploration on northern Crown lands was $1.6 billion, $1 billion of which was paid by federal grants.[55] So, Ottawa was sharing some of the pain.

The political results of the collapse were fairly immediate. 1982 elections were held in both Saskatchewan and Alberta. In Saskatchewan, in April 1982, Blakeney's apparently unassailable regime was defeated. It was more than defeated: the once-proud NDP government was thoroughly humiliated by the Tories. The Tories won 55 seats with 54 per cent of the vote, while the NDP were reduced to 38 per cent and nine seats, their worst showing since 1938.[56] The Saskatchewan separatists won only about three per cent of the vote.

The Tories swept the province on two issues: a promise, in a recession context, to put "money in the pocket" of the electorate to help deal with the crisis; and an attack on the NDP government for having betrayed the West, first, in the defeat of the 1979 Clark government (for which federal NDP MPs had voted), second, in the constitutional accord that had been largely authored by Saskatchewan's Premier Blakeney and Deputy Premier Romanow. The NDP in the

West, the Saskatchewan Tories argued, were just a bunch of closet Liberals, always eager to defend federal Liberal initiatives in the crunch. Upon victory, the Saskatchewan Tory government began to dismantle the edifice built by Blakeney during the resource struggle. The role of the crown corporations in resources was downplayed and their right to join any new investment was curtailed. Further, three months after victory, the new Saskatchewan Tory government gave the oil industry in the province a massive tax break: a one-year tax holiday on new conventional wells and a five-year holiday on deep wells.[57] Top employees of the crown corporations, and scores of civil servants, tainted with the socialist stigma, were fired. Arms were opened to private investors, apologies were made for the years of NDP socialist abuse, and Saskatchewan was declared unreservedly open for business.

In Alberta, the once-proud Lougheed, who had campaigned in two previous elections against the federal government's arrogance, was forced to fight the November 1982 election locally. He was no doubt haunted by the speed with which the Alberta electorate had turned against the Liberal government in 1921, the UFA government in 1935, and the Social Credit government in 1971. Blakeney's fate in April no doubt further concerned him. Lougheed campaigned on four issues: the use of the $11 billion Heritage Trust Fund for current expenditures like mortgage interest relief; his record; his eminently constructive views on Canada; and his economic recovery program. There was no fed-bashing, indeed, Lougheed was on the defensive as his critics argued that his oil-price agreement and support of the constitutional accord represented a caving in to Ottawa. Lougheed won his greatest victory — 63 per cent of the vote and 75 of 79 seats,[58] but, ominously the separatists won almost 12 per cent of the vote (though they won no seats, losing the seat won in a by-election in February 1981 in Olds-Didsbury). The Western separatists, plagued by a reactionary ideology (Trudeau was a communist, the social welfare system had to be dismantled, pure free enterprise was the way to go),[59] lost much of the confidence they had among the electorate. No matter how large the victory, Lougheed was on the defensive — about the oil agreement, about the constitution, about the recession, about his April gift of $5.4 billion to the oil industry in tax breaks.[60] The re-elected premier was a chastened man.

So ended the historic confrontation of the West with Ottawa over resources. Alberta, driven to the wall by a steep fall in world oil prices, was forced to go cap-in-hand to Ottawa to beg that the 75 per cent world price rule not be imposed, if this would lead to a steep fall in domestic oil prices. As the so-called "energy crisis" ended, Alberta found it difficult to sell its natural gas to the U.S. — the gas had become too pricey, according to the Americans. In Saskatchewan, the oil collapse had been accompanied by a fall in prices for uranium, potash, and wheat, confirming Blakeney's worst fears. The Blakeney government was replaced by a government willing to do virtually anything private capital wants in order to sustain development.

This general conservative turn in the West was dramatically confirmed in B.C. with the re-election of the Socred government on a platform of severe restraint and accelerated, large-scale resource development. NDP leader and former Premier Barrett's election campaign promising work and wages through a large-scale public works program, as well as his promise to back off from the heavy-handed wage controls Premier Bennett had imposed on public sector workers, failed to bring about what everyone initially believed would be an NDP victory. The 1981 re-election of the NDP in Manitoba clearly had not represented a trend, but rather had resulted from Tory Premier Lyon's harsh program of cutbacks and restraint.

The circle was now complete. The West once again was forced to seek development on any terms. Uncontrolled development, resource give-aways, foreign financed mega-projects were all again in fashion. Unbridled free enterprise again had become the solution to the crisis. The West, despite the great victories, was back where it had been in the 1960s, still destined as Clifford Sifton had so crisply said, to exploit "the wealth of the field, of the forest and of the mine... in vast quantities." The West's economic place in Confederation, in all essential respects, remain unchanged, despite the constitutional victory on the resource question. The West was still a hewer of wood and drawer of water — now and for the foreseeable future.

Ottawa proceeded to rub salt into the West's wounds with an announcement that would have been unthinkable during the West's boom. On February 1, 1983 federal transport minister Pepin announced that Ottawa was determined to dismantle the Crow Rate,[61] long a symbol of the West's struggle for concessions from Ottawa. First won in 1897, the Crow Rate, put into federal statute in 1926, cheapens the cost of transporting grain out of the West. In fact, Western farmers today pay only about one fifth of the actual cost of shipping their grain to market by rail. If the federal government succeeds, Western farmers will therefore be faced with paying up to five times the rates they now pay. The National Farmers' Union has estimated that a dismantling of the Crow Rate will result in an annual loss of over $500 million from the West. The Crow Rate had been put in place in recognition of the West's contributions to building Canada — through the give-aways to the railways, through the tariff protected prices they paid for Central Canadian industrial goods, through the vital importance of wheat as one of Canada's principal exports. Now, Ottawa is determined to end that concession. Once again, the Western provinces confronted the reality of federal power — Ottawa can give, but Ottawa can also take away. Ottawa had given the West what it wanted in the constitution on resources. Now Ottawa was determined to take away the Crow Rate.

Not very much had really changed.

9
Conclusion:
The Politics of Desperation

Although this book has focussed on the West, it is really about Canada. Can Canada survive as a federal state including such a persistently fractious region? Indeed, the West is only one of a number of increasingly fractious regions that constitute the Dominion. In this most recent series of confrontations, despite the amending formula and the stronger resource section of the new constitution, the West will not be satisfied. This latest confrontation remains only the most recent struggle to result in an unsatisfactory compromise. The West will want more, and more. And so too will Canada's other regions. Atlantic Canada, especially Newfoundland, will want more say in the fishery, in off-shore resources, and in tidal power. The separatist option will remain a major choice in Quebec politics forcing any alternative "pro-federalist" party to fight ever harder for Quebec's special status in the federation. And Ontario, behaving increasingly just like any other self-interested region, deeply worried about the future of the "national" economy, will undoubtedly become more insistently defensive about its special place within Confederation. Canada is, and will remain, in a bartering position: the stakes are and will remain nothing less than its survival and viability as a federation.

Canadian politics have never been more deeply poisoned by regionalism. Blind regionalism dominates our political debates to a point where no other option is heard. Lougheed bashes the "feds" and wins overwhelming mandates, while ignoring the fact that his provincial economy is the near-private preserve of the multinational oil companies, for whom he frequently speaks while posing as the West's champion. The premier of Ontario wins confidence in his province by bashing the West, making it clear that he will not let the "blue-eyed shieks" of Alberta take Ontario for a ride. Peckford of Newfoundland makes his name by standing up to Ottawa. Blakeney in Saskatchewan initially does well bashing the "feds," but upon his first accommodation his electorate punishes him, as the Tories accuse him of betraying the West. Bennett discovers that he is a militant defender of the West's interest, and wins renewed mandates. Trudeau, defeated by the regions in 1979, discovers the usefulness of regional politics and wins in 1980 by slamming the West, mobilizing Central and Atlantic Canada behind him. Meanwhile resource companies, oil men, and eager entrepreneurs in the West fund separatist organizations in order to battle federal interference in energy. In Ottawa, the federal Liberal government responds in kind. Assured of Quebec and a divided Atlantic Canada, the West is written off as efforts are made to win Ontario, the province that decides who will govern.

Are the West's Complaints Justified?

A strong current of opinion in analyses of Canadian history and politics views the rebellions of the West as the result of unfortunate and unsavory sectionalism. Blinded by purely local interest and grievances, such movements indicate an unwillingness on the part of Westerners to embrace the great task of nation-building. If only Westerners were able to see beyond immediate grievances to behold the great national vision that lies behind the Canadian project, we are told, their lamentations would subside as they accepted some discomfort as the patriotic price of building a great nation against impossible odds. The West's resistance to national policies, and its continuing fractiousness, have prevented the final realization of a united, vital, and strong Canada. If only Westerners would change their ways of thinking, see themselves as Canadians rather than Western Canadians, a great future for all would unfold. Therefore, though perhaps curiously understandable, the West's complaints have, the arguments go, been largely regrettable and ultimately destructive.

But history has largely vindicated the West's grievances. The genocide committed against the Métis nation, and the several Indian nations, now stands exposed as one of the monumental crimes of the 19th century. Canadians in the 1980s have recognized the injustices done. The complaints of the early farmers in the West were repeatedly vindicated by government investigation, and the list of concessions to Western grain growers are a testament to the nation's recognition of the justice of those complaints. The great agrarian crusade of the 1910s and 1920s, when a new vision of Canada was offered, again forced significant concessions conceding the justice of many of the grievances. The brave agitations of the Western working class, together with the efforts of workers all across the Dominion, have been vindicated by the fact that most of what they asked has been implemented. The agitations in the 1930s, led by the Social Credit party and the CCF, articulating a critique of capitalism and a new vision of Confederation more responsive to the needs of the common people, though failing to win the nation, modified the polity and the economy markedly. The record of concessions, including the most recent one on resources, more than anything else, vindicates the justice of the West's complaints. But the West was not merely seeking concessions, though those made were gladly accepted. The West was challenging the very nature of the political and economic structure of Confederation.

On no less than five occasions the West called on Canada for basic changes in national direction. In 1869-70, Riel and the white settlers of the Red River asked that the West not be unceremoniously incorporated into Canada as a colonial possession. The West ought to enter Confederation on the same terms as any other province, they argued. Further, the new nation ought not to be created by over-riding the Métis and western Indian nations. Rather these people should be embraced and helped to join the Westward expansion. The Dominion did not listen, creating the postage stamp province, retaining the remainder of the vast western territories as a colonial possession.

Riel called from the West a second time in 1885. Again he asked for recognition of the land claims of his people, a fairer deal for the Indian nations, as well as responsible government. Again he pleaded for help and support for his people to participate in the expansion. Again he asked for provincial status. He was again not heard and was sent to the gallows for his efforts. Provincial status for the rest of the Prairie West was denied until 1905. Control of natural resources was denied to the Prairie provinces until 1930. The Dominion justified this on the grounds that local legislatures might impede settlement and expansion. And when the provinces of Alberta and Saskatchewan were finally established, Western opinion was ignored as regimes loyal to the ruling Ottawa Liberals were put in office.

In the 1910s and 1920s the agrarians from the West, in union with organized farmers across English Canada, called for a less corrupt, more responsive political system and an economy freed from the control of the "Special Interests." Though they had a great impact, they were defeated. Two different voices emerged on the Prairies during the Great Depression — Social Credit and the CCF. Both asked for political and economic changes to humanize the political and economic face of Confederation and of capitalism. Again, though they had a great impact, they were defeated in their efforts to win national support.

None of these movements was primarily and singularly a manifestation of regional grievance. Riel's movements were fundamentally articulations of a national grievance by a people about to be crushed by Westward expansion. The organized farmer, Social Credit, and CCF agitations were primarily expressions of grievances from the perspective of "the middle sort" of farmer. Each of the latter three movements proposed alternative systems of economic organization and new terms for Confederation, more attuned to the popular aspirations of the common people. And each of the three presented itself to the whole Dominion in an effort to win the support necessary for the changes proposed.

In fact, the regionalization of the movements was imposed upon them by the structure of Confederation and of the national economy, which so clearly divided the economic interests of Canada's regions. Failing to win national mandates, the movements, in the case of the victorious Social Credit in Alberta and the CCF in Saskatchewan, retreated to provincial strategies as they struggled for political survival and economic improvement.

As the movements fought to win and hold office, increasingly they articulated their positions in regional terms. Thus the lowest common denominator in Saskatchewan and Alberta that united farmer, worker, and small businessman was a very real Western regional perspective: the bad treatment of the West in Confederation; the economic injustices perpetuated by Central Canadian interests; the need to diversify a vulnerable resource economy; the need to even out the "boom-bust" cycle; the need to fight Ottawa for more concessions; the need to give good, sound, Western-oriented government. As the movements failed to win nationally, and became increasingly confined in the West, this retreat to provincial strategies and regional perspectives became characteristic of all competing political parties in the region.

The resource confrontation of the 1970s confirmed that regional politics remain in command in the West. In the absence of structural changes to alter the West's place in the national economy, and its political weakness in Confederation, the West has been forced to continue to battle to defend its interests as a subordinate region. This is understandable. Despite all the concessions, despite all the booms and busts, including the recent resource boom, the Western economy remains vulnerable and fragile, rooted in the export of natural resources to uncertain world markets.

This fact is at the root of the West's continuing unhappiness in Confederation, an unhappiness that often intensifies during boom times due to resentment at missed opportunities. There is a sense of insecurity, of vulnerability. Good times are rarely enjoyed as Westerners wait for the inevitable bust. This structural economic inequality, built into the very fabric of the national economy, combines with the inevitable insecurity that haunts resource-based economies, to sustain an on-going sense of injustice in the West. Western disaffection, and its continuing expression in an increasingly regional politics, is the defensive reaction of the people of the West who have fought repeatedly for structural changes, only to be defeated each time. And each defeat has made an all-class regional sense of grievance the inevitable focus of electoral politics. Like separatism in Quebec, the West's sectionalism represents the politics of a disintegrating Canada, of a defeated national dream, a dream that frequently seemed to mock the West with the privileges and powers of the Ontario-based capitalist class as it imposed its will on Confederation, indifferent to the consequences for the West.

What Can Be Done?

Before we can contemplate solutions to the problem of the West in Confederation, we must frankly face that what we are dealing with is not merely a regional but a national problem. By focussing simply on the grievances of this or that region, and proposing half-measures and concessions to placate the West, to defuse resentment in Atlantic Canada, to undercut separatism in Quebec, the basic national problem persists. We are not just dealing with the continuing irrationality of Québécois nationalism, or the quaint complaints of Atlantic Canada, or the folksy alienation of the West. We are dealing with a nation that has no national politics. Western provincial governments, the government of Quebec, and the government of Newfoundland are no more guilty of regional self-seeking than Ontario. Though, due to its size and wealth, Ontario has often been successful in wrapping its own brand of sectionalism in the Canadian flag, governments of Ontario have nevertheless proven just as adept at playing the regional political game as have those of the West.

Regionalism dominates politics in every province and is used to mobilize the united opinion of people with quite diverse interests — businessmen, farmers, workers, the poor — in the ongoing battle of the regions. The Québécois worker, farmer, and entrepreneur are united to defend the nation from the abuses of English Canada. The Atlantic farmer, fisherman, worker, and entrepreneur, encouraged by the new potential of off-shore wealth, are united to enlarge the region's share of the pie. In the West, the farmer, worker, and entrepreneur, with the support of foreign capital in the resource sector, unite to battle the rest of Canada for control of the West's increasingly valuable resources. And in Ontario, the traditional big capitalist, rooted in Canada's large financial, commercial, and industrial enterprises, seeks support from the threatened farmer, worker, and small enterepreneur to defend Ontario's traditional privileges in Confederation.

The regional structure of the Canadian economy, as well as the political design of Confederation, makes such a squalid politics inevitable. Indeed, Canada's regions merely replay, again and again, the kind of bartering engaged in by the elites of the various colonies when Confederation was first bargained. Confederation began as a business deal among the elites of the colonies. And Canada remains a business deal among the elites of the various regions, bargaining and squabbling over sharing the wealth.

There is therefore no viable national politics in Canada. The successful politician — federal and provincial — is the one who can set one region off against the other in a bid for electoral power. There is no party of Confederation, there are only parties representing sectional interests and defending traditional ruling class privileges.

The federal Liberals pose as the party of Confederation merely because they win elections. The recipients of most of the support of big business and industry, simply because they alone seem able to provide stable government, the Liberals are able to win because their near-total hegemony in Quebec allows them to focus on appeals to Ontario. Atlantic Canada, deeply dependent on federal handouts, typically judiciously divides its loyalties between the two major parties — ensuring Cabinet representation no matter which party governs. In the 1980 election the Liberals won 42 per cent of their vote and 50 per cent of their seats in Quebec. And because of their additional success in Ontario, the party won 76 per cent of its vote and 86 per cent of its seats in Central Canada.

The federal Tories, justly deprived of any hope in Quebec because of its historical sins, have degenerated into a party that brings together (one really can't say unites) a whole series of contradictory regional grievances on the basis of the grab-bag of anti-Quebec sentiment, regional resource capitalist anger, and neo-conservative hysteria about big government. The party's sad efforts to unite the demands of the Alberta Tory regime for higher energy prices with those of the Ontario Tory regime for lower energy prices tore the Clark government to shreds in a few short months. In

1980 39 per cent of the Tory national vote, and 48 per cent of their federal seats, were won in the West, while the party won just over ten per cent of the vote and only one seat in Quebec.

Each major federal party is therefore locked into representing regional interests in national politics. Each shares Atlantic Canada. The Liberals dominate Quebec. The Tories dominate the West (though the NDP shares in that dominance). Ontario has therefore become the serene arbiter of who will govern the nation.

The NDP, as well, has become increasingly split along regional lines. Desperate for a national break-through, the federal party has tried to down-play its strong Western roots in a bid for electoral support in Ontario. Meanwhile the Western wing, which elects most NDP MPs, strives to retain its position as the reform voice defending the West in Confederation. Although the NDP won about 40 per cent of its vote in Ontario in 1980, this only netted five seats, while about 38 per cent of its vote won in the West took 26 seats. This discrepancy has increased the regional stresses in the party — the Western wing fears too many conces-sions to the Ontario electorate will lose the party its strong base in the West.

There is, therefore, no national voice in Canada's federal politics — just the continuing clamour of regional interests striving to win their way in each of the three main parties. This sad reality has convinced more and more Canadians of the need for basic politi-cal reform. Somehow the three major parties, it is argued, must find a way to ensure adequate political representation from all regions. Western Liberals ought to be represented in the federal Liberal caucus at Ottawa. Quebec Tories should have a presence among the federal Tory MPs. Ontario, Quebec, and Atlantic Canada NDP voters ought to have a bigger presence among that party's MPs. Generally, the regions, especially those excluded from the governing parties (the West when the Liberals are in power; Quebec when the Tories are in), must have more adequate political representation in the House of Commons and the Cabinet.

The most obvious way to ensure that our federal political parties begin to think federally and to create a truly national politics would be to abolish the present single-member constituency system of election in favour of proportional representation in the House of Commons based on a sharing of each province's seats on the basis of the parties' actual popular support. There would thus be MPs from all provinces committed to all parties. There would even be Liberal MPs from Alberta and a sizeable group of Tory MPs from Quebec under such a system! The advantages of the system are obvious: the true popular support for each party in the regions and in the nation would be faithfully reflected in the House of Commons. Each of the parties would therefore be forced to confront the particular problems of each region and develop national policies that attempted to seek a balance between conflicting perspectives.

Yet many argue that the main disadvantage of such a system is that Canada would never be able to elect a majority government, except as the result of an exceptional popular sweep by a party. Thus Canada would be plagued with political instability and uncertainty. But a case can be equally made that this vice is really a virtue. In Canada's history minority governments have had a consistently more responsive record than majority governments. Minority governments are forced to concede, to compromise, and to innovate. Majority governments, smug and secure in their mandates, need not remain responsive to the needs and aspirations of the people. And perhaps it is safer and more democratic to ensure that no government shall have a clear majority unless it has earned a majority popular mandate. Clearly proportional representation would not only go a great distance to reconciling Canada's warring regions, but to deepening our imperfect democracy.

There is, alas, very little support for thorough-going proportional representation among any of the established parties or the existing provincial regimes. This should not be surprising since the system would lead to uncertainty and the horrifying prospect of never having a comfortable majority. Our governments and politicians would have to work harder at governing better.

As a result the most commonly proposed reforms are considerably more modest. One proposal suggests retaining the existing system but attaching to it an additional group of Commons seats that would be distributed in each province based on popular support. This would ensure some representation from the regions for each party without being too messily democratic. Another proposal is to transform the Senate into a House of the Provinces, which would be composed of members appointed by each provincial government. It is indeed tempting to support anything to get rid of the wretched Senate, that lush pasture for defeated and worn out politicians, bagmen, and assorted political hacks. But the proposal of a provincially appointed House of the Provinces would solve nothing. It would be the worst sort of meaningless gesture, and would simply transform the Senate from its present sleepy uselessness to a futile debating ground where we could daily hear what we now are only subjected to at First Ministers' Conferences. If we are to retain the Senate as some sort of regional house, it ought at least to be selected by popular election and it clearly must have some meaningful powers to ensure a serious role in our political system.

None of these reforms will work, however, in the absence of a new national policy with deep popular support in each region. In the absence of that, no political tinkering in the world will change the regional impasse we confront.

A New National Policy

Canada desperately needs a national policy to articulate the aspirations of the regions in a new political and economic structure, while reflecting the desire of the people for a society based on economic and social justice. A vision of what Canada could be is urgently needed. It must be a vision that would begin to overcome the regional loyalties to which we have all been so well trained by our local political and economic elites. It must be a vision that allows us to break out of regional constraints in order to unite Canadians of all regions in a quest for a Canada able to survive and flourish in the next century.

The first step must be to open each region to the complaints and grievances of all other regions, to recognize the basic justice of the complaints of the regions. As a first principle, Canadians must declare a willingness to take the risks necessary to be generous to redress regional grievances as a matter of national policy. Quebec must be granted the unqualified right to self-determination, as well as the unquestioned right of special status, as the political expression of the

Québécois nation, in any new regime of Confederation. The West must be finally freed from the quasicolonial status that has haunted it since 1869, not just rhetorically, but with significant reparations in recognition of the costs the region has repeatedly borne in building Canada. The indigenous native nations must be granted forms of autonomy and self-government, at the same time as fair and generous settlements of all outstanding land claims are made. Atlantic Canada needs to be assured that extensive economic development will be fostered and supported by national policies. All Canadians, regardless of region of residence, must be assured that the nation is dedicated not just to a basic national minimum level of well-being, but to programs to lead to a genuine equality of condition for all. Such commitments will begin to remove the regional poison from our politics, allowing us to focus on the great general issues of social and economic justice, rather than on regional bartering and tradeoffs.

But such a new national policy would be worthless without a new economic strategy for national development. Canada, of all nations, due to the regional nature of its economy, needs serious economic planning and active government intervention at federal and provincial levels in order to achieve regional justice and balance. Such a strategy need not negatively affect Central Canadian industry. The tariff system is now largely gone, and Central Canadian industry is struggling to find its place in world markets. A new industrial strategy, building on existing strengths, is clearly essential if Central Canada is to resist further de-industrialization and if Canada is to retain its status as a major industrial nation. But surely a new industrial strategy can also focus on the beginnings of meaningful industrialization in the resource regions.

Let us be modest. The fisheries in Atlantic Canada and B.C. should be developed, modernized, expanded as a matter of national economic policy. There is no reason why Canada's fishing industry could not be among the greatest and most modern in the world. But it would require co-operative efforts between national and regional governments. The forestry industry in B.C. could be enhanced by national policies to encourage the production of more end products for world markets. The great agricultural industry in the West could be enhanced by national policies to encourage more processing and further diversification. Alberta could be declared the focus of a national petrochemical industry. Saskatchewan and Manitoba could be declared the focus of a national effort to expand food processing. Quebec's ailing industries could be replaced by new industrial growth that utilized its expanding resource sector and exploited its hydro-electrical potential locally. And who can say that it might not be wise in the long-run to declare Ontario to be the focus of a national effort to establish an integrated Canadian auto industry? In other words, through planning future economic growth deliberately to address the very real problems of the various regions, while retaining a commitment to exploit the existing economic strengths of the regions, Canada could develop an economic strategy not only to ensure its place among the advanced economies but also to begin an economic process to redress ongoing regional disaffection.

Such political and economic perspectives will not emerge either spontaneously or easily. Existing regional political and economic elites will resist them. The dominant capitalist class rooted in Ontario will resist them. Entrepreneurs, investors, and free enterprisers will wring their hands about government intervention. Such perspectives can only emerge if the people — farmers, workers, small businessmen, professionals — unite to sweep aside existing leaders and existing arrangements. The day will first have to come when the Ontario worker and farmer, the Prairie worker and farmer, the Atlantic Canadian fisherman, the B.C. logger, begin to realize that they have more in common with each other than they have with their existing regional leaders. It almost happened in the 1910s and 1920s. It almost happened in the 1930s. Perhaps it will happen in the 1980s or 1990s. Perhaps the Canadian people will come to realize once again that politics are too important to be left to the politicians, and that the economy is too vital to be left to the capitalists.

Sir Wilfrid Laurier was wrong. The 20th century will not be Canada's. We've needed it to work through the messy legacy of 1867. The 21st century could be Canada's, but first we must build a Canada that the regions will embrace.

Notes

Epigram

[1] P.B. Waite, *The Confederation Debates in the Province of Canada* (Toronto: McClelland and Stewart, 1963), p. 60.

Chapter 1: Introduction

[1] This and the following figures are based on 1982 estimates provided in *The Globe and Mail, Report on Business*, January 24, 1983. The figures have been rounded. The figures on GNP earned through exports and the resource share of those exports are from Paul Phillips, *Regional Disparities* (Toronto: Lorimer, 1982), p. 160.

Chapter 2: "The Last Best West"

[1] London *Times*, 13 April, 1865, quoted in P.B. Waite, *The Life and Times of Confederation, 1864-1867* (Toronto: University of Toronto, 1962), p. 323.

[2] Waite, *ibid.*, p. 329.

[3] The phrase appears in a letter from Macdonald to Captain Strachan, 9 February, 1854, see J.K. Johnson and Carole B. Stelmarl, (eds.). *The Letters of Sir*

John A. Macdonald, 1836-1857 (Ottawa: Public Archives, 1968), p. 202.

4 Stanley B. Ryerson, *Unequal Union: Confederation and the Roots of Conflict in the Canadas, 1815-1873* (Toronto: Progress Books, 1968), p. 276-77.

5 From an 1865 speech by Macdonald in the Assembly of Canada, reproduced in P.B. Waite (ed.), *The Confederation Debates in the Province of Canada* (Toronto: McClelland and Stewart, 1963), p. 39.

6 G.P. Browne (ed.), *Documents on the Confederation of British North America* (Toronto: McClelland and Stewart, 1969), p. 95.

7 *Ibid.*, p. 133.

8 *Ibid.*, p. 98.

9 *Ibid.*, p. 51.

10 D.G. Creighton, "Economic Nationalism and Confederation," in R. Cook (ed.), *Confederation* (Toronto: University of Toronto, 1967), p. 4.

11 M.C. Urquhart and K.A.H. Buckley (eds.), *Historical Statistics of Canada* (Toronto: Macmillan, 1965), p. 14.

12 Quoted in J.W. Dafoe, *Clifford Sifton in Relation to His Times* (Toronto: Macmillan, 1931), pp. 273-74.

13 These figures are from G.F.G. Stanley, *The Birth of Western Canada: A History of the Riel Rebellions* (Toronto: University of Toronto, 1936), p. 13.

14 New York *World*, 29 May, 1867, quoted in Waite, *The Life and Times*, p. 305.

15 *Parliamentary Debates* (1870), quoted in Lewis G. Thomas, *The Prairie West to 1905: A Canadian Sourcebook* (Toronto: Oxford, 1975), p. 80.

16 C.A. Dawson, and Eva R. Younge, *Pioneering in the Prairie Provinces* (Toronto: Macmillan, 1940), pp. 11-12.

17 Norman MacDonald, *Canada: Immigration and*

Colonization, 1841-1903 (Toronto: Macmillan, 1966), p. 187.

[18] W.A. Mackintosh, *The Economic Background to Dominion-Provincial Relations* (Toronto: McClelland and Stewart, 1964), pp. 30-32.

[19] Details on the CPR contract are provided in H.A. Innis, *A History of the Canadian Pacific Railway* (Toronto: University of Toronto, 1921), pp. 98-99.

[20] R.E. Caves and R.H. Holton, "An Outline of the Economic History of British Columbia, 1881-1951," J. Friesen and H.K. Ralston (eds.), *Historical Essays on British Columbia* (Toronto: McClelland and Stewart, 1976), pp. 152-66.

[21] Dr. John Sebastian Helmcken, quoted in Martin Robin, *The Rush for Spoils: The Company Province, 1871-1933* (Toronto: McClelland and Stewart, 1972), p. 46.

[22] Urquhart and Buckley, *ibid.*, p. 14.

[23] *Report of the Royal Commission on Dominion-Provincial Relations, Book 1* (Ottawa: King's Printer, 1940), p. 61. Hereafter cited as *Rowell-Sirois Report, I.*

[24] *Ibid.*, p. 57.

[25] All figures used on growth on the Prairies are from the *Rowell-Sirois Report, I.*

[26] *Ibid.*, p. 74.

[27] Quoted in *ibid.*, p. 73.

[28] Quoted in V.C. Fowke, *The National Policy and the Wheat Economy* (Toronto: University of Toronto, 1957), p. 66.

[29] Urquhart and Buckley, *ibid.*, p. 14.

[30] Robert A.J. McDonald, "Victoria, Vancouver, and the Economic Development of British Columbia, 1886-1914," W. Peter Ward and Robert A.J. McDonald, *British Columbia: Historical Readings*

(Vancouver: Douglas and McIntyre, 1981), pp. 369-95.

[31] A. Ross McCormack, *Reformers, Rebels and Revolutionaries: The Western Canadian Radical Movement, 1899-1919* (Toronto: University of Toronto, 1977), p. 4.

[32] The figures on homestead failures are from Fowke, *ibid.*, p. 285.

Chapter 3: Agitation and Rebellion

[1] A.S. Morton, *History of Prairie Settlement* (Toronto: Macmillan, 1938), pp. 93-95.

[2] Lewis G. Thomas, *The Prairie West to 1905: A Canadian Sourcebook* (Toronto: Oxford, 1975), pp. 96-97.

[3] E.H. Oliver, "Saskatchewan and Alberta: General History," in A. Shortt and A.G. Doughty, *Canada and Its Provinces, Volume XIX, Prairie Provinces — I* (Toronto: Glasgow, Brook and Co., 1914), p. 168.

[4] D.A. MacGibbon, *The Canadian Grain Trade* (Toronto: Macmillan, 1932), pp. 23-28.

[5] M.C. Urquhart and K.A.H. Buckley, (eds.). *Historical Statistics of Canada* (Toronto: Macmillan, 1965), pp. 14, 351-52.

[6] The following figures on wheat prices are from *ibid.*, pp. 41-44, and W.A. Mackintosh, *Economic Problems of the Prairie Provinces* (Toronto: Macmillan, 1935), pp. 283-84.

[7] Quoted in Oliver, *ibid.*, p. 168.

[8] Quoted by M. Chester, "Political History of Manitoba," in Shortt and Doughty, *ibid.*, p. 112.

[9] Morton, *ibid.*, p. 95.

[10] Quoted in G.F.G. Stanley, *The Birth of Western*

Canada: A History of the Riel Rebellions (Toronto: University of Toronto, 1936), p. 319. See also the highly sympathetic and moving account of Riel's struggles in Joseph Howard, *Strange Empire: Louis Riel and the Métis People* (Toronto: Lorimer, 1974).

11 George Woodcock, *Gabriel Dumont* (Edmonton: Hurtig, 1975).

12 Quoted in Stanley, *ibid.*, p. 395.

13 H.A. Innis, *History of the Canadian Pacific Railway* (Toronto: University of Toronto, 1921), p. 128.

Chapter 4: "The Man Behind the Plow"

1 Details on the early grain marketing infrastructure are from Harald Patton, *Grain Growers Co-operation in Western Canada* (Cambridge, Mass.: Harvard, 1928).

2 Details on early agrarian grievances are from Hopkins Moorhouse, *Deep Furrows* (Toronto: McLeod, 1918).

3 "Story of the Early Days — Hon. W.R. Motherwell, Regina," selections from the transcript of an interview by Hopkins Moorehouse in 1916, in *Saskatchewan History*, VIII:3, Autumn, 1955, pp. 108-9.

4 Quoted in Brian McCutcheon, "The Patrons of Industry in Manitoba, 1890-1898," in Donald Swanson (ed.), *Historical Essays on the Prairie Provinces* (Toronto: McClelland and Stewart, 1970), p. 115.

5 Paul Sharp, *The Agrarian Revolt in Western Canada* (Minneapolis: University of Minnesota, 1948), p. 33.

6 The activities of the Manitoba Patrons are outlined in L.A. Wood, *A History of Farmers' Movements in*

Canada (Toronto: Ryerson, 1924), pp. 123ff and in W.L. Morton, *Manitoba: A History* (Toronto: University of Toronto, 1967), p. 258.

7 Quoted in Edward and Annie Porritt, *Sixty Years of Protection in Canada, 1846-1912* (Winnipeg: Grain Growers' Guide, 1913), p. 407.

8 *Ibid.*, p. 440.

9 *Ibid.*, p. 435.

10 *Census of Canada, 1911*, Vol. IV, *Agriculture*, p.x.

11 Quoted in W.L. Morton, *The Progressive Party in Canada* (Toronto: University of Toronto, 1957), p. 298.

12 All information on the 1911 election is from Paul Stevens, *The 1911 General Election* (Toronto: Copp-Clark, 1970).

13 Porritt, *ibid.*, p. 4.

14 *Ibid.*, p. 15.

15 *Census of Canada, 1911*, Vol. 1, *Area and Population*, p. 530.

16 M.C. Urquhart and K.A.H. Buckley (eds.), *Historical Statistics of Canada* (Toronto: Macmillan, 1965), pp. 59, 351.

17 V.C. Fowke, *The National Policy and the Wheat Economy* (Toronto: University of Toronto, 1957), p. 72.

18 Quoted in Morton, *Progressive Party,* p. 300.

19 The following quotes are all from Moorhouse, *ibid.*, pp. 244-47, 281-86.

20 *Minutes*, 19th Annual Convention, Saskatchewan Grain Growers' Association, 1920, Saskatchewan Archives at Regina.

21 *First Grain Growers' Sunday of the S.G.G.A.*, 27 May, 1917, Saskatchewan Archives at Regina.

22 Moorhouse, *ibid.*, pp 289-90.

23 *Ibid.*, p. 292.

[24] All economic data is from the *Rowell-Sirois Report, I.*

[25] Quoted in Morton, *Progressive Party*, p. 43.

[26] *Ibid.*, pp. 302-6.

[27] Howard Scarrow, *Canada Votes: A Handbook of Federal and Provincial Election Data* (New Orleans: Hauser Press, 1962), pp. 34-35.

[28] See Patton, *ibid.*, pp. 389-90.

[29] Morton, *Progressive Party*, pp. 211-12.

[30] See Patton, *ibid.*, pp. 230ff and D.A. MacGibbon, *The Canadian Grain Trade* Toronto: Macmillan, 1932), pp. 343-44.

Chapter 5: Socialism and Syndicalism

[1] The characterizations here of early situations faced by Western workers, as well as subsequent struggles, is based on the following: David J. Bercuson, *Fools and Wise Men: The Rise and Fall of the One Big Union* (Toronto: McGraw-Hill, 1978); A. Ross McCormack, *Reformers, Rebels and Revolutionaries: The Western Canadian Radical Movement, 1899-1919* (Toronto: University of Toronto, 1977); Paul Phillips, *No Power Greater: A Century of Labour in B.C.* (Vancouver: B.C. Federation of Labour, 1967); Warren Carragata, *Alberta Labour: A Heritage Untold* (Toronto: Lorimer, 1979); S.M. Jamieson, *Times of Trouble: Labour Unrest and Industrial Conflict in Canada, 1900-1966* (Ottawa: Privy Council, 1968); Martin Robin, *Radical Politics and Canadian Labour, 1880-1930* (Kingston: Queen's University, 1968); Charles Lipton, *The Trade Union Movement In Canada, 1827-1959* (Montreal: Canadian Social Publications, 1967); Dorothy G. Steeves, *The Compassionate Rebel: Ernest E. Winch*

and His Times (Vancouver: Boag Foundation, 1960). Three articles in W. Peter Ward and Robert A.J. McDonald, *British Columbia: Historical Readings* (Vancouver: Douglas and McIntyre, 1981) were also useful: D.J. Bercuson, "Labour Radicalism and the Western Industrial Frontier, 1897-1919" (pp. 45lff); A. Ross McCormack, "The Industrial Workers of the World in Western Canada, 1905-1914" (pp. 474ff); and Stuart Jamieson, "Regional Factors in Industrial Conflict: The Case of British Columbia" (pp. 500ff).

[2] McCormack, *Reformers, Rebels, and Revolutionaries*, pp. 8-9 and Bercuson, *Fools and Wise Men*, pp. 2-4.

[3] This description of the 1906 streetcar strike is based on: D.J. Bercuson, *Confrontation at Winnipeg: Labour, Industrial Relations and the General Strike* (Montreal: McGill-Queen's, 1974), pp. 11-15 and Jamieson, *Times of Trouble*, pp. 84-85.

[4] Quoted in McCormack, *Reformers, Rebels and Revolutionaries,* p. 6.

[5] Quoted in R.C. Brown and R. Cook, *Canada: 1896-1921: A Nation Transformed* (Toronto: McClelland and Stewart, 1974), p. 116.

[6] This description of the strike is based on Jamieson, *Times of Trouble,* p. 123-26; Jack Scott, *Plunderbund and Proletariat* (Vancouver: New Star, 1975), pp. 82-84; and Phillips, *ibid.,* pp. 55-61.

[7] Quoted in Scott, *ibid.,* p. 84.

[8] R.E. Caves, and R.H. Holton, "An Outline of the Economic History of British Columbia, 1881-1951," in J. Friesen and H.K. Ralston (eds.), *Historical Essays on British Columbia* (Toronto: McClelland and Stewart, 1976), p. 152.

[9] *Census Reports, 1931.*

10 W.T. Easterbrook and H.G.J. Aitken, *Canadian Economic History* (Toronto: Macmillan, 1967), p. 564.

11 An estimate based on 1911 and 1921 census figures and G.V. Haythorne, *Labour in Canadian Agriculture* (Boston: Harvard, 1965), p. 9. For the 1911 and 1921 census figures see M.C. Urquhart, and K.A.H. Buckley (eds.), *Historical Statistics of Canada* (Toronto: Macmillan, 1965), pp. 351, 354, 355, 364. The 49,000 farm wage labour figure is a 1911 figure.

12 Quoted in L.A. Wood, *A History of Farmers' Movements in Canada* (Toronto: Ryerson, 1924), p. 104.

13 Quoted in W.A. McIntosh, "The United Farmers of Alberta, 1909-1920," M.A. thesis, University of Calgary, 1971, p. 32.

14 Quoted in Jamieson, *Times of Trouble*, p. 177.

15 Quoted in Steeves, *ibid.*, p. 273.

16 Brown and Cook, *ibid.*, p. 273.

17 J.H. Thompson, *The Harvests of War: The Prairie West, 1914-1918* (Toronto: McClelland and Stewart, 1978), pp. 160-61.

18 Information on events leading up to, during and after the Winnipeg General Strike was provided by the following: D.C. Masters, *The Winnipeg General Strike* (Toronto: University of Toronto, 1950); Norman Penner (ed.), *Winnipeg, 1919* (Toronto: Lorimer, 1973). Previously cited sources were also used.

19 Easterbrook and Aitken, *ibid.*, p. 569.

20 J.W. Scallon, President, Address to the 1920 Convention, United Farmers of Manitoba, *UFM Year Book, 1920*, Manitoba Archives.

21 J.W. Scallon, President, Address to the 1921 Convention, United Farmers of Manitoba, *UFM Year Book, 1921*, Manitoba Archives.

[22] *Farmers' Platform Handbook*, special issue of *Grain Growers' Guide*, 2 July, 1919, Manitoba Archives.

Chapter 6: Devastation and Protest

[1] *Rowell-Sirois Report, I*, p. 144.

[2] *Ibid.*, p. 150.

[3] *Ibid.*, p. 146.

[4] *Ibid.*, p. 149.

[5] Alberta, *The Case for Alberta: Alberta's Problems and Dominion-Provincial Relations* (Edmonton: King's Printer, 1938), Part I, p. 94.

[6] *Report of the Saskatchewan Reconstruction Council* (Regina: King's Printer, 1944), pp. 51 and 57.

[7] *Rowell-Sirois Report, I*, p. 168.

[8] Martin Robin, *The Rush for Spoils: The Company Province, 1871-1933* (Toronto: McClelland and Stewart, 1972), p. 235.

[9] E.J. Hanson, "A Financial History of Alberta, 1905-1950," Ph.D. thesis, Clark University, n.d.

[10] "Year by Year, the Load Grows Heavier," CCF party pamphlet, 1938 election, Saskatchewan Archives at Regina.

[11] W.L. Morton, *Manitoba: A History* (Toronto: University of Toronto, 1957), p. 429.

[12] *Rowell-Sirois Report, I*, p. 172.

[13] W. Allen and C.C. Hope, *The Farm Outlook for Saskatchewan* (Saskatoon: University of Saskatchewan, 1936), also cited by S.M. Lipset, *Agrarian Socialism: The Co-operative Commonwealth Federation in Saskatchewan* (Berkeley: University of California, 1971), p. 119.

[14] *A Submission by the Government of Saskatchewan to the Royal Commission on Dominion-Provincial Rela-*

tions (Canada, 1937) (Regina: King's Printer, 1937),
p. 148.

[15] *Ibid.*, p. 187.

[16] Alma Lawton, "Urban Relief in Saskatchewan During the Years of the Depression, 1930-37," M.A. thesis, University of Saskatchewan, 1969, pp. 46ff.

[17] *Rowell-Sirois Report, I*, p. 164.

[18] All per capita income declines are from *ibid.*, p. 150.

[19] *Case for Alberta*, part I, p. 6.

[20] Dorothy Steeves, *The Compassionate Rebel: Ernest E. Winch and His Times* (Vancouver: Boag Foundation, 1960), p. 87.

[21] L.M. Grayson, and Michael Bliss (eds.), *The Wretched of Canada: Letters to R.B. Bennett, 1930-1935* (Toronto: University of Toronto, 1971), p. 75.

[22] *Ibid.*, p. 160.

[23] Quoted in S.M. Jamieson, *Times of Trouble: Labour Unrest and Industrial Conflict in Canada, 1900-1966* (Ottawa: Privy Council, 1968), p. 217.

[24] The political events in Saskatchewan and Alberta leading up to and following the CCF and Social Credit victories are detailed in J.F. Conway, "To Seek a Goodly Heritage: The Prairie Populist Resistance to the National Policy in Canada," Ph.D. thesis, Simon Fraser University, 1979.

[25] *Journals*, Alberta Legislature, 1932, Vol. XXIX, pp. 6-10.

[26] Calgary *Albertan*, 21 January, 1932.

[27] Calgary *Albertan*, 23 January, 1932.

[28] Dean E. McHenry, *The Third Force in Canada: The Co-operative Commonwealth Federation, 1932-1948* (Berkeley: University of California, 1950), ch. I and

II. See also Walter D. Young, *Anatomy of a Party: The National CCF, 1932-62* (Toronto: University of Toronto, 1969), ch. 1 to 3.

[29] All quotations from the Manual are from Wm. Aberhart, B.A. *Social Credit Manual: Social Credit as Applied to the Province of Alberta; Puzzling Questions and Their Answers,* 1935, Saskatchewan Archives at Saskatoon.

[30] Aberhart promised all "bona-fide" citizens of Alberta a "basic monthly dividend." For those 21 years and older, it was to be $25; children up to 16 years old, $5; those 17 and 18, $10; those 19, $15; those 20, $20. Many detractors of Aberhart argue that this promise of monthly dividends won Aberhart the election. It doubtless helped but was not decisive. In 1940, after admitting he could not deliver the dividends, Aberhart was still returned as premier with a solid majority. See John Irving, *The Social Credit Movement in Alberta* (Toronto: University of Toronto, 1959) for an account of the Social Credit movement's drive to power.

[31] All election results are from Howard Scarrow, *Canada Votes: A Handbook of Federal and Provincial Election Data* (New Orleans: Hauser, 1962).

[32] *Financial Post,* 31 August, 1935.

[33] *Financial Post,* 19 September, 1936.

[34] Montreal *Gazette,* 12 May, 1938, quoted in J.R. Mallory, *Social Credit and the Federal Power in Canada* (Toronto: University of Toronto, 1954), p. 106.

[35] "Bankers' Toadies," Social Credit pamphlet collection, Glenbow Museum, Calgary. The text was also reproduced in its entirety in the *Financial Post,* 9 October, 1937.

[36] *Journals*, Alberta Legislature, 1940, Vol. XLI, pp. 6-13.

[37] Edmonton *Bulletin*, 22 February, 1940, quoted in J.J. Schultz, "A Second Term: 1940," *Alberta Historical Review*, X(1), 1962.

[38] Quoted in Schultz, *ibid.*

[39] *Financial Post*, 30 March, 1940.

[40] *Constitution and By-laws*, Farmers' Union of Canada, 1925, Saskatchewan Archives at Regina.

[41] D.S. Spafford, "The Origins of the Farmers' Union of Canada," *Saskatchewan History*, 28(3), 1965 and "The Left-Wing, 1921-1931," in N. Ward and D.S. Spafford (eds.), *Politics in Saskatchewan* (Toronto: Longmans, 1968).

[42] Quoted in David E. Smith, *Prairie Liberalism: The Liberal Party in Saskatchewan, 1905-1971* (Toronto: University of Toronto, 1975), p. 99.

[43] L.D. Courville, "The Saskatchewan Progressives," M.A. thesis, University of Regina, 1971.

[44] W. Calderwood, "The Rise and Fall of the Ku Klux Klan in Saskatchewan," M.A. thesis, University of Regina, 1968, and P. Kyba, "Ballots and Burning Crosses — the election of 1929," in Ward and Spafford, *ibid.*

[45] The record of the 1929 Co-operative Government is described in P.A. Russell, "The Co-operative Government in Saskatchewan, 1929-1934: Response to the Depression," M.A. thesis, University of Saskatchewan, 1970.

[46] United Farmers of Canada, Saskatchewan Section, *The U.F.C. Economic Policy and Convention Resolutions, 1932*, Saskatchewan Archives at Regina.

[47] Quoted in G.J. Hoffman, "The Saskatchewan Provincial Election of 1934," M.A. thesis, University of Regina, 1973, p. 50.

48 Quoted in G.J. Hoffman, "The Saskatchewan Farmer-Labour Party, 1932-34," *Saskatchewan History*, XXVIII(2), 1975.

49 Hoffman, "1934 Election," p. 278.

50 *Minutes*, First Annual CCF Convention, Saskatchewan, 1936, Saskatchewan Archives at Saskatoon.

51 *Program and Manifesto of the Co-operative Commonwealth Federation*, Saskatchewan Section, 1934, Saskatchewan Archives at Saskatoon.

52 Liberal party pamphlet collection, 1938 election, Saskatchewan Archives at Regina.

53 G.H. Williams, *Social Democracy in Canada* (Regina: McInnis Brothers, n.d. (1938?)), p. 32, Saskatchewan Archives at Regina.

54 "Is Social Credit Coming or Going?" CCF pamphlet collection, 1938 election, Saskatchewan Archives at Regina.

55 "CCF Debt Adjustment and Land Policy," CCF pamphlet collection, 1938 election, Saskatchewan Archives at Regina.

56 S. Silverstein, "The Rise, Ascendancy and Decline of the Co-operative Commonwealth Federation Party of Saskatchewan, Canada," Ph.D. thesis, Washington University, 1969.

57 Quoted in F. Steininger, "George H. Williams: Agrarian Socialist," M.A. thesis, University of Regina, 1976, p. 328.

58 See Martin Robin, *The Rush for Spoils: The Company Province, 1871-1933* (Toronto: McClelland and Stewart, 1972), ch. IX, "Business Government, 1929-1933," pp. 232ff; and Martin Robin, *Pillars of Profit: The Company Province, 1934-1972* (Toronto: McClelland and Stewart, 1973), ch. I, "Socialized

Capitalism: 1934-1937," pp. 9ff.

Chapter 7: Concession and Compromise

1 M.C. Urquhart and K.A.H. Buckley (eds.), *Historical Statistics of Canada* (Toronto: Macmillan, 1965), pp. 625-26.
2 Regina *Leader Post,* 31 October, 1938. My thanks to Professor M. Knuttila for drawing this poll to my attention.
3 United Farmers of Canada (Saskatchewan Section), *Applications for Reductions in the Tariff,* Regina, 1927, Saskatchewan Archives at Regina.
4 Alberta, *The Case for Alberta* (Edmonton: King's Printer, 1938), Part I, pp. 8-10.
5 All election results are from Howard Scarrow, *Canada Votes: A Handbook of Federal and Provincial Election Data* (New Orleans: Hauser, 1962).
6 Walter D. Young, *Anatomy of a Party: The National CCF, 1932-1961* (Toronto: University of Toronto, 1969), p. 110.
7 Roger Bothwell, *et al., Canada Since 1945: Power, Politics and Provincialism* (Toronto: University of Toronto, 1981), especially ch. 10, "Making a Better Country," pp. 99ff.
8 Social Credit Board, Alberta, *Annual Report, 1942* (Edmonton: King's Printer, 1943), p. 18. C.B. Macpherson, *Democracy in Alberta* (Toronto: University of Toronto, 1962) provides a good account of ideological developments in the Social Credit movement.
9 Speech from the Throne, *Journals*, Alberta Legislature, 1944, Vol. XLV, pp. 6-10.
10 Social Credit election advertisement, Edmonton *Journal*, 5 August, 1944.
11 From a speech by a Social Credit candidate, Edmonton *Journal*, 29 July, 1944.

12 From a speech by Premier Manning, Edmonton *Journal*, 22 July, 1944.

13 From a speech by a CCF candidate, Edmonton *Journal*, 27 July, 1944.

14 *Financial Post*, 19 August, 1944.

15 Edmonton *Journal*, 9 August, 1944.

16 *Financial Post*, 12 November, 1936.

17 *Ibid.*

18 Alf Hooke, *30 + 5: I know, I was there* (Edmonton: Co-op Press, 1971), p. 215.

19 Edmonton *Journal*, 15 August, 1935.

20 Edmonton *Journal*, 9 August, 1935.

21 "CCF Program for Saskatchewan," CCF pamphlet collection, 1944 election, Saskatchewan Archives at Regina.

22 *Ibid.*

23 CCF pamphlet collection, 1944 election, Saskatchewan Archives at Regina.

24 S. Silverstein, "The Rise, Ascendancy and Decline of the Co-operative Commonwealth Federation Party of Saskatchewan, Canada," Ph.D. thesis, Washington University, 1968.

25 T.C. Douglas, Premier, "Address in Reply to the Speech from the Throne," February 18 and 19, 1946, *Journals*, Saskatchewan Legislature, 1946, Vol XLV.

26 *Financial Post*, 3 July, 1948.

27 V.C. Fowke, *The National Policy and the Wheat Economy* (Toronto: University of Toronto, 1957), p. 93.

Chapter 8: Of Resources and Constitutions

1 Details of the deal are from Philip Mathias, *Forced Growth* (Toronto: Lorimer, 1971), ch. 6, pp. 124ff.

2 Details of the deal are from Mathias, *ibid.*, ch. 4, pp. 81ff.

3 Martin Robin, *The Rush for Spoils: The Company*

Province, 1871-1933 (Toronto: McClelland and Stewart, 1972) and *Pillars of Profit: The Company Province, 1934-1972* (Toronto: McClelland and Stewart, 1973).

4 Information on per capita incomes and provincial unemployment rates is from Canada, Department of Finance, *Economic Review*, 1982.

5 Canada, *Canadian Agriculture in the Seventies: Report of the Federal Task Force on Agriculture* (Ottawa: Queen's Printer, 1969).

6 *Parliamentary Guide*, 1969 and 1979.

7 Details on Western resource developments and controversies are from John Richards and Larry Pratt, *Prairie Capitalism: Power and Influence in the New West* (Toronto: McClelland and Stewart, 1979).

8 A. Blakeney, Text of a speech to the *Financial Post's* Conference, "Resource Development in Saskatchewan," August 29, 1979, Saskatoon.

9 P. Lougheed, Text of speech to Radio and Television Directors' Association, Edmonton, 20 June, 1981.

10 A. Blakeney, *Financial Post* Conference speech, August 29, 1979.

11 Data on the 1979 federal election are from *Report of the Chief Electoral Officer*, Ottawa, 1979.

12 An interesting account of Clark's period in power is contained in Warner Troyer, *200 Days: Joe Clark in Power* (Toronto: Personal Library, 1980). A better account, which provides a good description of how Clark was caught in the squeeze over energy policy is provided in Jeffery Simpson, *Discipline of Power* (Toronto: Personal Library, 1980).

13 *Globe and Mail*, 11 September, 1980.

14 *Financial Post*, 16 August, 1980.

15 *Globe and Mail*, 21 May, 1981.

16 *Globe and Mail*, 5 February, 1981.

17 All GDP figures are rough calculations based on data from the *Globe and Mail, Report on Business,*

"Outlook, 1981" series published during January, 1981.

[18] All per-capita income figures are from Canada, Department of Finance, *Economic Review, 1982*, pp. 140-41.

[19] *Report of the Chief Electoral Officer*, Ottawa, 1980.

[20] Canada, Department of Energy, Mines and Resources. *The National Energy Program*, Ottawa, 1980.

[21] Regina *Leader Post*, 8 June, 1981.

[22] Regina *Leader Post*, 6 May, 1981.

[23] Details on the constitutional struggle are available in David Milne, *The New Canadian Constitution* (Toronto: Lorimer, 1982).

[24] A. Blakeney, Text of speech delivered to law students at Queen's University, 10 April, 1980.

[25] *Globe and Mail*, 8 November, 1980.

[26] *Globe and Mail*, 11 November, 1980.

[27] Regina *Leader Post*, 1 November, 1980.

[28] *Financial Post*, 1 November, 1980.

[29] Regina *Leader Post*, 3 November, 1980.

[30] The study was done by the Sample Survey and Data Bank Unit, University of Regina, 1980.

[31] *Globe and Mail*, 17 November, 1980.

[32] Regina *Leader Post*, 2 January, 1981.

[33] *Globe and Mail*, 14 February, 1981.

[34] *Financial Post*, 28 March, 1981.

[35] Regina *Leader Post*, 8 April, 1981.

[36] Regina *Leader Post*, 25 April, 1981.

[37] Regina *Leader Post*, 6 May, 1981.

[38] Regina *Leader Post*, 17 January, 1981.

[39] *Globe and Mail*, 21 May, 1981.

[40] Regina *Leader Post*, 20 January, 1981.

[41] Regina *Leader Post*, 8 May, 1981.

[42] *Globe and Mail*, 2 June, 1981.

[43] *Globe and Mail*, 16 March, 1981.

[44] *Financial Post*, 21 August, 1982.

[45] *Globe and Mail, Report on Business*, 4 March, 1982 and *Financial Post*, 19 March, 1983.

[46] *Globe and Mail, Report on Business*, 6 November, 1982; 5 February, 1983; and 12 April, 1983.

[47] Regina *Leader Post*, 6 January, 1983.

[48] Regina *Leader Post*, 19 May, 1983.

[49] Regina *Leader Post*, 2 February, 1983.

[50] *Globe and Mail, Report on Business*, 17 August, 1982.

[51] *Globe and Mail*, 16 March, 1981; 23 January, 1982; *Financial Post*, 18 April, 1981; Regina *Leader Post*, 1 May, 1982.

[52] *Globe and Mail, Report on Business*, 16 March, 1981: Regina *Leader Post*, 1 May, 1982.

[53] Regina *Leader Post*, 3 September, 1982; 31 March, 1983.

[54] Regina *Leader Post*, 3 May, 1983.

[55] *Globe and Mail, Report on Business*, 17 September, 1983.

[56] *Report of the Chief Electoral Officer*, Saskatchewan, 1982.

[57] *Financial Post*, 24 July, 1982.

[58] *Report of the Chief Electoral Officer*, Alberta, 1982.

[59] *Globe and Mail*, 24 January, 1981 and Regina *Leader Post*, 27 January, 1981.

[60] *Globe and Mail*, 14 April, 1982.

[61] John Gallagher, *To Kill the Crow* (Moose Jaw: Challenge Publishers, 1983).

Other Books in the Canadian Issues Series

Oil and Gas
Ottawa, the Provinces and the Petroleum Industry
JAMES LAXER

For more than a decade, the oil industry and energy policy have been a central issue in Canadian economic and political life. *Oil and Gas* offers an overview of these turbulent years and fresh insight into the motives of the main players: Ottawa, Alberta and other producing provinces, the oil majors such as Imperial, the Canadian companies like Petro-Canada, the OPEC cartel and the U.S. government.

Women and Work
Inequality in the Labour Market
PAUL PHILLIPS and ERIN PHILLIPS

Why are women still second-class citizens at work? To answer this question, Paul and Erin Phillips trace women's involvement in the paid labour market, and in labour unions, throughout Canadian history. They document the disadvantages that women face today and examine the explanations that have been forwarded for the persistence of these problems. Chapters are devoted to the effect of technological changes such as the microelectronic "chip" on women's work and to proposals for bringing about equality in the labour market.

"A fine salute to the strong body of materials on women's work that has sprung into being in the last decade."
—*Toronto Star.*

Regional Disparities

New Updated Edition

PAUL PHILLIPS

This is the first and only book to address the perennial problem of the gap between "have" and "have-not" provinces. In this new updated edition of this popular study, Paul Phillips examines developments such as the National Energy Program, the Alberta-Ottawa oil deal, the industrial slump in Central Canada, and the increased prospects for economic growth in resource-rich provinces.

"A concise, convincing overview."
—*Quill & Quire.*

The New Canadian Constitution

DAVID MILNE

The New Canadian Constitution explains j
everyone wanted out of the constitution-ma
cess, who got what, and what the final result
Canadians. Of special interest is the conclu
ter, which examines the nature of the new c

in terms of both interests, issues and accidents that shaped it, and its own strengths and weaknesses.

"...a straightforward and comprehensive narrative."
—*The Globe and Mail.*

"Brisk and well-written."
—*The Vancouver Province.*

Industry in Decline

RICHARD STARKS

Summing up proposals from labour, the NDP, the business community and the Science Council of Canada, Richard Starks, a financial journalist formerly with *The Financial Post*, examines the growing consensus that Canada needs a new industrial strategy.

"The beauty of the book and its importance is its straightforward, uncomplicated, journalistic style, and its price."
—*Canadian Materials.*

y prices are so high today and
all about. The author defines
'cost-push" inflation and ap-
ituations.

ust what
king pro-
mean for
ling chap-
nstitution

ular economics. The book
ery elementary to the very
its readers along the way."